Kicking Habits

Welcome Relief for Addicted Churches

Thomas G. Bandy

Abingdon Press
Nashville

KICKING HABITS: WELCOME RELIEF FOR ADDICTED CHURCHES

This book is printed on acid-free, recycled paper.

Library of Congress Cataloging-in-Publication Data

Bandy, Thomas G., 1950–
    Kicking habits: welcome relief for addicted churches / Thomas G.
Bandy.
        p.   cm.
    Includes index.
    ISBN 0-687-03189-3 (pbk.: alk. paper)
    1. Church renewal.   2. Church management.   3. Church growth.
4. Pastoral theology.   5. United States—Church history—20th
century.   I. Title.
BV600.2.B326   1997
250'.973—dc21

96-48670
CIP

Scripture quotations are from the New Revised Standard Version Bible, copyright © 1989, by the Division of Christian Education of the National Council of the Churches of Christ in the United States of America. Used by permission.

00 01 02 03 04 05 06—10 9 8 7 6 5

MANUFACTURED IN THE UNITED STATES OF AMERICA

For
my parents,
Dorothy and Joseph Bandy,
and for my loving family,
Lynne, Lauren, and Joel

who experience with me
the whirlwind of God's grace.

I am grateful.

Foreword

You are about to embark on an incredible journey filled with metaphors and images that create an exciting experience in authentic Christianity. *Kicking Habits* is one of the best books in a long time. Every paragraph in this book is loaded with powerful imagery.

Tom Bandy is a gifted theologian, church consultant, pastor, master of metaphors, and trusted friend. I have seldom experienced as much theological depth and breadth and sociological acumen in a church consultant.

Kicking Habits describes a systematic approach to the organic transformation of congregations rather than a programmatic renewal and restructuring of institutional church life. It compares the Croquet game ethos of the Declining Church System—where people are required to jump through the hoops of political constraint—with the Jai Alai game ethos of the Thriving Church System, where all that matters is that the world is changed in the name of Jesus Christ through gifted, called, equipped, and sent people. Tom's uncanny visual graphs used to describe the two systems are alone worth the price of the book.

The genius of the book is Tom's use of pediatric and addictive metaphors to describe the condition of mainstream Protestantism. Mainstream Protestantism is addicted to many irrelevant "sacred cows." Addictive churches cannot be renewed. Like an addict, they must admit their addiction and be transformed. Their reason for being must be radically altered. "No programmatic change will overcome addiction. Only systemic change will overcome addiction."

This book is the call of a "sentinel" who is asking us to admit our addictions to institutional and programmatic educational systems and to embrace a ministry of transformation that finds its life and focus outside the institutional church among the "spiritual yearnings" of the public.

Tom uses the imaginary characters of Bob and Sally Public to caricature the differences between the Declining Church System and the Thriving

Church System. You'll laugh, cry, and celebrate as you follow their spiritual journey through the stale, debilitating ministry of the Reverend Enabler at St. Friendly-on-the-Hill Church to the life affirming, lay leadership of New Hope-in-the-Heart Church. You'll say "Aha!" when Tom writes about spiritual discovery versus the ecclesiastical informational highway, ecstasy versus just being happy, healing versus calling, being versus belonging or doing, resurrection versus the Cross, wholeness versus correctness, and environment versus ethics.

Bob and Sally Public are Tom's way of explaining why addicted mainstream churches have so much trouble finding volunteers, when the church down the street has so many volunteers. The educational, institutional, meeting-oriented model, instead of growing spiritual giants, drains Bob and Sally of everything spiritual, absorbing them as lifeless people who go around doing "church work" until they either burn out or become institutional junkies.

Tom contrasts the "belonging" emphasis of the Declining Church System with the "being" and "transforming" nature of the Thriving Church System. Whereas so many authors simply diagnose the disease, Tom offers a prescription for moving from the Declining system to the Thriving system. As we follow the spiritual journey of Bob and Sally Public, we learn that the primary issue in the transformation of systems is how the leaders relate to the question, What is it about our experience of Jesus Christ that this community cannot live without?

The number-one issue facing mainstream churches in the twenty-first century is how to say that Jesus Christ is Lord without being a bigot. Radical Christianity is all that transforms lives. There is room for only one addiction in the church—addiction to the grace of God through Jesus Christ. Anything less is nothing more than a club mentality that nurtures dues-paying members and sidesteps the publican and sinner on the streets. Tom hits this issue head-on in a way that will make your ears burn.

Tom attempts to jolt us out of our addictions into sobriety. He has the audacity to challenge the ability of the Cross to communicate with this postsecular society. In its place he begs us to focus on the "welcome relief" of the resurrection.

Warning. *Kicking Habits* may cause you to experience a transformation, not of your mind, but of your being! I dare you to read it to the very last sentence!

Bill Easum
Port Aransas, Texas

Contents

CONTENTS

Preface: The Challenge to "Thrive"

On the brink of the twenty-first century, the biggest surprise for declining North American denominations is *that there is a ferment of spirituality in the world!* The church has adjusted painfully to the fact that we are living in a post-Christendom age. The church has even begun to understand and accept that we are living in a postmodern age. The biggest shock, however, is that on the brink of the twenty-first century we are living in a *postsecular* age! The admission of Harvey Cox in the preface of his recent book *Fire from Heaven* (Addison-Wesley, 1995) should strike the church like a bombshell. The author of the landmark 1965 book *The Secular City,* who influenced two generations of church leadership to reassess church life and mission in the face of the relentless march of secularity, writes twenty years later: "Today it is secularity, not spirituality, that may be headed for extinction."

There is, indeed, a ferment of spiritual yearning that churches on both sides of the old polarities have failed to understand and engage. The twenty-first century is a postsecular age. Countless declining churches of North America (whether "conservative" and "evangelical," or "liberal" and "mainline") are failing to grasp that single essential fact. They still function as if they were defending a doctrinally pure heritage against the rising tide of atheism; as if they were preserving the last example of healthy community life in the midst of a violent, anonymous, and selfish society; as if they were proclaiming the last call for true morality and correct ideology into the raging storm of materialism, capitalism, and self-interest.

It is not merely that the church placed itself in a confrontational mode with society, it also accepted the reality that it was losing the confrontation. In the paradigm of *The Secular City,* church decline verified our religious identity. "If we are declining, we must be on the right track!"

11

Yet there is a new paradigm emerging. It recognizes the ferment of spiritual yearning among the public and has engaged that yearning in vigorous conversation. Growing numbers of thriving churches have managed to break loose from old assumptions, liberating themselves from chronic, self-destructive behavior patterns, to discover a whole new life.

I always want to use the word *growth* in connection with these churches, but the word has come to have negative connotations in the ethos of "the Secular City." People seem to understand *growth* as an industrial metaphor. It refers to numbers and statistics. It describes the number of units stored in the warehouse, or the number of widgets produced in the factory. Such an understanding of *growth* does not fit the church. I use the word *growth* as a *pediatric* metaphor. It refers to the healthy development of a child. It describes the expansion of activity and interest of a living organism. "Growth" occurs when a living organism truly "thrives."

For example, within weeks of the birth of our first child, our family physician began to become alarmed. She regularly compared the height, weight, and physical development of our infant daughter to charts tracing typical development. Our daughter was always lighter, shorter, smaller, and generally "atypical." We were worried. In the language of the pediatricians, our little girl was "failing to thrive." After several months of this, our family physician sent us to the famous "Sick Children's Hospital" in Toronto. Expert pediatricians used even more sophisticated diagnostic tools to examine our daughter. We sat in the waiting room and worried even more. At last, the chief pediatrician came into the room. She had a big smile on her face. "Congratulations, Mr. and Mrs. Bandy!" she said. "After extensive tests we have determined that your daughter *is not failing to thrive . . . she is naturally petite!*"

Thriving congregations described in this book do not have to be big. They may be petite or small. They may be any number of sizes, and this characteristic is often influenced by the demographic realities of the population.

Large, small, or in-between, this new breed of church that is emerging on the brink of the twenty-first century is engaged with the public in a new way. They do not see themselves as "prophets" in confrontation with society. They see themselves as "sentinels" sharing a vision that sustains and nurtures new life. Even in regions where the population is declining, they are in vigorous conversation with the fastest-growing segment of that population, namely, the spiritually yearning and institutionally unhappy public.

A "Thriving Church," no matter what size, is doing four things.

1. *They are increasing the participation of the public in church life.* Membership statistics are irrelevant to them. They are busy designing a multitude of ways in which the spiritually yearning, institutionally unhappy public can "connect" with some aspect of church life that helps them address their spiritual yearning.

2. *They are deepening the spirituality of adults, both within the church, and beyond in the community.* Doctrinal or dogmatic agreement is unimportant. They are busy coaching adults (and yes, youth and children) to explore their experiences of God with integrity, profundity, and self-discipline.

3. *They are multiplying the opportunities for discipleship.* Institutional mission agendas are abandoned. They are busy helping people discern their gifts and callings, training them with necessary skills, and then releasing them into hands-on, personal mission for which they have unbounded enthusiasm.

4. *They are maximizing the impact of the gospel on the world.* Mere philanthropy is not enough. They are busy combining justice advocacy and personal faith-sharing, through personal initiatives next door and across continents.

These thriving churches may be very large or naturally petite. Each will look uniquely different. Some may tend to appear more "liberal" and some more "conservative," although the diversity of people involved in the church makes such political, traditional categorizations difficult. Some churches may or may not hold certain doctrines, celebrate more or fewer sacraments, or associate with this or that public issue. Each thriving church has a unique character, but they all essentially do these four things.

The "pediatric" understanding of "growth" is vital for the church of the future because it helps us understand the real meaning of *change* in the transition of the church from the twentieth to the twenty-first centuries. For example, a pediatric nurse related to my congregation asked me to visit the hospital and see a newborn baby. Pleasant as that task would be, it seemed like a rather ordinary thing for a minister to do. I went. I watched. The baby was lovely. He appeared to be in the best of health, sleeping peacefully in the bassinet. A crowd of cooing adults gathered at the observation window, admiring this perfect child.

Within a few moments, however, the baby awakened. He began crying with a power I had never seen. Writhing, twisting, bending in agony, the baby screamed and screamed. The cooing crowd of adults drifted away, leaving us alone. The nurse who had invited me to the hospital appeared with a hypodermic needle. She injected the baby, who again became peaceful.

"The mother of this child was a heroin addict," the nurse explained to me. "The baby is an addict also—without knowing it or being responsible for it. We are slowly trying to ween the baby from the addiction. Only then will he truly thrive."

As a church consultant and church planter, this experience revealed for me a hidden depth to the challenge of church transformation. I had always believed in the power of "strategic planning." I had always assumed that what was needed to help a church really "thrive" was a winning combination of well-designed programs, well-chosen leadership, high-quality, format-ted, liturgical worship, and appropriately renovated and located facilities. If you could just show people, educate people, or explain to people the right course of action, they would undertake it. If you could just enlighten people about the process of planning and development, they would pursue it. If you could just learn from, and borrow, the experiences of a church "over there," and import it "over here," a church could be changed. If the denomination could just perfect the formula, thriving churches could be born over and over again. This was the world of "Church Renewal."

But already I had begun to suspect that "Church Renewal" was not preparing the church for the twenty-first century! "Winning combinations" in strategic planning seemed harder and harder to find. No amount of education or explanation seemed to motivate people to change. Even when a church began a good process, it always seemed to fail. Congregations would spend months writing a new Mission Statement—only to discover five years later that nothing had changed! The denominations planted new churches amid great celebration, only to discover five years later that the new church had peaked with 250 members, the minister was burning out, they were in financial trouble, and the neighborhood public didn't know (or care) that they were there.

The inability of declining churches to change has deeper, and more troubling, roots. *The declining church is an addict.* Churches are addicted to habitual, self-destructive behavior patterns *which they do not even recognize!* No matter how well-meaning, sincere, and spiritually sensitive the church is, members still cannot bring themselves to admit or see the inner addictions that dictate church life and mission. No matter how earnest or energetic they become to plan their future, they always seem to return to the same old ways. And perhaps the hardest lesson of all is this: Addictions are passed on from mother to child! New congregations are, in fact, rarely a beacon of hope for the denomination. They unconsciously perpetuate the same habitual, destructive behavior patterns of the parent.

Addiction is the great barrier to the church on the brink of the twenty-first century. The church cannot simply be renewed—it must be transformed. No programmatic change will overcome addiction. Only systemic change will overcome addiction. The real beacons of hope for any denomination are not the strategically planned new churches birthed by the institution, but the "maverick," "fringe," "adventurous" established churches that have the courage to travel a radically new path.

Although the new generation of "thriving churches" is very diverse, they are almost always in tension with their parent denominations or sponsoring bodies. Moreover, while their life and mission will vary enormously, it is possible to trace common patterns and purposes. They may not share the same programs, but they do operate within a distinct *system* of church life. They have overcome the addictions that beset the whole system of past church life, in order to live with new health in an entirely new system of church life.

Unless declining churches are willing to confront the depths of their systemic addictions, they learn very little from observing thriving church life. For example, in the first flush of enthusiasm, local church leaders simply try to memorize every detail of a specific thriving church and reproduce it in their own situation. Often the radical change is initially received with great excitement, and there is a short-term spurt in congregational energy and community participation. The response to every new issue is to recycle "how they did it over there." Yet it is impossible simply to reproduce the experience of one regional context in another local situation. Eventually the questions and issues that arise in one's own situation will demand a depth of creativity and a richness of vision that is unique and distinct. In such a crisis of creativity, when only originality will do, the church unconsciously returns to its old habits, and repeats its addictions. In this case, the learnings from the thriving church are like the seeds Jesus describes, which land on rocky soil and spring up quickly. Yet when the realities of life in their situation bear down upon them, habitual responses take over, and their efforts for church transformation wither (Matt. 13:5-6).

Or for example, with greater caution and deliberation local church leaders selectively "borrow" and "adapt" programs, ideas, or methods from a specific thriving church for their own situation. Again, for a time the local church may experience a renewal of life, often among the youth, singles, young mothers, or some other target group in the community which previously had not been well integrated into the mission of the church. What they experience, however, is short-term renewal, rather than long-term transformation. The system of their local church life remains essentially unchanged. They remain addicted to policies, structures, assumptions, or methods that have no place in the thriving church that has been their mentor. These addictions eventually choke the new life of the church, even as the seeds sown among thorns are gradually overwhelmed (Matt. 13:7).

The consequences of these false starts are severe. Stress, conflict, and confusion beset congregational life. The congregation responds to the inevitable budget crises that always accompany church transformations, not with prayer, perseverance, and vision, but with acrimony and recrimination. Often old traditions and authorities return with the sevenfold vengeance that Jesus described, leaving the church worse off than before (Matt. 12:43-45). The participation of the new target groups from the community fades again, this time leaving behind a cynicism any church in the community will for years find hard to overcome. Finally, and most sadly, the situation may lead to the departure of the ordained ministry leader and key lay leaders.

The whole purpose of this book is to avoid these false starts, and their consequences, so that the learnings from thriving churches can fall upon "good soil" to bring forth abundant fruit for the long-term life of the local congregation. I find that four things are needed.

First, the people of God need to capture (or be captured by!) the *Vision*. Before they study any of the details of thriving church life, and before they try to borrow, adapt, or devise new ideas for their own situation, they need a concrete image that embodies the *Vision* that motivates and guides them. The uniqueness of their own situation will call forth creativity in method and program for which there will be no existing pattern to imitate. The first, and greatest, difficulty church people have is to grasp some initial image of what in heaven's name thriving churches are *talking* about and *aiming* to accomplish.

Second, people need to understand *Systemic Change*. Instead of inserting pieces of a new paradigm into the system of the old program church, they need to perceive how the entire *system* of church life (leadership, organization, stewardship, finance, worship, mission, etc.) needs to be radically changed. Transformation of worship, for example, is interconnected with transformation in leadership expectations, in Christian education strategies, in property management, and all other facets of church life. The church is not a collection of programs, but an organic whole, and people must grasp the larger picture of how the whole system succeeds or fails.

Third, people need to identify the *Key Corners* their congregation must turn in order to thrive in the twenty-first century. This is not a matter of tactics, but of strategy; it is not a matter of program, but attitude. Thriving congregations may actually do many different things, and initiate any number of unique ventures. Their programmatic direction will largely depend on local needs and dreams, and the particular set of gifted people with whom God has blessed any given place. They will have diverse "missions." Nevertheless, they will have certain key attitudes and strategies which they hold in common.

Fourth, people need to *Plan for Stress*. This is a whole new, blossoming paradigm of what it means to be a "church." It is as if a seed from the first century of the Christian Era had been trapped in amber and preserved through all the mutations and changes of 2,000 years, and then released and planted again. It both resembles all species and is radically different from all species. In the same way, both traditionally "mainstream" and "liberal," and traditionally "evangelical" and "pentecostal," churches will have trouble understanding and living the new paradigm. Transition will be stressful, but thriving churches have learned that you can plan for it, address it in stages, and not be overwhelmed by it.

Church transformation is the great task for the church of our time. It is the hope of victory over the destructive addictions which rob our church life of meaning and our church mission of relevance. Perhaps our choice at the end of the twentieth century is similar to the choice of the faithful from the first century.

On the one hand, we can choose to be the "kin of Qumran." We can be the perpetual adversaries of culture. We can retreat into the wilderness, not because we have been pushed there, but because we have chosen to live there. We can recruit the few who agree with us, but intentionally remain the "righteous remnant" of the doctrinally pure or politically correct "priests" and "prophets" of an elder time. We can record our predictions on parchment or computer chips, so that one day some stray shepherd boy will throw a stone into our former cave and discover the documents which declare to a puzzled public "We told you so!"

On the other hand, we can choose to be the apostles of a new age. We can be in a vigorous conversation with the yearning public of our day, learning and sharing together. We can relocate into the coffee shops and public places of our day, not because we have been manipulated there, but because we have chosen to live there. We can welcome the many who also share transforming experiences of God, and help them discover the meaning of an ever-deepening mystery—we can be the sentinels of a future time. We can leave a trail of healing in a hurting world, making sense out of those unsettling words of Paul:

> I have become all things to all people, that I might by all means [rescue] some.
>
> (1 Cor. 9:22)

The Church Addiction Test

Get a grip on your hidden institutional addictions! Score your anxiety in response to each of the "Top 20 Shocking Truths Thriving Churches Have Learned." Then turn the page to learn the positive discoveries thriving churches have made, and identify those areas where you will find the greatest difficulties or best opportunities for church transformation.

Top 20 Shocking Truths Thriving Churches Have Learned

No Anxiety							High Anxiety		
1	2	3	4	5	6	7	8	9	10

1. The youth are *not* the future of your church! _____

2. Nobody cares about the mere presence of God! _____

3. "Friendly churches" are the dinosaurs of the twenty-first century! _____

4. "Good enough" is just *not* good enough! _____

5. Most people don't like organ music! _____

6. Debt freedom *always* leads to church decline! _____

7. Consensus management *kills* churches! _____

8. It does *not matter* what people *know* following the service! _____

9. It is *not* the pastor's job to visit the hospitals! _____

10. Few lay leaders have *any business* managing the church! _____

11. Church membership is *unimportant!* _____

12. If you want action, *never* form a committee! _____

13. Self-sacrifice is the *wrong* message! _____

14. God and the Holy Spirit are *not enough* for the coffee shop public! _____

15. Church insiders are the *least able* to predict the church's future! _____

16. Sunday school is *no longer* the cornerstone of Christian education! _____

17. Finance committees *should not* talk about money! _____

18. *Nobody has time* to hold church offices! _____

19. Strategic planning is *overrated!* _____

20. When it comes to mission, if you can say it all with words, *you've missed the point!* _____

Top 20 Positive Discoveries Thriving Churches Have Made

Compare these top 20 positive discoveries with the foregoing shocking truths that reveal your institutional church addictions. Then discern your areas of greatest difficulty or opportunity for church transformation.

1. *Transformed adults (ages 18-40) are the future of your church.*
   Adults who are changed, gifted, called, and equipped will take care of the kids—and everything else!

2. *Everybody wants to be touched by the healing power of God.*
   The publics of North America are desperate to be changed, different, and liberated from their hurts and addictions.

3. *Churches that provide multiple opportunities for intimacy are the new "species."*
People want to go beyond the coffee urn to bare their souls with a deeply trusted few.

4. *God expects every Christian to be on a constant crusade for excellence.*
Training one's God-given gifts to a high standard of performance is both fulfilling and effective.

5. *Most people like contemporary music with strong melody and lots of rhythm.*
Percussion, guitar, creative instrumentations, and small group ensembles get people's attention.

6. *Sound debt management is the key to thriving church development.*
People multiply their investments in clearly beneficial missions and are motivated to assume the debts of mission-driven institutions.

7. *Streamlined, high-trust organizations grow churches.*
Church management is best done by a trusted, gifted, and equipped few.

8. *What matters most of all is how people feel following the worship service.*
People want to "feel better" or "feel healthier" for worship, and be motivated to learn and serve through the week.

9. *It is the pastoral leader's job to train gifted laity in pastoral care.*
Clergy are trainers, motivators, and visionaries who equip others to do ministries.

10. *It is the volunteers' business to actually do ministry.*
Every layperson is called to discover and exercise the spiritual gifts God has given.

11. *Participation in any aspect of congregational life and mission is everything.*
Hands-on mission work and involvement in ministry is more meaningful than mere belonging.

12. *If you want action, find a gifted and called individual and turn that person loose.*
Trained laity, who are free to take initiative, will find whatever help they need.

13. *Self-affirmation is the right message.*
People seeking self-worth give generously to express and celebrate their inner value.

14. *Christ is that revelation of the Trinity which directly addresses transformation.*
The church best engages the public when they talk about their experience of Jesus Christ.

15. *People on the fringe of church life are key to discerning the future.*
Biblical visions are most often perceived by those who have been marginalized.

16. *Small groups are the cornerstone of Christian education.*
Groups in any configuration, meeting during the week in homes, promote Christian growth.

17. *Finance and administration leaders talk mostly about mission.*
Church boards only exist to empower people to walk in mission with the risen Lord.

18. *People make time to deepen self-awareness and exercise spiritual gifts.*
In the rat race of daily life, people will take the time to do things that are really meaningful.

19. *The anticipation of the unpredictable is the art of thriving church life.*
Spontaneity, flexibility, and planned stress management are part of authentic visions.

20. *Motivating visions are always a "Song in the Heart."*
They are best shared without words, to get the blood of church participants and utter strangers pounding.

Adding Up Your Addictions and Counting Your Opportunities

Add your scores in each of the following areas. Higher numbers indicate areas where you will find it difficult to understand or implement change. Lower numbers indicate possible "entry points" to initiate church transformation. *Remember that the statements overlap, because from one direction or another, sooner or later, transformation touches the whole system of church life.*

Organization and Structure
    Statements 7, 12, 15, 18 total: _____

Worship and Spirituality
    Statements 2, 5, 8, 13 total: _____

Vision and Systemic Clarity
    Statements 1, 11, 14, 20 total: _____

Leadership Expectations
    Statements 4, 9, 10, 19 total: _____

Education and Nurture
    Statements 1, 3, 11, 16 total: _____

Stewardship
    Statements 6, 13, 17, 18 total: _____

Chapter 1

Discerning the Spirit

Distinguishing Between Authentic Calls and Destructive Addictions

The Basic Problem

It is no secret that church transformation on the brink of a new millennium faces many hurdles. No sooner has a congregation leaped over one barrier than they encounter another. The real hurdle that causes church developments to stumble, however, is not about finance, aging property, or diminishing volunteers; it is not even about articulate mission statements. Even before a congregation confronts the need for a mission statement—and long before it must tackle issues of finance, property, and leadership—the congregation must have a *vision.*

The difficulty with perceiving a *vision,* is that too often the congregation is unable to discern between an authentic calling of Jesus Christ, and its abiding addictions to past ideals, forms, and procedures. *Addiction* is the right word. Just as an alcoholic, smoker, or drug abuser chronically denies the destructive impact of certain habitual behavior patterns, so also congregations simply cannot "see" that the demise of their congregational health is directly connected to their dogged and misplaced loyalty to the "sacred cows" of former ideals, forms, or procedures. Just as an addict dimly perceives the truth, but then rationalizes that a "gradual" change in the behavior pattern will "eventually" lead to freedom and health, so also many congregations only pretend to transform their church. They "play" with new mission statements, with restructuring the official board, or with experiments in worship, allowing these exercises in futility to deceive their constituency into thinking a genuinely authentic *vision* has replaced their destructive addictions. "We'll be really different—next year!"

The publics of North America, of course, are not stupid. They know an addict when they see one, and they go and get their religion someplace else.

Spiritual Gifts

The spiritual gift to "discern between spirits" has fallen on hard times at the end of the twentieth century. Before we can know what to do about it, it may be helpful to know how it happened, and, more important, how it happens among mainstream churches in North America.

The earliest Christians organized congregational life into nine "charisms" or spiritual gifts. Paul listed them as "wisdom," "knowledge," "faith," "healing," "miracle working," "prophecy," "tongues," "interpretation of tongues," and "discernment of spirits" (1 Cor. 12:7-11). Knowing how fractious egocentric Christians can be, Paul urged that the gifts be evaluated and exercised using the "more excellent way of love" (meaning especially patience, kindness, and humility).

As the church became institutionalized, "charisms" were replaced by "offices." Presumably, "elders" or "presbyters" would be assumed to be gifted in wisdom, knowledge, and interpreting the faith; "deacons" would be gifted in healing and miracle working for personal and social change; "prophets" would be gifted in anticipating the consequences of present folly; and "members" would be gifted with ecstasies and their meaning. "Discernment of spirits," however, seems to have been reserved for the apostles themselves, and, with their deaths, the discernment fades.

The "mainstream" Protestant church of the postwar twentieth century, in a fervor of minority consciousness and distrust of institutional leadership, has carried the process farther. "Charisms" that were formerly replaced by "offices," are now replaced in our time by "standing committees." The nine spiritual gifts may now be divided among multiple bureaucracies, but the peculiar gift of "discerning spirits" is left to the consensus of the congregation. This is a profound moment in the life of the church. For the first time, *vision* of the authentic call of Jesus Christ becomes the task of a group, which then requires allegiance from individuals, rather than being the task of an individual, who then shares the vision with the group.

Assigning the "discernment of spirits" to group process, rather than to individual inspiration, marks a significant turning point in congregational life. The very fractious, egocentric spirit, identified by Paul long ago, remains active today, but the resolution offered by the postwar twentieth-century church is not the way of love, but the way of perpetual consultation, general church meetings, and popular vote. It is no accident that churches today spend enormous energy writing consensus "mission statements" that change nothing, and fail to be gripped by motivating visions from vision champions that can change everything.

Since the late 1960s, congregations of mainstream churches in North America have tended to assume that the "charism" of "discerning between spirits" can be experienced through layers of accountable government, due process, parliamentary procedure, and the eventual consensus of the people. Trust, personal initiative, spontaneity, and the inbreaking of God are verbally praised, but structurally discouraged, in an effort to enforce whatever is "politically correct" or "loyal to our heritage."

Again, the publics of North America are not stupid. They perceive that the expectation that a congregation can be gripped by a vision of church transformation, *through consensus,* is like expecting an alcoholic to be gripped by a vision of health through consultations with his drinking buddies at the local bar. It's possible, but unlikely.

Institutional Addictions

What are some of the destructive addictions which masquerade as authentic calls of Jesus Christ? Here are eight examples.

The Addiction to Vision by Committee. This is the assumption that visions come from inside the church, at the top of the hierarchy, to an officially designated committee. The committee goes away on retreat, collectively defines the institutional vision, and returns to inform the rest of the people about the direction of God's call. The vision becomes a "construction," rather than a "revelation." It is notable more for its continuity with the past, than for its originality toward the future.

The authentic call of Christ from the experience of the earliest church would be *revealed.* The revelation would be to an *individual.* The individual would almost always be *from the fringes or margins of institutional life.* The vision would be notable for its discontinuity with the past and its *originality for the future.* The authentic "charism" of discernment is given to those farthest from the controlling center of institutional life.

The Addiction to Mission by Task Group. This is the assumption that mission can best be accomplished by elected or appointed representatives who work in behalf of congregations, but who are not integrated with a specific congregational life. It is the assumption that congregations pay for mission, task groups plan the mission, and professional experts do the mission. Mission becomes an activity, not of the congregation, but of "salaried accountable staff," "higher courts," "advocacy groups," "agencies," or "institutions." As a result, the social service network expands, while the congregation declines.

The authentic call of Christ from the experience of the earliest church would be for congregations themselves to finance, plan, and perform ministry using the "charisms" given the various members of the church. In this way, individuals experience a spiritual process to discover their gifts, an educational process to understand their personal calling, a training process to gain the skills to employ their gifts with integrity, and are then trusted, financed, and "turned loose" to do mission themselves. They do not "do good" because "it is a good thing to do," but they "do good" because "Jesus Christ has called me to do it," and because this church has equipped them to do it personally.

The Addiction to Redundant Management. This is the destructive strategy of multiple layers of overlapping decision making, all of which are designed to reduce risk, avoid controversy, and maintain control. This coincides with the addiction to nominating offices of the church. Church "offices" are abstractly defined, and people are recruited to manage ever smaller pieces of the mission agenda of the institution. As bureaucracy grows, the final manifestation of this addiction is the destructive behavior that postpones any action until nearly unanimous agreement has been achieved. The larger the circle of management becomes, the more insulated the institution is to change.

The authentic call of Christ from the experience of the earliest church is for a trusted, gifted few to give rapidly responsive leadership. The "charisms" of church life will always be risky, often controversial, and exercised through personal initiative. For this reason, the spiritual gift of love (including forgiveness for mistakes and a robust sense of humor) is foundational to all other gifts. Meanwhile, individuals are not recruited into the mission agenda of the institution, but into the fulfillment of their spiritual gifts.

The Addiction to Acceptable Mediocrity. This is the destructive attitude that accepts the best that ill-equipped people can offer. It measures the success of any program, ministry, or other initiative by focusing on "input." That is, the church celebrates the number of people involved, or the amount of production energy required, rather than the quality or the efficacy of the final result. The church values ministry in behalf of the institution that is "good enough," rather than ministry in the name of Jesus Christ that is excellent.

The authentic call of Christ from the experience of the earliest church is always a call to excellence. It measures the success of any program, ministry, or initiative by measuring "outcomes." The success of the "Gifts of the Spirit" (wisdom, knowledge, faith, healing, miracle working, prophecy, etc.) is revealed by the advance of the "Fruits of the Spirit" (love, joy, peace, patience, kindness, generosity, faithfulness, gentleness, and self-control—Gal. 5:22). The only acceptable ministry is excellent ministry, and the church motivates and trains people to attain it.

The Addiction to Debt Freedom. This is the assumption that debt is a debilitating evil, while debt freedom is a sign of spiritual success. Change only occurs with cash-in-hand. As the costs of property acquisition and renovation, and personnel salaries, go up, and as the needs of the community become ever more expensive to address, congregations are perpetually saving and never spending. They become tolerant of nonfunctional facilities and content with "Band-Aid" missions. They are debt-free, but filled with bored or inactive members. The addict is always saving "for a rainy day," without ever realizing that it is already raining outside.

The authentic call of Christ from the experience of the earliest church would be not to debt freedom, but to careful debt management. It is the result of the genuinely pentecostal experience of "selling all you have" to follow Christ. To be in debt is the norm for the church, rather than the curse of the church, because the congregation is perpetually risking its very life on the "charisms" given to the members. It assumes that the financial future of the church rests not on the pledging campaign to support countless standing committees and building repairs, but on the individual members exercising their spiritual gifts among the public, which in turn attracts new members who will also be gifted, educated, trained, and sent out.

The Addiction to Worship as Information Event. This is the assumption that social and personal change will happen through better education. People come into the presence of God in the belief that the good they wish to do, can be done, if only they are better informed about the meaning of biblical texts, the needs of the world, or the opportunities of service through their church. Hence, the worship service includes very scholarly preaching, didactic liturgies, children's messages for less articulate adults, prayers primarily designed to instruct the people praying, and code words used as a shorthand to express complex institutional data. There will also be a multitude of bulletin inserts.

The authentic call of Christ from the experience of the earliest church would be for worship to be a transformational and motivational event in which the "charisms" are revealed as gifts of grace that change how people behave. In this way, people come into the presence of God in the belief that they may know the good but cannot do the good, unless an encounter with God changes who they are and equips them to accomplish a specific goal. The worship motivates them to do the necessary learning and training the other six days of the week. The challenge to worship leadership is not to alleviate terminal boredom, but to channel all the ecstasy into productive mission.

The Addiction to Burdening the Youth with the Future of the Church. This is the assumption that the Sunday school is somehow the future of your church. Tremendous energy is given to education for children, and much anxiety is devoted to "reaching the youth." Such is the chronic panic over Sunday school staffing, and the periodic euphoria over a youth group that survives longer than six months, that the nominations process resembles an addict looking for a "fix." Of course, the real goal here is not the future pursuit of the gospel witness to a changing public, but the preservation of the heritage of the children's grandparents. The future must include the old property relatively unchanged and the old habits relatively untouched.

The authentic call of Christ from the experience of the earliest church would be to place the burden of the future on transformed adults. Church energy is given to help adults encounter God, discover their "charisms," and be educated and trained to use their gifts. These adults will educate the children, although the primary vehicle for this may not be Sunday morning in the basement of the church. Instead, it may be Saturday morning around the home kitchen table. These adults will also be educating children, not to preserve the heritage of their grandparents, but to discover and utilize their own spiritual gifts. The children of these adults grow up feeling free to change, tear down, or relocate the building, not because the past was evil, but because the ministry of Jesus Christ has moved forward to the future.

The Addiction to Parish Chaplaincies. This is the assumption that the role of congregational leaders is to take care of the folks on the inside, while busily telling the folks on the outside what they are doing wrong. Like an addict who can never get enough, leaders must visit, visit, visit, comforting every individual through all of life's stages. Or, like an addict with strong opinions about what is wrong with the world, and who seeks to deflect attention from what is wrong with herself, church leaders are always warning, criticizing, rebuking, or chastising the public. Memorializing the saints and rebuking the government, the parish "chaplaincy" attracts few newcomers. It is the "Righteous Remnant" in group therapy.

The authentic call of Christ from the experience of the earliest church would be for congregational leaders to be visionaries, trainers, and motivators. In this way, they help other individuals discover the "charisms" for healing or prophecy (plus other gifts as well), and then educate, train, and motivate them to use their gifts. It is the many gifted and trained members who do the caring for one another, and many other gifted and trained members who pursue a multitude of ministries in the community. Meanwhile, the public is beckoned neither to feel guilty, nor to enter therapy, but to experience a change of life that will give them new meaning and purpose. The leaders are "pastors," rather than "chaplains," who mediate the encounter with God and then freely release individuals to go wherever the Spirit leads them to exercise their gifts.

The Changing Spiritual Yearning of the Public

Destructive addictions can be very subtle. They warp every program of the church and are the real problems hidden behind a multitude of conflicts or crises. If church members have a chronic controversy or problem which they just cannot seem to solve, chances are the problem, however large or small, is but a symptom of an addiction. It is as if an otherwise praiseworthy individual has trouble keeping jobs, often quarrels with others, and suffers frequent indigestion. Career counseling, conflict management, and medical treatment don't help—and then one day someone awakens him to the truth. He is an alcoholic.

The crucial point is that *the awakening does not come from within the circle of addiction, but from beyond the circle of addiction.* A leader who is seeking to "discern between spirits" in order to distinguish between addictions and authentic callings, will waste her time if she stays within the sphere of church life. She must go beyond church life. She must go where the Holy Spirit goes. She must go among the publics of the community.

The "charism" to discern between spirits is not revealed to a leader in the context of church committees, church bureaucracies, or even church associations and prayer groups. It is revealed in the coffee shop, the sports arena, the workplace, or the community center. To those who patiently listen and observe, the changing spiritual yearning of the public will be revealed. This spiritual yearning will test the possible callings of the church for authenticity. If the calling is authentically of Christ, it will address the spiritual yearning of the public directly, clearly, and powerfully. On the other hand, if the "calling" being articulated by the church does *not* address the spiritual yearning of the public, then it is an addiction. It is an addiction to an agenda irrelevant to the movement of the Holy Spirit among the public, an agenda meaningful only to those within the inner circle of addiction.

The changing spiritual yearning of the public on the brink of the twenty-first century can be summarized in the categories of "being" and "doing." A descriptive "profile" follows.

Twentieth-Century Assumptions	**Twenty-first-Century Assumptions**
Being	Being
Who I Am	*Who I Can Become*
Union with Meaningful Traditions	*Freedom from Destructive Addictions*
Personal Loyalty	*Personal Integrity*
Making Sense of the World	*Appreciation of the Universe*
Personal History	*Personal Destiny*
Friendship	*Intimacy*
Happiness	*Ecstasy*
Christian Contact: "Following the Cross"	*Christian Contact:* "Walking with the Risen Lord"
Doing	Doing
Restructuring Society	*Transforming People*
Doing Good Because I Want to Be Good	*Doing Good Because I Am Good*
Committee Work	*Personal Work*
Holiness Through Righteousness	*Righteousness Through Holiness*
Life Should Be Moral	*Life Is Ironic*
No Funny Business	*Funny Business*
Confidence in Professionals	*Confidence in Grace*
Christian Contact: "Do It in Order to Be Like Christ."	*Christian Contact:* "Do It in Order to Be with Christ."

"Freda and Fred" and "Bob and Sally" are typical contrasts of the changing spiritual yearning of the public. Freda and Fred grew up in the sixties and seventies wondering who they were. Bob and Sally grew up in the eighties and nineties knowing who they are, but wondering what they can become. Freda and Fred buy name brand products and go every week to a "name brand" denominational church; Bob and Sally buy no-name products and go every Friday night to Alcoholics Anonymous. Freda and Fred have each been married only once, have researched their family tree over several generations, and eat supper watching CNN news. Bob and Sally have been married three times, speculate about reincarnation, and eat supper watching "Star Trek." Freda and Fred belong to three clubs and have innumerable friends who share their many interests. Bob and Sally belong to no clubs, and enjoy small groups of very close associates with whom they each readily share their innermost feelings. Freda and Fred have lived most of their lives together in the same neighborhood, and want to be contented and happy. Bob and Sally have each moved twelve times, delight in being restless, and are looking for high emotion and ecstasy.

Freda and Fred represent a context of spiritual yearning the church once addressed. They take civic responsibility very seriously, and serve on a community task force to combat racism. Bob and Sally represent a context of spiritual yearning that Freda and Fred cannot understand. They are cynical of politicians, and more interested in befriending the Vietnamese family across the street. Freda and Fred fight for fair housing, feeling chronically guilty that they themselves live so well. Bob and Sally take hammers in hand to help build houses as participants in Habitats for Humanity, in celebration of their conviction (born of several years in psychotherapy) that they are each "O.K." Freda and Fred know parliamentary procedure and represent their church at denominational meetings. Bob and Sally hate parliamentary procedure and consider denominational meetings a complete waste of time.

Deep in their hearts, Freda and Fred believe there is an answer for every question, and that life should make sense. They take life and religion very seriously, and their humor is always in good taste. They believe in their doctor, their lawyer, and their minister. Bob and Sally, on the other hand, gave up believing that life makes sense long ago. Life is always ironic, and often unjust. They don't take life or religion too seriously, and their humor is often in bad taste. They have little confidence in experts, but they always look forward to pleasant surprises and believe that "things will come out all right in the end." Freda and Fred are always trying to imitate Christ. When one of them dies, the church will call them a "saint." Bob and Sally want to be "with" a Higher Power on an hourly basis. When one of them dies, friends will call them a "seeker."

Facing the Truth

The "charism" to discern between spirits is similar in nature to the ability to distinguish between "the speck in your brother's or sister's eye" and "the log in your own eye." It is relatively easy for the church leadership generation trained in the 1970s and 1980s to criticize the church leadership generation of the 1950s, for their addictions to hierarchy, sexism, black Geneva preaching robes, and complex truths. It is much more difficult for congregational leaders today to acknowledge their own addictions to bureaucracy, trendiness, white cassock albs, and complex feelings. It is easier to criticize the meaningless jargon of a previous generation, than to acknowledge the meaningless jargon in one's own generation. Just as the removal of the log from one's own eye depends upon the wisdom and action of someone other than oneself to do the removal, so also liberation from destructive addictions within the church depends upon interaction with the public beyond the church.

The changing spiritual yearning of the public will test the authenticity of the "callings" to which the church gives energy. If the "callings" to which the church gives energy only lead people to

friendship,
happiness,
and
heritage,

then the church is most likely only repeating destructive addictions from the past. It is addressing the spiritual yearnings of those people already inside the institutional church. It is not that these yearnings have no legitimacy in themselves. Freda and Fred have places in the Body of Christ, too. The addiction is that such yearnings cannot be legitimately imposed on others. On the other hand, if the "callings" to which the church gives energy lead people to

intimacy,
ecstasy,
and
destiny,

then the church is most likely perceiving an authentic calling of Christ. God calls the church *into the public,* not into its own world. Churches oriented around friendliness, happiness, and heritage tend to deceive themselves into thinking that they are faith communities inviting and open to public participation—and they "just can't understand" why nobody comes. Churches oriented around intimacy, ecstasy, and destiny accept the spiritual reality that *their* tastes, interests, and talents are *secondary* to the development of their spiritual gifts. The truth is that "gifts" are intended—not for "keeping"—but for "giving." If you are not addressing the spiritual yearnings of the public, just what do you think Christ does call you to do?

The most difficult thing an addict must do is admit it. Denial is a chronic condition of the local church, though that denial is often projected with anger onto the denominational or judicatory leaders. Congregations can go on retreats, establish visioning committees, restructure the Board, and direct truly sincere people to investigate the authenticity of their calling, *and still miss the truth.* Even when serious dialogue with the spiritual yearning of the public points toward their addictions, congregations may still respond, "No! It can't be!" or "Well, after all, the public are sinful and ideologically wayward, so why should we listen to them!"

The courage to admit addiction is the first sign of the "charism" to discern between spirits. With great respect for Bill W. and Dr. Bob, I have a rather fantastic image of congregations who have been blessed by Christ with the "charism" to discern between spirits. They gather together in presbytery, diocese, or conference, and one by one introduce themselves. "Hi! We're Bill and Ethel from St. Matthew's Church, and we're addicts." To this admission, the others respond, "Hi, Bill! Hi, Ethel!" The meeting begins with the twelve steps congregations might use to distinguish authentic callings from destructive addictions:

1. Admit we are powerless over our addictions, and that our institutions have become unmanageable.
2. Affirm that only a Higher Power greater than our congregation can restore us to sanity.
3. Decide to turn our corporate will and corporate lives over to the care of God.
4. Make a searching and fearless inventory of our congregational life.
5. Admit to God, to ourselves, and to the public the exact nature of our wrongs.

6. Affirm that we are entirely ready to have God remove these defects in our corporate character.
7. Humbly ask God to remove our shortcomings.
8. Make a list of all persons our corporate addictions have harmed, and be willing to make amends to them all.
9. Make direct amends whenever possible.
10. Continue a corporate discipline to distinguish between destructive addictions, and the changing calling of Jesus Christ, revealed in the changing spiritual yearnings of the public.
11. Seek to improve constant contact with God, praying only for knowledge of God's will and the power to carry that out.
12. Carry the message of reawakening to other congregations, and practice these principles in all our church life.

Only when this spiritual discipline has worked itself deep into the "bone marrow" of church life, will the church in fact be ready to talk about mission statements, new constitutions, or restructuring the Board. In such a climate of healing and listening, authentic visions of congregational life and mission will emerge. They will emerge, not because group process has created consensus, but because individual women and men of all ages have begun to stand up in ecstasy and dream dreams.

Part 1

THE SYSTEMS
OF CHURCH LIFE

Allow me to introduce you to "Bob and Sally Public." Their real names may be Boris, Juan, Said, Hung, or Takemura, and Mariska, Maria, Linh, or Zarpana. They may belong to any number of North American subcultures or "publics." They may be married, divorced, divorced for the third time, single, living together, parenting their own children, or parenting children from their present partner's past partnerships. They may be any age, at any economic level, and have any educational background. Whoever they may be, they share five things in common:

1. Bob and Sally are simultaneously bored and frantic.
2. Bob and Sally wrestle with low self-esteem and broken relationships.
3. Bob and Sally wish they had a better life without knowing what it would be.
4. Bob and Sally usually do not leave home Sunday mornings unless it is to play softball or buy the morning paper.
5. Bob and Sally live next door to you.

Bob and Sally represent the fastest-growing segment of the North American population. They are the "Gentiles" of the new millennium. They are the spiritually yearning, institutionally alienated public.

Bob and Sally have changed forever the meaning of that simple phrase "going to church." It used to mean an intention to attend worship an hour a week, and a commitment to support a charitable institution. In the new millennium, it means a yearning to experience God through the week, and a covenant to be involved in Christian mission.

Bob and Sally probably cannot accurately describe in advance what they are seeking in a church. They may only be "church shopping," and their "shopping list" may well not reflect the spiritual foods that in the end will truly satisfy and fulfill. Their list may include:

> "center aisle sanctuary"
> "good nursery"
> "low financial expectations"
> "friendly people"
> "nice minister"

but in the end they may well gain all of these things *and still drop out of the church.* It is the system of church life that will be crucial to Bob and Sally. It is the whole flow of spiritual experience that will be vital. It is the coherence and value of the whole movement from seeker to servant, and from healing to healer, that will hold them in the life of the church. Their initial shopping list will fade into secondary importance. What will determine their future participation is whether or not the church has helped them go deeper, soar higher, see farther, reach wider, and live better one day at a time.

Chapter 2

The Declining
Church System

Bob and Sally Public have come to St. Friendly-on-the-Hill Church with their young family. A lay greeter welcomes them as they enter the narthex, and provides them with directions to the coatracks and washrooms. The greeter also gives them "Newcomer Name Tags" and introduces them to other members of the church, and eventually, to the minister.

"Reverend," Sally says, "we're new in the neighborhood, and we would like to make friends in the community. We also want our kids to start learning Christian values in your Sunday school—and, oh yes!—our new baby has not been baptized."

"Fine, fine," replies the Reverend Enabler. "Here's a booklet about our church and denomination. There just happens to be a Baptism Class beginning this week for six sessions, so we can discuss it. Now let's introduce the kids to their Sunday school teacher, and then grab some coffee."

In due course, the kids are enrolled, the baby is baptized, and Bob and Sally become recognizable figures during coffee hour. Soon people know them by their first names. Before long speculation begins as to Sally's suitability for nursery care leadership, and Bob's potential for the Property Committee. (It turns out he is an electrician! Hooray!)

A year later Bob and Sally have "gone missing." It happened slowly. First they only appeared in worship every other week—then the kids began appearing in Sunday school every other week. Then less. Elders visitation reported how busy a dual career couple could be, and how hard it was to attend regularly with young children. They appeared again at Christmas— then the pledge was discovered to be in arrears.

"No, no," said Sally on the telephone with the church secretary. "There's no problem. We really love you folks. You're so friendly. Everything's fine—we're just so busy!" And yet, a year later, Bob and Sally have vanished into the spiritual fog.

Church decline is not a programmatic problem—it is a systemic problem. St. Friendly-on-the-Hill Church has tried all kinds of programmatic changes and improvements to "keep" Bob and Sally Public in the congregation. They created friendly greeters to meet them at the door! They posted signs all over the building to inform strangers where the washrooms and coatrooms were located! They created intergenerational worship services so that the family could stay together—and have a few laughs at the same time! They even paved the parking lot and built a drive-in canopy to allow Bob and Sally Public to unload their children from the minivan without getting wet! They have a new curriculum in Sunday school, a terrific membership training class, and new hymnbooks to supplement the old ones. Yet, despite all this, they are declining. Bob and Sally just don't "stick" with the church.

Again, the problem with St. Friendly-on-the-Hill Church is not programmatic. It is systemic. They unconsciously live within a church system that cumulatively fails to address the spiritual and cultural situation of Bob and Sally Public. The diagram of the declining church system describes the "Home Plate" of the St. Friendly-on-the-Hill Church system. That is to say, it describes the basic orientation, attitude, philosophy, and behavior pattern, which remains constant behind all the programmatic changes they initiate. It is this essential system of church experience and congregational mission that remains untouched by all the "improvements" and "perfections" of the church—and which is the real reason Bob and Sally disappear in the spiritual fog. Soon Bob and Sally will be on an "Inactive List." They will likely never be actually taken off the rolls of membership, but they will never really be involved—and their friends, relatives, and neighborhood associates will never attend. Let's discover why this church is systematically declining, even if Bob and Sally stick it out and stay awhile longer.

Enrolled

The initial mistake of St. Friendly-on-the-Hill Church is that it takes Bob and Sally at their word and assumes that they have come to church in order *to belong*. Church members assume that "belonging" to the institution is the vehicle through which Bob and Sally will discover profound religion. Therefore, they have greeted Bob and Sally personally, issued them name tags, called attention to their presence as strangers, and generally embarrassed them with all the attention.

DECLINING CHURCH
"All About Belonging"

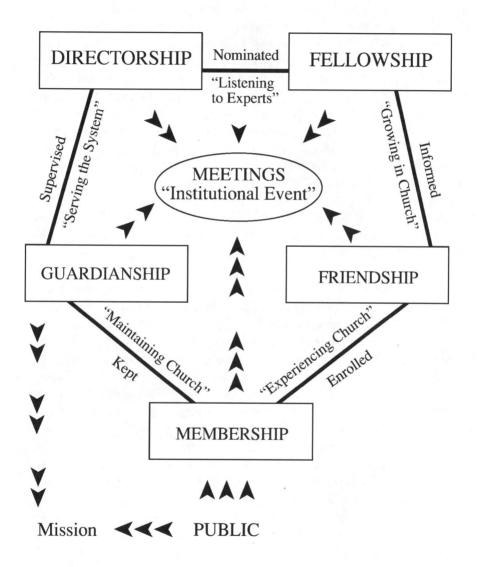

To involve them in the friendly in-group of the institutional church, the congregation has front-loaded all the educational expectations. Bob and Sally must go through "hoops and hurdles" of education. They attend baptism and membership classes. They are presented with a booklet to understand how the congregation and denomination are organized, the beliefs to which Bob and Sally will be asked to give assent, the structures of decision making in which Bob and Sally will need to participate, and the unified budget which Bob and Sally will feel obligated to support.

Just to enter church life, Bob and Sally will need to learn many things. They need to learn where they can park and cannot park. They need to learn where they can sit in the sanctuary, and where they dare not sit in the sanctuary. They will learn all the code words of the church. They will learn what a "narthex" is, what a "Gloria Patri" and a "doxology" are all about. They will learn when and how often the committees meet, how large the deficit is, who holds power in the congregation—and who *really* holds power in the congregation. They will also learn the limits beyond which the behavior of their children dare not go—and they will begin to perceive the denominational agenda toward which their time, energy, and money will be devoted.

All this they will be expected to learn very quickly in their church experience, if they hope to earn the friendliness of the folks in the church. The worship service itself will be an "informational" experience. The bulletin will contain from two to five pages of inserts listing the meetings, concerns, and announcements of church life. In some congregations, it will need to be stapled together. A tablet will be passed down the pews requiring Bob and Sally to register their attendance. They will soon learn when to stand and when to sit, which hymnbook or liturgical resource is intended by the abbreviations in the bulletin, and what the Christian year, liturgical colors, and strange clothing of the worship leaders are all supposed to mean.

In short, Bob and Sally have been "enrolled" in the institutional assimilation process of being the church. What they know about the church is all important, because without the knowledge of how to be a part of the institutional church culture, they will potentially embarrass themselves: standing when they should be sitting, confusing Advent and Lent, forgetting which committee does what, and mistakenly assuming certain people don't hold power when they really do. They will also fail to advance toward the inner circle of church life. That seemingly simple "friendliness" around the coffee urn following church, is in fact won by an educational process that is largely unconscious, but already exhausting. "Is it worth it?" Bob and

Sally are asking themselves deep in their hearts. Is the achievement of being able to converse with Elder Fred and Deacon Julie about community life, and the achievement of being able to joke with the pastor about "those crazy kids" during the children's story, really worth the intensive information assimilation that has taxed their minds?

Perhaps more important, Bob and Sally begin to wonder if it is worth the *time* they have invested so far. Notice that everything in this declining church requires *meetings*. Most often, these are *evening meetings*. Going to meetings is the method by which they gain needed information, and by which they are "tested" by the congregation to determine if they truly "own" the institutional ethos. For some congregations, the physical attendance of Bob and Sally in meetings is enough to convince them that they are truly "one of the family." For other congregations, the quality of Bob's and Sally's interaction in these meetings will be the measure of their acceptance. Do they have "crazy ideas"? Are they too aggressive? Do they accept the "rulings" of the patriarchs and matriarchs—and will they acquiesce when it is clear that they are in the minority?

Finally, if Bob and Sally stick it out, they come to know the liturgy, the parliamentary procedure, the organization, and the community customs of St. Friendly-on-the-Hill Church. Fellowship is their reward. They will sit solemnly and meditatively during the worship service, enduring the pre-children's-story anxiety of what on earth their six-year-old might say or do, celebrating the post-children's-story contentment knowing that embarrassment has been postponed for another week, and then break forth in smiles around the coffee urn greeting old friends. They are now ready to go deeper into the life and mission of the congregation.

Informed

"Going deeper" for adults in the declining church largely means more animated discussion about institutional church or community life around the coffee urn, and disciplined faith education for children and youth. The kids go to Sunday school. Indeed, the whole church is passionate about children's Sunday school. After all, aren't they the future of the church? In the declining church system, less than 1 percent of the adults are involved in any planned faith development or spirituality group during the week. Oh yes, they do attend meetings! The meetings begin with a rather benign prayer and sometimes include a reading from the lectionary passage for that week, but as soon as the conversation turns to intimate sharing or puzzled discussion about the Bible, the chairperson will always be ready to "call them back to their real purpose" and get on with the institutional agenda.

While the children go to Sunday school, the flow of information increases for Bob and Sally. Their "consciousness will be raised" regarding an increasing number of ethical or ideological issues. This information will be given to them through newsletters, special mailings, additional inserts in the worship bulletin, and, yes, additional evening meetings they will be encouraged to attend.

The declining church system may encourage information-sharing between the children in the Sunday school classes and the adults around the coffee urn. For example, the lectionary readings of the service may be integrated with the curriculum of the Sunday school. Again, adults may be encouraged to read some printed resource which is being used by the preacher to expound a text or a topic. The family will be encouraged to discuss the insights they have gained through their separate information-gathering experiences. Unfortunately, in the declining church system, there are few incentives and little training to enable this sharing to occur. It peaks around the family Sunday lunch table during grades 4-6, when the kids are in their most curious and conversational life stage, and then fades quickly.

The declining church assumes that the information itself will be sufficiently interesting to generate conversation at home. Unfortunately, the realities of today's social experience betray that assumption:

a. More than half the congregation are single, and will have no opportunity to discuss with any child the learnings of the Sunday school.
b. The couples among the remaining half of the congregation have seen their children leave home already.
c. Most families rarely eat meals together, and certainly not on weekends.
d. Parents of young children generally feel so confused about Christian faith and values themselves that they are uncomfortably helpless when their children do want to talk about the learnings from Sunday school.
e. Communication between parents and children regarding school ("public" or "church") is never about information sharing anyway, but always about problem solving.

In short, the assumption by the declining church that families will discuss religion at home, and that the primary purpose of such a conversation will be to clarify and reinforce beliefs and values in the children, has left Bob and Sally very uncomfortable. The energy they are investing to learn how to belong to the institutional church, just doesn't connect with the energy the kids are investing to learn basic beliefs and values. When Bob and Sally hear a question from their ten-year-old, they are motivated to reply, "Why don't you ask your Sunday school teacher (or minister) that question, Dear?"

Although Bob and Sally have small children, they have made friends with families and with teenagers in the congregation. In part this has been driven by the desperate need to find capable baby-sitters to allow Bob and Sally the freedom to attend those evening church meetings (among other things). The tales they hear from the teens fill them with anxiety.

The declining church system always has a "boom or bust" youth ministry. The youth groups are strong for about two years and then become almost nonexistent for several years. The trend in the declining church is that the periods of "bust" become longer, and the periods of "boom" become shorter. Occasionally the congregation can boast about their "youth program" to the community (and ecumenical colleagues), but more often they repeatedly lament the absence of youth. They may hire a part-time youth minister, but the results are most often disappointing. The teens either don't respond, or they respond too energetically, disconcerting and conflicting the church. Dismissal of the youth minister, alienation of the youth, and a longer period of "bust" follow.

The declining church always assumes that the solution to youth ministry is programmatic. If only they could get a good leader! If only they could find a great curriculum! If only they could renovate a room in the building for youth meetings! They fail to recognize that the solution to youth ministry, like the solution to decline in general, is systemic.

First, the number one reason youth groups fail is that the adults themselves are not involved in regular faith development groups through the week. Less than 1 percent of the declining church adults are involved. Many of the adults (even those who are members of the official board), attend only one in three worship services during the winter, and one in four worship services during the summer. If it is not important for adults, why should it be important for teens who are yearning to be adults?

Second, the real reason youth groups succeed in the declining church is that the right young men and young women are dating each other. It has little to do with curriculum, leadership, or private space (unless the youth room can be dimly lit). It has almost nothing to do with information sharing. Teens and young adults are primarily concerned with relationships (authentic friendship, intimacy, personal acceptance, and, yes, sexuality). If the youth meeting agenda cannot address the issues of relationships, or cannot be sabotaged or circumvented to address the issues of relationships, then the youth will not be interested. This is not to say that other topics of faith, justice, and living are not important, but that such topics will only be embraced enthusiastically if they are addressed in the broader matrix of relationship building. Indeed, it is no accident that the activities and topics most energetically pursued by youth groups will be those that are "relational" in character, rather than simply doctrinal or ideological.

Third, although the declining church constantly declares that "the youth are the future of the church," teenagers vigorously refuse to be burdened with the future of the church. They are not interested in perpetuating the heritage of the institution, and they are not motivated to assimilate "information" about the history, systematic theology, and ethical perspectives that shape the institutional church. In other words, although the declining church is all about belonging to the church, the teens are not in the least interested in belonging to the church. At first glance, they are interested in:

Sports! Youth groups thrive around organized, informal team sports that involve friendly competitiveness, fun, and opportunities to relate easily with newcomers.

Clubs! Youth groups thrive around clusters of special interest, no matter how "secular" those interests may be, which allow teens to explore their collective enthusiasms.

Music! Youth groups thrive when most of the time together is devoted to listening, performing, and experiencing contemporary music forms.

A deeper look will discover that teens have powerful and profound interests in spirituality, the supernatural, world religions, and personal faith experiences (often associated with health and healing). These will be explained more fully as we explore the Thriving Church System.

Finally, the "boom" or "bust" cycle of declining church youth ministries is characterized by the constant burnout of the adult leaders. Call them "supervisors," "counselors," or "advisors," these adults flourish for a time, suddenly vanish, and frequently disappear from church life as a whole while they recover from the experience. If the youth ministry fails, they know that they have disappointed the declining church at the point of its most vocal yearning. They will be criticized for poor leadership, inappropriate behavior, or nonmagnetic personalities. On the other hand, experience suggests that if they succeed, the ensuing tensions and conflicts within the congregation will require that they assume stressful roles of mediation, interpretation, and negotiation for which they were never equipped. They are torn between the institutional agenda of the congregation to train the next generation to perpetuate the glorious heritage of the church, and the dynamism of youth that shatters old forms.

The understanding of what it means to belong to the church has been deepening for Bob and Sally. They now participate in the annual stewardship visitation. Not only do they know more and more about the organization, mission, faith, and activities of the church, but they have also assimilated an understanding of the "dynamics" or "ethos"—the unspoken rules for community behavior. As they seek to move closer to the center of church life, they know precisely the operational deficit, and they are better able to weigh the risks and opportunities that surround their conversations and actions.

The coffee urn fellowship enables them to perceive one more reality of the declining church. There are not many single young adults in the fellowship. There are many in the outside world, but few within the church. The constant references to the "church family" begin to carry a deeper significance. The experience of marriage and children is central to the identity of the church. "Matchmaking" jokes may pursue those few young singles active in the church. Divorce or separation almost always leads to the disappearance of one or both of the adults from the fellowship. Adult socializing revolves around "couples clubs," groups of women who devote time to "wifely" tasks of preparing food and doing crafts, or groups of men who do "husbandly" tasks of consuming that food and renovating property. Bob and Sally learn that the fact that they are *together* is just as important to belonging in the church as their individual talents.

Bob and Sally have been accepted into the church community. Most people know them by sight, if not by name. They hold church envelopes, receive the church newsletter, attend church meetings, and seem relaxed and comfortable during coffee hour. They use institutional jargon and "code words" appropriately, worship at least twice a month, and interact reasonably with others. Congregational members have learned their occupations, perceived at least some of their main hobbies or interests, and mentally "located" them in the matrix of congregational talents and needs. They are now ready to move forward into the system of church life.

Nominated

Bob and Sally have noticed that the pressure to join various committees, groups, or projects has been increasing. The bureaucratic nature of the program church model (official board, executive, and multiple standing committees, and various ad hoc committees) requires that 20 to 25 percent of the congregation must be recruited to serve in various offices. These people will form the core group of volunteers who manage and direct church life.

Bob and Sally know that they have crossed a central threshold of belonging in the church, when a well-respected leader of the church approaches them during coffee hour, places a symbolic arm around their shoulders, and says: "Congratulations! You have been nominated to the official board!" It is a sign of respect, acceptance, and trust. It is also a sign that the inner circle of church life, represented by the nominations committee, is confident that they can offer new vitality to church life without changing the ethos, heritage, or basic identity of the congregation.

The pinnacle of congregational involvement is the experience of church management. Bob and Sally are not being asked to do ministry, but to manage ministry. The core volunteers of the congregation will devote between 60 and 100 hours a month, simply to attend meetings and manage the affairs of the congregation. Church management will include:

—giving or withholding permission for new projects and ideas;
—shaping and interpreting church policy;
—supervising the people who are doing ministry;
—raising money for other people doing mission or ministry;
—maintaining or improving property, equipment, or resources;
—recruiting and training new members into the life of the organization;
—monitoring the processes and procedures of church life.

The key vehicle through which Bob and Sally "belong" to the church will now shift its orientation away from the Sunday worship service, toward meetings of committees and official board. Church leaders may attend worship services only once a month, but they will never miss committee and board meetings. Church leaders may regularly disappear on holiday for two months in the winter and summer, but they never miss a congregational vote. For Bob and Sally, institutional meeting agendas now begin to replace spirituality as the center of church life.

Bob and Sally will be assigned to a committee which can best utilize their talents or occupational skills for the agenda of the institution. The committees will have carefully designed, "prescriptive" mandates, which will be occasionally reviewed and ratified by the congregational meeting. These mandates will "prescribe," or list, all the activities the committee can or must do. If Bob and Sally suggest any initiative that does not clearly appear on that list, the board will likely appoint an ad hoc committee to explore and recommend whether or not permission should be granted.

Church management in the declining church is not only hierarchical, but more significant, it is purposely redundant. Decisions will actually be made over and over again, as many as four times, by different management bodies, who will review and discuss the same information and the same proposal. Thus, a committee will recommend to the executive, who will recommend to the board, who will refer to an ad hoc committee, who will recommend back to the board, who may defer to a congregational meeting. The process is redundant in the belief that such consensus-building will identify and lower the potential risk of any idea or initiative. Action will be taken only if no one is upset, and only if the heritage of church life is not compromised.

The purpose of church management in the declining church system is "preservation." Bob and Sally belong to the organization. That membership, that "belonging," gives them meaning and purpose in life. The organization can be enhanced, of course, but it certainly must be preserved. If the character of the church is compromised, "belonging" will no longer be meaningful, people will leave, and the organization will collapse. Therefore, nothing Bob and Sally do in church management should cause anyone to leave. The withdrawal of people from church life, either through conflict or mere indifference, is always a sign of failure. It is always an incentive to "clamp down," "control the system," "bring it back to its roots," and generally work harder to articulate and preserve the heritage or ethos of the church, which, after all, motivated the people inside church life to join in the first place.

Oddly enough, the declining church has anticipated twenty-first-century business and politics in recognizing that true power lies in control of information. The ultimate impact of the hierarchical, redundant management strategy is not that it builds consensus, but that it controls information. Congregational annual meetings, sessions, or conferences in the declining church are notoriously dull, and usually poorly attended by anyone outside the inner circle of the hierarchy. Most people of the congregation recognize that information has been selectively disseminated, that recommendations have been checked at least four times and carefully orchestrated, and that the board is committed to the preservation of the institution. Indeed, heated debate in the annual meeting usually arises only if the congregation doubts the sincerity of the board's commitment to institutional preservation, or if "due process" has not been followed. The fact that annual meetings are dull and poorly attended verifies that the church is on course.

Bob and Sally enter a world in which discussion will be endless, but actual decisions few. Information will be carefully sifted and weighed, and compared with church life as it has been over the years. Sally will quickly learn that the congregation has always "done that before and it didn't work," as people refer to a fund of information to which they have fairly exclusive interpretative access. Bob will quickly learn that "this is the way we do or do not do things around here," as people refer to a complex organizational mythology which sets their assumptions and directions.

Bob and Sally will be asked to be official board members of the church. They are initially anxious that they have no clear sense of pastoral calling, nor any clear awareness of their spiritual gifts, but they are assured that their role will not be to do ministry, but to manage ministry. Their key responsibility as church leaders will be to communicate information. They will deliver newsletters; they will visit or telephone a list of members to pass on news of the monthly deficit, upcoming meetings or fellowship opportunities, or significant events of joy or sorrow; and they may occasionally make announcements in church, or read prepared statements about the mission of the denomination.

Bob and Sally fill a "liaison" role between the community, the congregation, the board, and the minister. They will listen to ideas, concerns, or complaints, and forward them to the appropriate committee or officer, or to the minister or pastor of the church. Their sense of priority and appropriateness will significantly influence who does or does not receive ministry, what does or does not receive funding, and which information receives the greatest attention.

The role of the communicator is not only to ensure that information is shared but that the "right" information is shared. Correct perspectives or interpretations will be important. There will be some matters, perhaps related to finance or personnel, which can only be shared with reserve, or not at all. Since many people never fully understand the complexities of the committee structure, committee mandates, or decision-making process, Bob and Sally become authorities for the people on the leaders' visitation lists. They are numbered among those who are knowledgeable about church life, who can guide people as needed through the complexities of the organization. Their opinion about all matters of the church carries a new weight. After all, they are in the inner circle of church life—surely, they should *know* what is best!

Bob and Sally, in company with other members of the board, begin to feel increasingly uncomfortable. First, their immersion in literally every decision and every issue in congregational life, forces them to attend even more meetings, and offers little extra time to ponder deeper issues of long-range strategy. Second, the management of ministry offers them little opportunity to experience personally and appreciate the details of what ministry is all about. Third, they find themselves in a seemingly impossible dilemma, namely, that it is more important to the church to keep people than to welcome people. Bob and Sally begin to experience a friction with the staff, lay colleagues, and the public that they never knew before. They really don't have a vision for the long-range future of the church; they don't really understand how the minister spends her or his time; and they can't reconcile the seeming friendliness of the congregation with the obvious fact that the public by and large is not interested in the church.

Since Bob and Sally do not do ministry, but manage others who do ministry, the natural solution to these dilemmas is to invite experts to tell the official board what to do. These experts will come from within the denomination, or from social service, business, and artistic groups in the community. The degree of helplessness in the official board will usually determine the size of the honorarium paid to these experts. The higher the anxiety, the more ready they will be to pay large fees or salaries. The list of consultations will include:

a. Youth ministry: How do we "bring in" the youth?
b. Fund-raising: How do we cope with our growing deficit?
c. Conflict management: How do we resolve disputes with our staff?
d. Recruitment: How do we increase membership in the organization?

There may be additional consultations with experts regarding property renovation, Sunday school curriculum, or choir music.

The experts who have the most impact on the declining church board, are always those with the most practical tips to resolve the issues here named. The declining church board is only interested in *programmatic* change. It is never interested in *systemic* change. In other words, board members want the experts to give them tips, keys, ideas, or programs that will help the existing *system* of church life work more effectively. It is always best that the tips or programs not cost too much *financially,* but it is crucial that the tips or programs not cost too much *psychologically.* The basic system of the church must be preserved.

Bob and Sally find that they spend a great deal of energy restructuring the board. The constitution is rewritten, the committee mandates are redefined, staff job descriptions are rewritten to lower apparent "hierarchical" distinctions, and budgets are redrawn. They spend months painstakingly building a new mission statement through the various levels of bureaucracy in the church. Each of these achievements is celebrated with great fanfare in the congregation—but two years later it is apparent that nothing has really changed. Those outside the inner circle of the official board do not feel that the church is any different, and, for many, that is a welcome relief. Programs come and go, but the essential issues, problems, and dilemmas remain. Decline continues unabated.

Bob and Sally, along with the rest of the board, have tried every programmatic trick in the book to invite the interest of the public and recruit new members into the church. They even created an evangelism committee, which sponsored community social events, increased parking, invested more money in advertising, and placed signs all around the building. However, the evangelism committee members discovered that they were far more articulate about their organization's structure than they were about their individual faith, and that they were far more sensitive to their institution's needs than they were to the spiritual yearning of the public. Eventually the evangelism committee was merged with the membership committee.

Bob and Sally may now be on the brink of burnout. Even after countless meetings and management changes, the beloved church in which their belonging means so much, continues to decline. They may rotate to different committees; or they may finish their term of office and take a sabbatical leave from leadership (and church attendance); or they may place the blame on society. This last option requires some explanation.

Bob and Sally become annoyed with the community beyond the church doors. They begin to believe that the publics of the community are not interested in religious matters at all. They begin to think that people "out there" are spiritually indifferent, materialistic, lazy, and godless. Despite every invitation, they refuse to "come to church." The rapidly growing segment of the population that seemingly prefers softball, coffee shops, or sleeping in, to church attendance, must be either doctrinally "sinful" or ideologically "incorrect." Bob and Sally do not wish to be snobs. They would not describe themselves as elitist. Indeed, they continue to take pride in the friendliness of their congregation. Nevertheless, they begin to understand themselves to be a kind of "righteous remnant" in a sinful world. They are different from the people outside. Their church decline is but a sign of the growing spiritual darkness that is overtaking the community.

Supervised

If Bob and Sally have not burned out yet with too many meetings and administration, they continue to gain seniority in church management, and eventually move to the innermost circle of control. They join the finance committee, the personnel committee, the trustees, or the monitoring committee supervising the clergy. It happens so naturally in the system, that neither Bob nor Sally realizes that another corner of church involvement has been turned.

The most fundamental task of lay leadership in the declining church system is to raise money, in order to pay somebody else to do ministry and mission. Bob and Sally find themselves monitoring the growing deficit: organizing rummage sales and church bazaars, marketing chocolate and greeting cards, promoting special offerings to denominational projects, and canvassing the congregation for higher annual pledges. The cynic might accuse Bob and Sally of simply trying to maintain the property, but this is unfair to their real purpose. They are simply trying to maintain an organization through which selected, trained experts can do ministry and mission.

The largest portion of money they help raise will finance staff salaries. They will also raise money which, in combination with other denominational or government funding, will finance the salaries of assorted social workers, counselors, advocates, and missionaries. Finally, the work of selected volunteers will be subsidized (Sunday school teachers, group leaders, social service workers, and others). Bob and Sally do not find fund-raising to be easy. They are not trained to do it. They are not aware of possessing any particular spiritual gift to do it. They would not really describe the task as a "calling." It is a necessary task to sustain the institution in which their "belonging" is so meaningful.

Fund-raising leads Bob and Sally to become supervisors. In their "heart of hearts," Bob and Sally think: "If I have spent all this energy raising money, and the poor church people have given so sacrificially, then we had better make sure that we get the most ministry out of every penny we raised." I use the word "penny" advisedly. The declining church system quantifies everything in small amounts. The board will debate for hours decisions regarding photocopying that may ultimately make only about a hundred dollars difference to the budget. More important, efficient time management will become an ever-larger issue in the supervision of support staff. Secretaries and custodians will be asked to squeeze more work into less time, and do quality work with cheaper and fewer resources.

Supervision for the minister (or salaried pastoral leadership team) is a much more ambiguous and difficult matter. The difficulty is that Bob and Sally don't really know what a minister does. They are church managers, but one cannot seemingly "manage" a minister in the way that others manage store clerks, hospital technicians, or athletes. Conversations about "time management," "job performance," and "efficiency" seem to lead nowhere; and yet conversations about "stress management," "spirituality," and "quality" seem to plunge into depths that Bob and Sally can never quite comprehend. The minister always seems to have it backward. Somehow the spontaneous one-minute conversation in the grocery store has more pastoral significance than the scheduled one-hour tea with the oldest member of the church. On the other hand, somehow the twenty-five hours of marriage counseling that still ended with a divorce, seem more important than the two-hour "Couples' Club" dinner that always raises money for the youth group.

Bob and Sally feel their supervisory responsibilities deeply, but they are ill-equipped for the task. Their energies in the system have been devoted to learning the right institutional information, understanding the organization, and preserving the traditions and ethos of the church which have made their "belonging" meaningful. Preoccupied with fund-raising for the present and immediate future, they have had little time to ponder the emerging needs of the next decade. They are utilizing their occupational skills in behalf of the congregation, but they are not quite clear about the relevance of "gifts" and "calling" for their lives. True, the letterhead from the church office refers to the salaried staff by name, and proclaims that the "Ministers" are "All of Us." Yet no one really believes it. Everyone knows that the great majority of church people are not directly doing ministry, but are involved primarily in fund-raising or church management. If anyone wants "ministry," he or she *will* go to *the* "minister"—and Bob and Sally aren't sure whether they should be relieved or troubled by that fact.

The declining church often finds itself burdened with what might be called *"C.P.D.,"* or "Chronic Personnel Dissatisfaction." It is a constant undercurrent of discontent, criticism, cynicism, or negativity regarding the salaried pastoral leadership of the church. It is a thread running through conversations in the couples' clubs, women's groups, and coffee hours. It surfaces in meetings of committees and boards in hints, suggestions, and vague rumors regarding the feelings of unnamed people. If the salaried pastoral leadership has the support of key lay church managers, or is particularly diplomatic, or is able to tap additional resources of energy to "track down" and "chase after" the hidden sources of discontent, the pastoral relationship remains fairly stable. On the other hand, declining churches will increasingly find themselves experiencing "Acute Personnel Dissatisfaction" *(A.P.D.)*, involving highly emotional conflicts, the withdrawal of key lay church managers from active participation, and the intercessions of the personnel committee and denomination.

"You attend to the work of the Lord, Reverend Smith," say Bob and Sally and their colleagues, "and leave all the administration to us." Since Reverend Smith has been trained to be an enabling caregiver, and does not have any particular training for administration anyway, this appears to be a good division of labor. She devotes herself to pastoral care, advocacy, liturgy, and teaching. Unfortunately:

a. Bob and Sally are no better equipped for the unexpected complexities of administration, and Reverend Smith finds herself surreptitiously doing it anyway, feeling guilty about it, and anxiously expecting criticism at any moment.
b. Reverend Smith discovers that the power to do anything significant in pastoral care, advocacy, liturgy, or teaching lies in administration, so she would do better to get involved in it deeply.
c. Bob and Sally discover that church administration is dull, time-consuming, and meaningless to a volunteer.

Supervising the salaried pastoral leadership uncovers the hidden, corporate codependency of declining church life. They *say* that they are all "ministers," but in fact they simply manage an institutional organization that pays experts to do ministry. They *claim* to be individually "called," but in fact they merely staff institutional offices, the work of which seems remarkably unfulfilling. They *give* their time and talent, but the resulting good fellowship seems an increasingly shallow reward.

"Acute Personnel Dissatisfaction" erupts for two basic reasons:

Clergy Burnout. The declining church tries to squeeze ever more ministry out of the minister. Simultaneously, they will reduce pastoral leadership staff or freeze salaries. The minister will visit, visit, visit, and visit again the inactive, the elderly "high givers," the youthful "low givers," the newcomers. The minister will be asked to preach better sermons, design more-exciting services, personally lead youth groups, attend more meetings, appear in more fellowship gatherings, and be more available to the Sunday school—while always being readily available in her office for anyone who drops by to talk. At the same time, she will be asked to reduce time with mutual support groups (denominational or ecumenical organizations), withdraw from controversial activities (advocacy, social service, evangelism), and reduce time away from the church (vacations, days off, continuing education, guest speaking). Faced with increasing demands and higher expectations, diminished peer support, and fewer opportunities to release her deepest pastoral passions, she becomes physically weary and psychologically defensive. Growing cynicism toward the church undermines her attitude, and she begins to contemplate a disability leave.

Irreconcilable Tension Between Creativity and Maintenance. As more and more energy is required to preserve the traditions of church life to which the membership has found it so meaningful to "belong," there is less and less time or tolerance for anything new. Conflicts between congregation and minister often find congregational members declaring that they "want to have their church *back again*." Creativity undermines the ethos of the church. It is not that any given program is particularly radical. Indeed, the precarious nature of the congregation's negativity is revealed when they cannot point to any one thing that is significantly disliked. Items of contention may appear to an outsider remarkably trivial. It is the ethos of church life which has been changed by too much creativity. It is the alarming change in attitude which appears to favor welcoming people over keeping people. It is failure to maintain the ethos of church life, even though no one can define exactly what that ethos is.

It is crucial to note, however, for the sake of Bob and Sally, that chronic or acute personnel dissatisfaction is but a symptom of a deeper identity crisis among the declining church laity. The declining church system in which Bob and Sally serve is a system based on mutual accountability. As the decline accelerates, Bob and Sally feel increasing pressure as well. They sense the grumblings of members. They hear criticisms. They serve multiple offices, attend more meetings, control more work, consult with more experts, labor more intensely to raise money and cut costs. They debate with each other more heatedly, perhaps split into factions. Staff supervision becomes ever more reactionary and directive, and inevitably becomes more confrontational. The very fellowship which was the bedrock of their "belonging" to the institutional church may begin to shake. Bob and Sally experience acute *personal* dissatisfaction:

Laity Burnout. Bob and Sally are also in danger of burning out, as the church tries to squeeze more and more service from fewer and fewer lay leaders. The multiple responsibilities, increasing meetings, and stressful interpersonal relationships begin to weary them. They, too, become increasingly cynical, negative, and defensive. Administration and decision making become ever more complex, burdened by subtleties and nuances that are often surprising. Bob and Sally feel hurt as they are unfairly criticized, and guilty as they unintentionally hurt others. As factions multiply, it is more and more difficult to keep clear just what the ethos of the church is to which "belonging" is so meaningful. Bob and Sally begin to contemplate resignation—and a "sabbatical leave" from church life.

Irreconcilable Tension Between Office Holding and Spirituality. The worship service itself is no longer the central, unifying experience of church life. Board and committee meetings become the central experiences of church life. So much time is spent with the bureaucracy that they complain that they have lost the ability to pray. They feel distant from the "Spirit." The offices they hold bear less and less resemblance to biblical leadership roles. They feel an emptiness and aimlessness in church life. For the first time, Bob and Sally may begin attending another church on Sunday evenings or through the week. It may not in fact be any more "spiritual" than their home church, but the anonymity and freedom from responsibility they experience when attending these alternative services allow them to focus again on faith.

Fortunately, Bob and Sally know that the system they have served places a higher worth on keeping people than on welcoming people. If they withdraw from active church participation, they can count on being missed. They know *the* minister will come to them, or that the system will do everything possible to adjust itself to meet their "belonging" needs. The church simply cannot be seen to fail Bob and Sally, because that would cast doubt on its very institutional identity.

Kept

If chronic personnel dissatisfaction never truly becomes acute, Bob and Sally avoid burnout and irreconcilable tensions with spirituality. Their commitment to the church system remains strong. Their struggles in the "directorship" of church life, serving the system and supervising ministry, have helped them define clearly the essence of church life to which "belonging" is so meaningful. They may retire from active church management, to a more passive and more potent church management. They may become "guardians" of the ethos of the church. Indeed, their opinions, views, and perspectives may become synonymous with the ethos of the church. They may become the "eldest members" who cross the floor during coffee hour to embrace another "new" person, to give such people the glad tidings that they have been nominated to the official board. Their patronage of emerging ideas, programs, and volunteers becomes crucial to the decision making of congregational meetings.

Bob and Sally may become what passes for "evangelists" in the declining church. Their own appreciation of the joys of "belonging" is so profound that it overflows in a desire to include others in the same blessing. Free from the many meetings of directorship, they are responsible for bringing selected newcomers into the church. They often serve as sponsors for teenagers being confirmed. They open their homes to fellowship gatherings, remind the ministers to visit nursing homes, and attend funerals regularly. They have a reputation for warmth, and frequently invite neighbors, friends, and business associates to church.

Nevertheless, Bob and Sally *are selective* about who they welcome into the church. Their goal is not to "convert" in any traditional sense of evangelism, but to "recruit" valuable new members into church life. Their lives have been immeasurably enriched through belonging to their church. What could be better than to assist others to experience the rewards of "belonging," *while at the same time* giving longevity to the institution they love by recruiting new members who will preserve its essential ethos? Bob and Sally assume newcomers will be enriched by "belonging" even as they have been—but they also understand that not everyone should "belong" to their particular church. They will be looking for potential recruits who are "our kind of people," who will fit into the system of church life without causing too much stress.

Declining churches are remarkably homogeneous. The lack of diversity in race, culture, language, economic background, formal education, and age is a direct result of the system in which they live. The sameness does not necessarily imply any conscious bigotry, class consciousness, or racism. Newcomers simply must adjust themselves to the system; the system never adjusts itself for the newcomers. Those newcomers who can best adjust themselves to the system will resemble Bob and Sally. The more dissimilar newcomers are to Bob and Sally, the more difficult it will be to fit into the system.

Even as "recruitment" is a primary goal for the declining church, authentic "evangelism" is the hidden enemy of the system. The church never quite knows what to do about evangelism. They establish "evangelism committees," which never accomplish anything and are later merged with a "membership committee." No one seems to know exactly what it is about individual faith that urgently needs to be shared; and no one has the courage or the training to risk sharing that faith. The truth is, no one really wants evangelism to succeed for the church. The last thing the declining church system wants is a radical diversity of newcomers who will redefine the homogeneous church ethos. Church members are so busy trying to maintain what they have, that they view potentially creative ideas with positive dread. There just isn't enough time or energy for the additional meetings that would be required of their system for it to adopt radically new initiatives.

Therefore, declining churches rarely go out among the public. They are even wary of advertising. They prefer to wait at the doors for the public to come to them. Their highly trained greeters and ushers are ready to engage in information sharing as soon as newcomers walk into the building—but they must first *walk into the building*. The very act of *walking into the building* is a sign that they are willing to adjust themselves to the system of church life. Once inside, newcomers will be informed, inspected, and tested to determine their worthiness to be a part of the church. Newcomers must "be prepared" to become a part of the church: multiple classes and meetings for weddings and baptisms; multi-week courses in membership training; home-study disciplines reviewing printed information. They *join the church*. The church never joins them.

It may be that fewer and fewer people will be interested in joining the church. Bob and Sally feel sorry for them, but a drop in potential recruits is paradoxically affirming for them. It makes the system to which they belong even more precious—and motivates them to be even more careful to preserve it unchanged for the future. "One day the public will come to its senses," say Bob and Sally to themselves. "And we will still be here, waiting for them, ready to embrace them like prodigal children come home."

Postscript: Whatever Happened to Mission?

The diagram of the declining church system illustrates what happens to mission. It spins right out of the church. For example:

A congregation in a large city realized in the late 1970s that it was seriously declining. Financial contributions were down, worship attendance was down, membership was aging, nominations were a nightmare. They consulted with experts. In an effort to find that program, idea, or project that would communicate with the public and rescue the church, they went door-to-door surveying the community. "What do you need?" they asked. They received a long list of requests, including food banks, counseling centers, addiction recovery groups, child daycare centers, and more. "We'll do it," said the church. They set aside space in their building, raised money for social service ministries, and hired staff for the various agencies.

First, they discovered that their space was inadequate. Aside from being inaccessible for the elderly, young parents with strollers, and people using wheelchairs, they never had enough storage space. Support groups meeting downstairs filled the sanctuary with tobacco smoke. The women's group complained that strangers were using their dishes. The secretary worried that there were weird people in the building. Community people walked the hallways, whom church members did not know by name. Precious things were broken or stolen. "Outsiders" seemed to control the time and use of "church space." So, they leased commercial space and relocated their mission agencies into the community.

Second, they discovered that no one inside the church could actually lead the missions. Indeed, they understood their role as raising money to pay experts to do ministry. So, they hired counselors, social workers, nurses, and other professionals to run the mission.

Third, they discovered they couldn't afford their mission. Leased space and salaried experts were expensive. They applied for federal, provincial, and municipal funding. Soon their own church financial contribution was a mere drop out of the bucket—and was dropped from the budget.

For a time, the church appointed its own members to the governing boards of the various charitable agencies it had created. This was in keeping with the members' general assumption that their role was to manage and supervise ministry. However, before long the salaried experts complained that they needed board members with specialized expertise. The community complained that they wanted board members who actually lived in the neighborhood. The various funding bodies complained that they couldn't allow outsiders to control the disbursement of their money. And the church itself complained that it needed key leaders to spend more time in meetings directly related to the church. Church members were withdrawn from the boards and advisory committees of the charities.

By the 1990s, "missions" had become "agencies." Mission had spun right out of the church. The publics of the community were not stupid. They realized that they could gain access to the mission of the church, without ever becoming involved in the church. The church itself was irrelevant to the mission. The property, leadership, organization, and financial support of the church were unimportant to the mission. More significant, the worship and spirituality of the church were unimportant to the mission. The city was deeply appreciative of the long list of important social services that the church had helped create. The denomination is in the process of closing this church.

What happened? The declining church system is not really designed for mission. It is designed for self-preservation. If large numbers of people join the church, a surplus of energy and resources can overflow into mission. Mission is a kind of side effect; a fortuitous, secondary result of institutional vitality. However, if large numbers of people cease joining the church, there is no surplus of energy and resources. Indeed, the whole process reverses itself. Continued maintenance of the church becomes so desperate that it begins to siphon energy and resources in the community *away* from mission in order to sustain the viability of the church.

Imagine the declining church system to be a remarkably inefficient water pump. Such a pump requires immense quantities of "fuel" to pump the surplus water from inside the well, outside into the village water tanks. As the "fuel" is cut, the pump not only stops working, but it reverses itself. It actually begins sucking in water from the water tanks in the village outside. In the same way, preoccupied with its own survival, the church sucks in resources that might otherwise have been invested in the greater well-being of the community, using them instead to preserve the institutional church.

Thus, step-by-step, the system works against mission:

1. Bob and Sally are welcomed, not to address their own needs, but to address the institutional needs of the church.

2. Bob and Sally are nurtured, not to discover their own faith, gifts, and calling, but to understand and contribute to the organization.

3. Bob and Sally are encouraged, not to probe the boundaries of creativity, but to accept the friendly consensus of the bureaucracy.

4. Bob and Sally are trained, not to do ministry, but to raise money and manage an institution that will pay and supervise somebody else to do ministry.

5. Bob and Sally are devoted, not to welcoming people, but to keeping people; their priority is not to care for the world, but to take care of each other.

In short, the declining church assumes that Bob and Sally will find meaning and purpose in life through "belonging" to the church; and that preserving the institutional church so that others can "belong" to it in the future is their most important task.

Chapter 3

The Thriving
Church System

Bob and Sally Public have come to New Hope-in-the-Heart Church with their young family. One child each from previous relationships and a new baby have them thinking about a formal marriage to each other. A lay greeter welcomes them as they enter the foyer, and personally introduces them to the trained nursery staff who will care for their toddler, and the trained children's ministers who will lead the Sunday school. The security system to keep the children safe is briefly explained. Bob and Sally are then led back to the foyer where they already hear loud, rhythmic music and singing. "Just go on in and sit where you like!" says the greeter. "It's great to meet you!"

As Bob and Sally walk toward the worship center, they see all around them visual displays of missions, adult faith development opportunities, and spirituality groups that are available. The worship experience is fast-paced, dramatic, visual, and requires no printed helps. The message-sharer seems to be speaking directly to them. Trained lay counselors around the room occasionally interact with participants with a laugh, a hug, or a conversation. And the music never stops. Bob and Sally feel glad they are here.

During refreshment time, one of the lay counselors talks with them. "We used to go to St. Friendly-on-the-Hill Church," says Sally with some embarrassment. "The truth is, we lied to them . . . or maybe we lied to ourselves. Anyway, we told them we wanted to make friends, but the truth is we already have a great bunch of friends in the softball league." Here Sally takes a deep breath. "And we told the minister that we wanted our baby baptized, but the truth is I WANTED TO BE DIFFERENT."

A year later Bob and Sally still do not know everyone by first name, but they attend a small, intimate, spirituality and faith development group every week in a participant's home. Neither Sally nor Bob belong to any committee and rarely attend church meetings, but each is passionately involved in a mission. People who know them say they have changed. They never miss a worship service, even during the summer.

New Hope-in-the-Heart Church is thriving. It is thriving not because it has some clever new programs, or an incredibly fine building with accessible parking, or better Sunday school curricula and hymnbooks. It is thriving because it is living in a whole new *system* of church life. Bob and Sally find church participation as necessary to their life and well-being as eating breakfast, jogging, family time, and watching the sun rise. They find in the thriving church system an ever-deepening experience of personal discovery, an ever-growing intimacy with motivated seekers, and an ever-multiplying opportunity to do meaningful mission. Bob and Sally don't just "stick" with the church. They are delighted with the church, and they tell people about it.

The diagram of the thriving church system describes the "home plate" of New Hope-in-the-Heart Church. It describes the basic orientation, attitude, philosophy, and flow which remain constant behind all the experiments and creative initiatives of the congregation. It is not a blueprint for success, which, if faithfully duplicated, will allow any congregation in any context to grow. The details, groups, and activities will vary enormously from place to place. It is the essential system which effectively attracts Bob and Sally's continuing involvement in the "religious enterprise" of life.

Changed!

New Hope-in-the-Heart Church has discovered that the fundamental reason new people come to church is not to *"belong"* but to *"be changed."* Of course, this is not always what they say when they come to church. They often say that they have come to make friends, enroll the children in Sunday school, or have their baby baptized. They say this because:

—that is what they believe the church wants to hear, since it affirms the corporate identity and makes it easier for Bob and Sally to gain entry into church life;

—that is the function the church traditionally fulfilled for Bob and Sally's grandparents in the prewar "rural" days of few socializing structures, and Bob and Sally's parents in the postwar "resettlement" days with scrambled populations; and

—that is the myth Bob and Sally want to maintain, lest they confront the realities of their own emptiness, addiction, and relational confusion.

THRIVING CHURCH
"All About Changing"

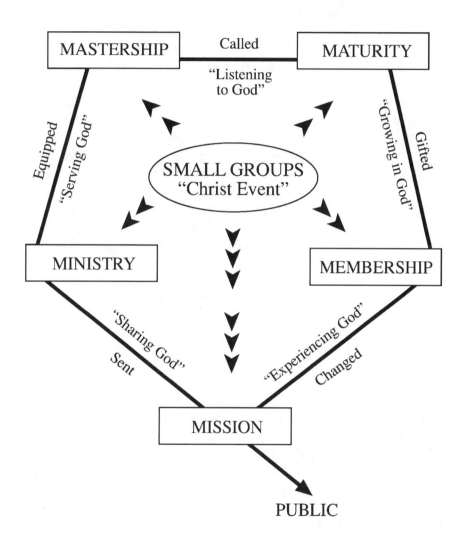

Bob and Sally are very private and very proud. They are not going to share their innermost longings, doubts, and self-destructive, sinful habits with the complete stranger at the church door, knowing that they may be in a political and organizational relationship down the road. Why reveal yourself too candidly to people who will have some measure of control or influence over your life? Paradoxically, they will share their innermost longings, doubts, and struggles to overcome self-destructive habits with a complete stranger in the coffee shop, knowing that they may never see that person again.

Therefore, the leaders of New Hope-in-the-Heart Church prioritize most of their time to be purposely spent, not in meetings, but in the coffee shop, in the public crossroads of life. They are listening to people like Bob and Sally, who are speaking candidly in an anonymous atmosphere free from fears of future organizational "blackmail." They are listening to the longings of the publics of the community. They are "reading between the lines" of conversation to discern the doubts, self-recriminations, and dreams of the people. They are open to the discovery that the longings and dreams of Bob and Sally *differ* from the longings and dreams of their parents and grandparents. Indeed, they are aware that the needs of one "generation" are radically different from those of another "generation" just eight years younger or older. After they spend time listening in the coffee shops and public places, they pray, weep, and laugh about all that they have experienced.

The leaders of the thriving church have discovered that in the twenty-first century, *nobody cares about the Presence of God!* The Presence of God is a widely accepted, and universally irrelevant assumption. Almost everybody believes that some kind of God exists, and that this God organizes the universe in some fashion. They know that God is everywhere—in the taxicab, in the park, at work, in the den where the multimedia computer is, and on the lake where you go fishing. Therefore, since you are going to be with God wherever you are, you may as well be where you want to be (i.e., in the park, in the den where the computer is, or on the lake fishing)—certainly not in church.

Thriving churches have discovered that, although nobody cares about the Presence of God, *everybody cares passionately about the Healing Power of God.* The fact that the healing power of God can deliberately and directly affect my life, and your life, and the life of my family, friends, community, and world—*that* is something people are longing to experience. They are desperately interested in the healing touch of God, something that can transform dull, impotent, sick, meaningless routine into vibrant, useful, healthy, and purposeful living. To connect with the healing power of God, they will not only go to church, but they will make time in busy schedules to attend support groups during the week.

When Bob and Sally appear at the church door, the lay greeters have been trained to respect Bob and Sally enough never to take them at their word. Bob and Sally are not seeking to belong to an organization. They are seeking to *be changed.*

"I want to be different," says Bob or Sally Public. "I feel empty inside. I am locked into a job that I hate, and a marriage that is rocky. I am addicted to alcohol, sex, cigarettes, materialism, and a hundred other self-destructive habits I haven't even identified yet. My kids ask me questions I can't answer, my parents tell me to do things that are pointless, and my company may lay me off at the mere hint of a recession."

"I want to be different," says Bob or Sally Public. "I want to be changed, whole, healed, healthy, and full! I want to feel like somebody special! I want to like myself for a change! I want to be going somewhere valuable, doing something important, and personally connected with an enduring meaning! I want a 'fresh start,' so that I can 'boldly go' wherever I am 'meant to be'! I want to be transformed!"

This is no mere "psychobabble" begging for attention. It is the exclamation of people who are simultaneously frantic and bored, burdened by low self-esteem and broken relationships, who desperately want a better life. Bob and Sally are not even sure what that "grace" will look like that *can* transform their lives. The people of this church, however, understand all of this. They also urgently believe that they share an experience of God that will help Bob and Sally immensely. Therefore, the lay greeters will make sure that Bob and Sally are confident that their children will be absolutely safe and positively nurtured, freeing Bob and Sally to attend to their own adult needs for transformation.

There are no "hoops," "hurdles," or "barriers" of any kind that Bob and Sally must negotiate in order to become involved in the church. There are no membership classes, no baptism preparation sessions, and no orientation groups. There are no worship bulletins to read, no books to juggle, and no information to digest. There is no specialized church language to memorize, like "narthex," "doxology," "hymnal," "gloria," and so on. They do not have to sit in any special place, be identified in any special way, or synchronize their sitting, standing, or kneeling in any corporate manner. They are instantly and completely welcome, comfortable, and "at home" in the church.

The worship service they experience aims at their hearts, not at their heads. The music that never stops has basically the same style and rhythm as the music they love to hear on their car radio. The words to songs are simple, everyday words projected on readily visible screens. Prayers are original, authentic, and sincere. Visual pictures describe scenes and human needs they can identify in their own neighborhood, and which they can own in their personal experience. The atmosphere is celebrative, positive, thankful—and electric with anticipation.

Bob and Sally's introduction to the church is an experience of expectation for change. They look about them and see people emotionally, as well as intellectually, engaged with the service. With tapping toes, nodding heads, and flashing eyes, people feel free to stand or sit or kneel. The leaders will help people focus on one or more themes or issues. From time to time, some people will weep, laugh, smile, or clap. Bob and Sally can see people experiencing God in profound ways. The overall message is the same: *Healing!* The healing touch of God can bring new health, wholeness, balance, purpose, wisdom, courage, confidence, and self-worth.

Occasionally, people will feel too overcome to continue in the service, and exit to the foyer. There, trained counselors will meet them for conversation, support, or prayer, and they will return to the service. No one ever pretends that all one's problems will go away like magic—but all are discovering new sources of strength to cope with whatever burdens they bear. Bob and Sally may or may not experience God's touch in any dramatic way. However, they will feel generally encouraged, strengthened, and motivated for another week. Something has happened to Bob and Sally. Something has changed them, uplifted them, and taken them outside their old selves. It is what the Bible means by "ecstasy."

By the end of the service, Bob and Sally may not remember any particular scripture or idea. They may not "know" much more about doctrines, ethical demands, political ideologies, or organizational practices than they did before. New Hope-in-the-Heart Church doesn't care about that right now. The point is that Bob and Sally have begun to observe, and to personally experience, the transforming power of God that can change people. They already know the power that addictions have in their lives. They know that all the education, all the self-help reading, all the good intentions, and all the best wishes of friends have been powerless to rescue them from the addictions that destroy meaningful, healthy living. They have begun to see that only a Higher Power can bring them new life.

This is not the only worship service offered by the church. It is simply the one Bob and Sally most likely first attend. There are other services that may be more traditional and educational, and there may be still other services that may be quite liturgical and sacramental. Each will be distinct, each will nurture church participants in various stages in their deepening spiritual lives, and each will appeal to varieties of musical taste. Every one of them will nurture positive personal change, and every one of them will motivate people like Bob and Sally to disciplined learning, sharing, and mission through the week.

In the present moment, Bob and Sally have not thought about any of this. They are simply and sincerely *glad they came to church.* They feel different. It is not that they "feel good" but that they "feel better." They feel stronger, kinder, gentler, and healthier. They feel *joy!* Restlessness stirs in them. Yearnings that lie in their hearts beckon to them. Their eyes see the realities of pain and suffering around them, and their hearts dare to believe that there can be hope. "I am glad we came!" say Bob and Sally to each other. "It has made a difference."

Gifted

The spiritual rapport that is beginning to build with the congregation does not end at the church doors. Within a week, a flowering plant is left at their front door with a note of welcome from the church. Within ten days, a trained layperson drops by to greet them personally. She or he assures Bob and Sally of continuing prayers, affirms that they should feel free to participate in any way they wish, stays only a few moments on the doorstep, and purposely says absolutely nothing about the organization and financial support of the church. Still later, the same visitor may return for a longer conversation. Bob and Sally are impressed:

—that the minister thankfully has *not* visited them, and that this personable layperson, who is volunteering precious time, *has* visited them;
—that the lay visitor spends the most time listening, rather than talking, and is clearly more interested to learn how the church can help Bob and Sally, rather than to explore ways Bob and Sally can help the church;

—that the lay visitor has himself or herself experienced God's transforming touch, but is neither pushy and boastful, nor embarrassed to acknowledge and talk about it.

Bob and Sally realize that they have gained, not an "institutional pilot" who can guide them through the intricacies of the church organization, but rather a "trusted, sensitive friend" with whom they can reflect on their experiences of God.

Bob and Sally continue to experience worship every week, and sense that their lives are changing. Perhaps change is emotionally dramatic, as they make a startling discovery, break through to a new attitude, or find themselves suddenly liberated from a burden. Perhaps change is emotionally cumulative, as they slowly evolve toward a new lifestyle, comprehend a complex idea, or build confidence that the power of God's grace is real. During refreshment time, Bob and Sally are struck by the fact that the animated conversations they overhear are not only about the mundane details of life (weather, relatives, sports, politics, etc.), but also about the real struggles and joys people are experiencing in their Christian living and personal mission. People are naturally, spontaneously, and unself-consciously talking about Jesus Christ—even after the worship service is over!

At some point, Bob or Sally or both may want to experience baptism, or reaffirm and celebrate their baptism which has only now gained meaning. In the thriving church system, adult baptisms happen as frequently as infant baptisms. There is no "class" to attend, nor is there any long study program. The pastoral leader will simply counsel with them about the life changes they are experiencing, and the connection between these changes and the person and work of Jesus Christ. The goal is not that they digest quantities of historical and doctrinal information, but that they simply link the experienced grace with the profound presence of Christ. The thriving church strategy is always *first* to experience healing, and *later* seek to comprehend what happened. The baptism will be celebrated in any number of ways, but always with intense joy as a primary focus of worship.

It may take weeks or years, but one day Bob and Sally say to each other: "I am a different person, but I don't know why and I don't know what to do about it. I am experiencing healing in my life, but I really don't understand what is happening to me. God has changed my life, but I really don't know who or what God is. I do know that I am so appreciative of what is happening to me, that I would like to do something in return. I want to go deeper into this experience." The thriving church system of New Hope-in-the-Heart Church is ready to move them deeper into faith.

As Bob and Sally make known their desire to understand more deeply the changes that are happening to them, only now does the church talk to Bob and Sally about membership. Membership is the covenant through which the church will help Bob and Sally go deeper into their faith. Membership in the thriving church means something different from its meaning in the declining church. Its purpose is not to provide Bob and Sally with a vote in congregational meetings, or permission to hold offices and to serve on committees, or the means to make financial pledges to pay somebody else to do ministry. The truth is that Bob and Sally have felt that they have always had a sufficient voice in church life from the very beginning. They have always felt welcome to become involved in any project. And they have been giving to a variety of church missions with increasing generosity using credit and debit cards.

Membership in the thriving church is a covenant of a unique kind. The church commits itself to assisting Bob and Sally to go deeper into their Christian faith and to discern their spiritual gifts and callings. The church also commits itself to doing everything possible to equip Bob and Sally to fulfill their personal mission to which they are called by Christ. In return, Bob and Sally commit themselves to an intentional discipline of adult faith development, which will ultimately lead to their personal involvement in mission and faith-sharing. In other words, this church is not interested in investing time and energy nurturing people who have no intention of doing anything for anyone else. The covenant Bob and Sally make is that they will ultimately be active "givers of life," rather than merely passive "receivers of life."

The last thing the church wants is for Bob and Sally to be sidetracked into organizational committees and meetings, or to think that membership means simply making regular financial contributions to the church. They become members in order to engage in a guided spiritual discipline. It is a process through which they will come to understand what their continuing experiences of God's healing touch *mean*. Along the way, they will begin to discern their own God-given abilities (spiritual gifts), and their own God-given ministries (spiritual callings). In the end, they will discover that the experience of the healing touch of God is only fulfilled in themselves, when they share the fruits of that experience to improve the lives of others. "God has been good to me," Bob and Sally say to their mentor and friend. "How can we appreciate, celebrate, and share that goodness?"

Of course it may take a long time for Bob and Sally to fulfill their covenant with the church. It may take years of searching and exploring to discern their gifts and callings. It may take even more time to gain the skills and expertise necessary to do it. However, the church is with Bob and Sally "for the long haul," because the church believes that every single human being is gifted and called by God to do ministry. If Bob and Sally are not exploring, training, or doing ministry, then the church is failing them—because Bob and Sally are failing to live and work with Christ.

In contrast to the declining church system, in which less than 1 percent of the adults were involved in faith development experiences, in the thriving church system more than 85 percent of the adults are involved in faith development experiences. Spirituality is the essence of church life. All subsequent activities, missions, or services will encourage deeper personal spirituality, and ever-deepening spirituality will carry individuals into appropriate and meaningful activities.

The first step will be an intensive "Spiritual Gifts Discernment" process. This process will involve prayer and Bible study, helping Bob and Sally discover how each can become a "channel" for God's energy, strength, or wisdom. Bob and Sally are invited to engage with counselors using a "Spiritual Gifts Inventory." The inventory is similar to a Myers-Briggs or Enniogram personality inventory, in that the participant responds to a number of key questions that are then grouped and evaluated by the counselor. Personality inventories reveal the dispositions and characteristics of the individual. Spiritual gifts inventories help Bob and Sally discover the inner, and often hidden abilities with which God created them.

Spiritual gifts may be defined using biblical terms from Isaiah 11, 1 Corinthians 12, or Romans 12, which may be described in more current language. These may include gifts of wisdom, understanding, counsel, fortitude, or reverence (based on Isa. 11:2-3). They may include prophecy, mercy, teaching, hospitality, prayer, exhortation, shepherding, healing, administration, and others (based on 1 Cor. 12:7-11 and Rom. 12:6-8). Generally speaking, a spiritual gift is simply that which engages your passion, which intuitively you seem to do excellently well. Gifts are abilities that are often unrecognized, hidden by low self-esteem or poor self-awareness. They may be unused or underdeveloped, treated as irrelevant to the career or employment path of the individual, and treated as irrelevant to many declining church committees.

Once discovered, however, Bob and Sally can begin to develop and use them. The process may even lead to career and employment changes, as they realize why their work is not fulfilling, or to lifestyle changes, as they realize why life has been boring. However professionally skilled they might be, their work simply does not allow them to express their authentic, God-given, inner nature. However secure and comfortable their lifestyle has been, their daily routine simply does not allow them to give energy toward what they really enjoy. People who live and work solely within the context of their professional training often become bored and restless. People who live and work within the context of their spiritual gifts never "burn out."

Bob, for example, is trained as an electrician. The declining church of St. Friendly-on-the-Hill had recruited him into the property committee. However, Bob actually found his professional skill remarkably unfulfilling. It brought him a stable income, but he was frequently bored and frustrated. His presence on the property committee made sense to the church, but it didn't help Bob. At New Hope-in-the-Heart Church, Bob discovered that he had spiritual gifts that he had long devalued. He had an inner wisdom and sympathy for teenagers that made him a perfect "mentor." His greatest satisfaction in the workplace, he realized, came not from electrical work, but from the long supportive conversations he had with young apprentices and trainees with whom he worked. He could spend hours in intense conversations regarding all of life, and his perceptiveness and down-to-earth understanding gained the respect of his rebellious younger colleagues. He was a lousy group organizer, a talented and bored electrician, and an amazingly good friend and colleague. It was the exercise of this gift of wisdom that sent him home whistling with satisfaction.

The second step for Bob and Sally will be a deeper intimacy with companion seekers. Most of the young adults (ages 20-45) are involved in small groups. These groups begin as "affinity" groups, but grow to be spirituality cell groups. Bob and Sally have been aware of these small groups for a long time, since the refreshment area at the church is surrounded with pictures and stories about their activities. The small groups are incredibly diverse, ranging from the seemingly shallow "Joys of Fly-Fishing" group to the clearly profound "Survivors of Divorce" group.

These small groups combine mutual support, topical discussion, and Bible sharing in a matrix of spiritual enrichment. The groups never exceed ten participants, and meet regularly (usually weekly) in participants' homes for a set period of time. Participation is a short-term, or at least "renewable" commitment. After nine months to a year, the group strategically divides, or multiplies, to shift in other topical directions. Some participants might continue to be enthusiastic about the existing group, while others may feel called to explore other interests. Meanwhile, new participants will continue to join the group. The group does not exceed ten to twelve persons, because this is the maximum number that still permits the intimacy that is crucial to the small group. The direction they go will emerge from their continuing spiritual discernment, in which they uncover their gifts and begin to listen for God's call to use their gifts in specific ministries.

This is a process in which seekers like Bob and Sally can share intimately their struggles and questions, learn about the Bible and their faith, and discover a deeper connection with God through prayer. The affinity, or topical interest, that has brought them together is not incidental, but central, to the process.

First, it grounds their deepening spirituality in their real, day-to-day lives. Their deepening spirituality is not something that stands outside their enthusiasms, tastes, enjoyments, interests, and routines. There is no artificial barrier between the sacred and the ordinary experiences of life. Their deepening spirituality permeates all of their day-to-day living. It heightens their appreciation of their interests, and guides them in their enjoyment or exercise of their passions. Sally finds herself using biblical images and pictures in her computer programming at work. Bob finds himself compelled to kneel at the goal line in prayer the moment after an exhilarating touchdown. Wherever there is joy, there is God.

Second, the affinity of the group becomes a vehicle through which Bob and Sally begin to understand their spiritual gifts. Their very passion for their topical interest, whatever it might be, suggests fruitful directions to discover the inner abilities with which God created them. They seek deeper self-awareness, not by standing apart from life but by becoming involved in life with newly opened eyes. What topics grip my imagination? What activities fill me with excitement? What issues compel my attention? Wherever there is intensity, there is God.

The affinity will vary, but the matrix of spirituality in which an affinity is discussed or experienced will be the same in every small group. Every group will spend much of the time talking about whatever it is they eagerly want to talk about. Yet every group will also do four things.

1. *They will pray together.* This may be as informal as silence with an occasional single spoken word; or as formal as unison, responsive, and single-voice prayers. Prayers will always focus outward; that is, they will be prayers for others.

2. *They will read and talk about the Bible.* This may not be a formal Bible "study," but simply a time of reading significant portions of Scripture, and discussing what passages mean for the participants. Or, it may evolve into a more structured "study" program.

3. *They will share ever more intimately with one another.* As mutual trust builds within the group, they will share honestly their feelings, personal struggles, and faith questions, and help one another find healing, resolution, or answers. They will help one another discern ever more clearly their spiritual gifts.

4. *They will become involved in a common mission activity.* The group builds a shared enthusiasm for a mission activity which arises from their own mix of gifts, interests, and dispositions. They do something in addition to their regular meetings that is "mission" or a "ministry," be it as simple as washing dishes following church fellowship times, or as complex as caring for the terminally ill.

What brings them together is an affinity stemming from common interests. What keeps them together is mutual support for personal and spiritual growth. What eventually scatters the participants to become involved with other groups is the growing awareness of multiple spiritual gifts and specific calling into ministries that exercise them.

Of course, such groups demand high-quality, trained leadership. These are lay "shepherds," "pastors," or "elders," whose own gifted and called ministries are to mentor small groups toward greater spiritual maturity, and motivate individuals to become involved in their own called ministries. These leaders are trained by New Hope-in-the-Heart Church in a "relationship-building" process (involving listening, conflict resolution, communication, and group dynamics), and in a "faith-building" process (involving questioning, prayer, Scripture, and discernment of gifts and callings). They also have a topic of great interest which they love, and they actively seek out others who share that interest, and who are interested in pursuing it in a spiritual context. Such group leaders are themselves part of a continuing mutual support and training program of the church, periodically meeting with the staff to discuss common problems and emerging directions.

For example: It happens that Bob and Sally are fascinated by model railroads (one of the fastest-growing hobbies in North America). Bob applies his electrical know-how to the minute intricacies of wiring track, sound systems, and lighting. Sally loves the artistic challenges of creating landscapes and scenery. One day during refreshment time, someone approaches them. She (or he) is gifted, called, and trained by the church to small-group leadership. He, too, loves model railroads. "I'm gathering a group together," he says to Bob and Sally, "and I understand you share this interest."

Bob and Sally join the group. They meet on Wednesday evenings, sometimes including dinner. Most of the time, they talk about railroads. They also pray and read the Bible. The group leader enables them to know and trust one another, and in time they are sharing ever more deeply with one another. "I'm having trouble at work . . . ," says one. "There is a continuing argument dividing our family . . . ," says another. "Is there anything after death . . . ?" asks a third, grieving for the loss of a loved one. They comfort and support one another, but more than this, they affirm one another in having valued spiritual gifts, and begin listening for a call into some mission or ministry activity.

Eventually, they build on Bob's gift for mentoring, and other individual gifts in helping and teaching—combine these with their skills in electricity, art, carpentry, and organization—and hear a call from their prayer life to be sensitive to kids eight to fourteen in their neighborhood. They decide to lease a small property with an empty building, and start building a group model railroad layout for which they invite any and all kids in the neighborhood to contribute. They provide a safe, healthful activity for youth in which they can teach basic skills in electricity, art, small engines, and on and on—in the context of which they can mentor young people in their basic values, beliefs, and experiences of God in the midst of life.

In years to come, the Youth Railroad Ministry involves countless kids from the neighborhood. The small group itself changes and evolves. Some stay with the group for a long time, passionately called to this ministry. Others move on. One joins a small support group for unemployed adults. Another joins an alcohol addiction support group, while a third joins a group studying the historic doctrines of the church. Bob has been coached by the leader of the group to enter training as a group leader. He will soon be equipped as a shepherd himself.

Here is an interesting conclusion to the story. When Sally's mother dies in a nearby nursing home, her primary emotional support comes from her small group. In fact, she does not turn to the pastoral leader ("minister") of the church to conduct the funeral service. She turns to the small-group leader ("shepherd"). The small-group leader designs and leads the funeral service, and provides additional counseling before and after the experience.

Although adults in the church commonly grow in spirituality and faith through joining small groups, this is by no means the only vehicle. There are adults, many over forty years old, who do not like small groups. There are more complex mission projects for which several small groups will organizationally cluster together. There are Sunday school, music, or youth initiatives that are less easily adapted to the small-group process. Therefore, the thriving church will offer other options for nurturing faith: large groups for women and men, weekend retreats, traditional Bible study groups, and Sunday school classes. The matrix of spirituality, however, will consistently be the same. The goal is to be more than a civic club, educational event, or fellowship gathering. The goal is always to deepen faith, and multiply opportunities for ministry through the discernment of gifts and callings.

The covenant of membership is moving Bob and Sally to "Christian maturity." Of course, this is difficult objectively to measure. The maturity of today may seem but youthful exuberance from the perspective of future growth. However, maturity can broadly be described thus:

a. Bob and Sally better understand what has happened to them in the experience of healing and grace, and the nature and loving purpose of God revealed in Jesus Christ.

b. Bob and Sally better understand how their personal story, the biblical story, and the stories of Christians through the years, are all part of a single movement of the Spirit.

c. Bob and Sally are able to articulate their faith aloud, and are motivated and prepared to share their faith story with others.

d. Bob and Sally have a growing sense of connection with God through intentional worship and prayer, and affirm that they daily seek to walk with the risen Lord.

e. Bob and Sally know that they are not perfect, but are involved in a process of continuing discovery and growth.

f. Bob and Sally are aware of the spiritual gifts with which God created them, and they know that God calls them personally to be in ministry.

g. Bob and Sally are committed to being responsible, and to taking responsibility, in a network of mutually supportive Christians, who are incredibly diverse, but one "Body of Christ."

h. Bob and Sally have an inner sense of worth and joy, and are motivated by a deep appreciation for God's grace, to seek ways to share healing and faith with others.

Maturity is never an end in itself. It is, rather, yet another new beginning. The real sign of Christian maturity is that Bob and Sally are now restless and eager to *do something!*

Called

The process of listening for the calling of God has already been going on in the small groups in which Bob and Sally have participated. Their group came to recognize God's call to ministry using the various gifts, interests, and personalities of the group, and they initiated various activities. The growing spiritual maturity of Bob and Sally, however, leads them in an even more intentional process to hear God's call more personally.

New Hope-in-the-Heart Church recognizes that very few people are actually called to church management. Some clearly discern spiritual gifts for administration, and they may be called to exercise that spiritual gift in the organizational life of the church. Only a few are needed. Others with the gift of administration may be called to organize and supervise a variety of charitable or community organizations. The point is that spiritual maturity does not lead to management, but to ministry. It does not lead to bureaucracy, but to some form of activism.

Spiritual discipline becomes more intense and more exciting. Bob and Sally are searching for their spiritual "vocation," the ministry or mission, simple or complex, which God is asking them to do right now. Bible study and prayer become even more vital, because the "calling" is not constructed by the individual but revealed by God. They are in a time of waiting and listening. They literally pore over the newspapers and watch events in their community and world intently. Perhaps their gift is "helping" and their call will be to work in the soup kitchen or drive meals-on-wheels to the housebound. Perhaps their gift is prophecy, and their call will be to some social justice advocacy in their region. Perhaps their gift is healing, and their call will be to visit the terminally ill.

New Hope-in-the-Heart Church does not claim to know what that calling should be. Their staff and their administrative board do not set the mission agenda of the church. The mission agenda of the church is set by the Spirit calling out the special gifts of ordinary people. The church never says to Sally, "We need you to do this, or we want you to do that." Instead, the church prays and listens with Sally, and says, "When you know what God wants you to do, tell us, and we'll do all in our power to help you do it."

Creativity is at its maximum in this stage of the thriving church system. The church knows all about "burning bushes" and seemingly impossible tasks. It also knows that, where committees may not be able to move an inch, motivated individuals can move mountains. The people are not in the business of maintaining institutions but of birthing new ministries. They are "midwives" for the progeny of the Spirit and faith-filled Christians. There-fore, even the craziest ideas will be given serious consideration. They will test each calling for authenticity:

—Does it contradict our basic vision, values, or beliefs? If not, no matter how crazy it is, let's try it.
—Does it address the real needs and spiritual yearnings of the public? If so, no matter how creative it is, let's do it.
—Does it emerge from the spiritual maturity of an individual who has been changed, gifted, and called by God? If so, let's trust it.

Questions of finance, organization, and accountability are vitally impor-tant—but they are, after all, secondary. The thriving church is not trying to protect and enhance a heritage dating back one hundred or more years. It is trying to imitate the church experience of the first century: risking, trusting, proclaiming, sharing, exploring, and advocating the Way of Christ in a morally turbulent and spiritually hungry world. Survival is not its concern, for "whether we live or whether we die, we are the Lord's" (Rom. 14:8).

The thriving church can never anticipate or predict the callings of Christ. Neither the board, nor the staff, nor the denomination sets the mission agenda. They can describe in enthusiastic detail what the mission agenda *is,* but they can never really describe what the mission agenda *should be.* The mission agenda emerges only as the Spirit calls forth the gifts of individuals and small groups. *Therefore, there will always be gaps, and there will always be risks.* Certain needs or issues which the denomination, the government, or society deem important, may not be met immediately by the church. Certain emerging ministries may seem too crazy, too expensive, too politically suspect, or too doctrinally ambiguous to the denomination, the government, or society. Yet society does not set the mission agenda of the church; God sets the mission agenda of the church. The church does not recruit Bob and Sally to do what society or the institution thinks should be done; the church takes the risk of equipping Bob and Sally to do the mission God calls Bob and Sally to do.

For example: Bob has grown spiritually through his small-group partici-pation. He has combined his passionate interest in model trains, his profes-sional skills as an electrician, and his spiritual gift for mentoring, in a creative mission activity with the small group. The experience, however, has led Bob to care deeply about the growing number of kids involved in their ministry who are experimenting with drugs and alcohol. He was shocked and deeply disturbed to discover that several twelve-year-olds in the model railroad club were in fact addicts. He shared this in the intimacy of his small group. He and his friends prayed about it, and shared the Bible together with a new perspective. Bob began to reflect in fresh ways on the addictions from which the healing touch of God had liberated him. Bob talked with his pastor, school counselors and teachers, and community leaders. He began to hear a call and consider a new personal mission.

Bob goes to the church and says, "I believe God is calling me to develop a ministry for young teenage drug addicts to help them be free from addiction." The church says, "That's great, Bob. How can we help you?" The very first step is to train Bob in small-group leadership, so that he can use his spiritual gift in mentoring to its fullest potential. Bob joins a new company of intimates, who together share a passion for youth ministries. He is trained in all the skills that allowed his own former small-group leader to work so effectively with him. His new small group includes two or three young teens from the railroad club, and it begins to grow and mature. The church holds itself in readiness to support whatever new directions Bob's mission may take.

Or, for example: Sally has grown spiritually through her small-group participation. She has combined her interests, artistic talents, and spiritual gifts for organization in the mission of the small group. The sensitivity and support of her intimate friends has touched her deeply during her grief for the death of her mother; and it now helps her cope with the discovery that her aging father has Alzheimer's disease. Sally becomes increasingly frustrated with the lack of elder day-care programs in her community. She and her friends pray about this and share the Bible with a new perspective. Sally begins to reflect in fresh ways on the healing power of God that helps her daily to care for her father. She talks with nurses and doctors, and the directors of various charities. She begins to hear a call and consider a new personal mission.

She goes to the church and says: "I believe God is calling me to organize and direct an elder-care ministry specializing in day care for people with Alzheimer's disease. It would be sponsored by this church, and be run using our Christian beliefs and values. It will require leasing or building a new facility, and building a trained staff of spiritually gifted people." The church takes a deep breath. They say: "That's great, Sally. How can we help you?" The first step is to cultivate Sally's spiritual gifts in organization. They pay part of her registration and tuition fees to attend a community college course for social service and charitable organizations. They help her promote the vision in the church and build a small group of people with a similar passion—and they help her identify potential sources of fund-raising. The church staff holds itself in readiness for whatever new directions this initiative may take.

The spiritual callings discerned by the members of New Hope-in-the-Heart Church are not all as complex or expensive as these examples might suggest. Spiritual callings will be incredibly varied, and may seem very simple. Others in the model railroad group will continue doing just what they have been doing. Some church members will be called to be greeters or counselors in the transformational church services; others will be called simply to wash the dishes after fellowship dinners. Some will be called to traditional activities, such as teaching a Sunday school class, visiting newcomers, visiting hospitals, telecare and telephone communications, and secretarial support. Still others will be called to more surprising activities, such as lobbying local governments regarding environmental standards, or supporting antiracism groups in the city. The calling for some will be local; the calling for others may take them to other nations and other continents. Whatever the callings, three things will remain constant:

1. *The church values every calling equally.*
2. *The people called are motivated by their own experience of the transforming power of Jesus Christ, and their own awareness of inner abilities given by God.*
3. *Every calling, great or small, will be pursued only when the people who are called can do it with excellence.*

The vision of New Hope-in-the-Heart Church is not for people to be Christian, but for people to live a Christian life. Therefore, it is not enough for people to experience the healing touch of God. It is not enough for people to discern their gifts and mature in their faith. It is not even enough for people to hear their call and to become involved in mission and ministry. If God's power is to be shared in the world by faithful human beings, it must be done with integrity and skill.

Equipped

New Hope-in-the-Heart Church believes in excellence. They may not be able to do everything, but what they do will be done well. No one will be released into ministry until that person can be the best minister that she or he can be. Opportunities to upgrade skills and improve performance will be offered regularly.

Training, of course, will vary according to the nature of the calling. Those who are called to teaching in the Sunday school may train for several weeks or months in communications, methods, curriculum, crafts, and so forth. Those who are called to child care may train extensively in health and safety, child psychology, playtime as education, or helping children overcome family crises. Counselors, greeters, helpers in the kitchen—every calling, simple or complex, will receive careful preparation, because every calling is equally important.

Much of the training will be done by staff or volunteers within the church. Indeed, part of the membership covenant foundational to training in a ministry is the promise to help equip others for the same ministries. For example, one woman who believes she is called to a ministry with meals-on-wheels may be coached by another volunteer to improve driving skills in poor weather conditions. An elderly woman called to a ministry of communication may be trained by another in effective telephone calling. Pastoral leadership staff may train lay ministers extensively in pastoral care and counseling, hospital visitation, worship leadership, wedding and funeral planning.

Some training may need to be done by professionals from beyond the local church. Bob, for example, will be trained by pastoral leaders within the church to be a small-group leader and mentor for young teenagers. However, the church may also help him obtain training from private or government drug rehabilitation programs. Sally, for example, will be coached by other volunteers within the church in pastoral care with the elderly, but she will also be sent by the church to a community college for courses in management for social service agencies.

New Hope-in-the-Heart Church does not raise money to pay others to do ministry, but it will be highly motivated to raise money so that it might equip *its own people* to do ministry. Professionals are contracted, not to do ministry, but to do training. The goal of the church is that all of its ministries will be done with the same (or better) standards as any comparable service in the community. Religious education for children will aim for as much quality in teaching as public education for children. The ministries of Bob and Sally will each match in quality the comparable services sponsored by secular agencies. The pastoral caregivers released into hospitals, nursing homes, and the community at large will have training comparable to the pastoral leader's own training at seminary.

Professional training, however, is not the only training received by the people who are changed, gifted, and called through New Hope-in-the-Heart Church. Unique though each ministry may be, all ministries will have certain things in common.

First, *all ministries will involve people.* Therefore, lay ministers will be equipped to understand and demonstrate the values the church holds dear. They will understand the urgency for equality of race and gender, or multicultural and interfaith respect. They will be coached to be sensitive to special needs, to create safe environments for children, or to protect the safety and health of all personal relationships. They will become alert to the potential for hidden abuse or subtle prejudice, and learn how to interact with the public in ways that encourage trust and respect.

Second, *all ministries will share faith.* Therefore, lay ministers will be equipped to understand their own beliefs. They will be coached to be confident, but open to dialogue. They will be equipped with communications skills to articulate their faith clearly, and to listen to the spiritual journeys and yearnings of others. They will be encouraged to explore the spiritual dimensions of any practical ministry in which they are involved.

Third, *all ministries reflect the basic vision of the church.* Therefore, lay ministers will be guided to understand how their calling is connected to that larger vision which is the "song in the heart" of the congregation. They will be coached, not to place their ministry in a hierarchy of bureaucracy, but to locate their ministry in the organic unity of the "Body of Christ."

It is true that this stage of involvement in church life and mission may lead to meetings, classes, or seminars. However, the purpose of such meetings is not *governance,* but *preparation for ministry.* They are time-limited, and dedicated to a specific, practical purpose. They do not replace the small-group participation that will continue to be the core of growth in spirituality and faith of the individual.

Those who are outside the thriving church system may wonder where Bob and Sally and all the other people find the time to be so involved in spiritual development and personal mission. Certainly Bob and Sally have their own careers, a young family, and private lives that are all very important. St. Friendly-on-the-Hill Church discovered that Bob and Sally were "too busy" to get deeply involved in the church. What makes the difference now? Why are Bob and Sally, and many others like them, ready to give so much extra time out of their busy schedules? In addition to worship and small-group gatherings, Bob spends every Saturday morning with his ministry among young addicted teens, while Sally spends every Tuesday night for six months taking a community college course. Why?

The answer is that they are *motivated*. They do not have time for consensus bureaucracies, meetings about governance, fellowship gatherings that lead nowhere, or information events about things the institution believes to be important. They will make time for intimacy, opportunities to deepen spirituality, and experiences that will help them make life truly meaningful and exciting. They will give priority to whatever time is needed to be equipped to share new life and help others, in some practical way that they thoroughly enjoy, and to do it with excellence. Their own continuing experience of the transforming power of God, which is releasing them from destructive addictions, and filling their lives with purpose and meaning, motivates them to celebrate and exercise this new life, in an overflow of generosity. In short, people don't give time to an institutional agenda, but will give time to a personal agenda. People won't give an evening to things that are dull and meaningless, no matter how obligatory such things are made to seem. Yet they will give Saturdays, weekends, and even blocks of their vacation time to hands-on ministries that are meaningful, profound, and fulfilling.

Sent

New Hope-in-the-Heart Church has helped people be changed, gifted, called, and equipped. Now these people are ready to be released into a high-quality ministry. Such ministry will be the fulfillment of the experience of grace from the start of their church involvement. Such ministry will also continue to enrich their understanding of that grace, and continue to deepen their spiritual growth. Ministry for these people is an expression of self-affirmation, not an act of self-sacrifice. They know that by giving, they themselves will be enriched. Unless the joy that they have received is in some way "passed on" to benefit others, that joy will begin to diminish in their own hearts, and they will slide back into the destructive addictions that previously robbed life of meaning.

Although it may seem surprising, the thriving church system assumes that the primary, foundational motivation to do ministry is *not compassion* but *celebration!* People have been changed, and they want to do something about it. People discover spiritual gifts, and they want to fulfill their potential. Ministry is that which results when people experience the transforming touch of God, discern the spiritual depths within their own selves, hear divine calls to live out their thanksgiving to benefit others, and equip themselves to share new life in practical ways with excellence.

It may take time for the experience of transformation to bear fruit in ministry, but thriving church leaders have the patience to work with people over time. They are opportunists who can help others grasp any event, good or bad, large or small, as a moment of insight and growth. This is why three words spoken in earnest during a chance encounter in the drugstore, can be more powerful than any number of prepared sermons. Once another person has been changed, gifted, called, and equipped, the most important task of leadership is simply to get out of the way.

In the thriving church system, the number of possible outreach ministries able to be undertaken simultaneously is without limit. Small or large, complex or simple, they all assume two basic principles:

1. *Social service and sharing faith occur simultaneously and deliberately.* The act of ministry, and the rationale or motivation of the ministry, are equally important and mutually supportive. To do ministry without sharing the story of spiritual transformation which motivates it, prevents others from sharing the fullness of new life. To share the story of spiritual transformation, without actually doing something of practical significance to better another's life, prevents others from hearing their own calling. The point of any ministry is to transform "seeking recipients" into "thankful givers" in their own right.

2. *The practical and spiritual needs of the public are more important than the practical and spiritual needs of the church.* The equipped ministers of the church do not primarily serve the system of the institution, but they address the real yearnings of the community. Similarly, they are not concerned to recruit new members for the church, but to enable members of the public to experience the healing touch of Christ in whatever form is most relevant for that person.

Evangelism is at the heart of all ministries, great and small. The vision of the thriving church is not that its people will be "inside" the church thankful that God is in the world, but that they will be perpetually "beyond" the church walking and working with the risen Lord.

Postscript: What Happened to Mission?

The diagram of the thriving church system illustrates what happens to mission. The mission of the church never "spins out" of the system but remains central to the identity and work of the church. Indeed, *the mission of the church IS the church!* This is because it is more important for this church system to welcome people than to keep people. They have learned that in order to welcome people beyond the church to share an experience of Jesus Christ, they must *send* people beyond the church into the context of public need.

Therefore, as the members-ministers of the church are released into the community to do whatever it is God has gifted and called them to do, they move through the doors of the church to be wherever the public is gathering: coffee shops, sports arenas, and shopping malls; offices, assembly lines, and workplaces; neighborhoods, friendship groups, and family gatherings. Wherever the public is, these motivated and equipped church people are joyfully exercising their spiritual gifts and callings.

The social services, agencies, and support groups, which "spun out" of the declining church system, remain within the thriving church system. The property is never valued as a heritage but only as a vehicle for mission. It is readily rebuilt, reshaped, or even relocated to adapt to the changing missions of the church. Outside experts are never hired to do the ministry, because the thriving church trains its own experts to do ministry. Outside funding for most ministries is never required, because the thriving church has abandoned unified budgets, and raises more money through diversified stewardship opportunities that encourage people to give to the specific missions that move their hearts. More than this, the thriving church is unafraid to be in debt in order to be in mission. They understand that debt-freedom is a sign, not of fiscal responsibility, but of mission irresponsibility. The church may enter partnerships with other churches, municipalities, or government agencies for large and expensive projects, but only if their partners will acknowledge that the project will operate within the basic vision, basic values, and basic beliefs of the church.

For example, we have followed Sally through her experience of the thriving church system. She faced the fact that it was not her toddler that needed to experience the transforming grace of God but she herself. She experienced change in her life through the worship services and felt rescued from destructive addictions and the abyss of meaninglessness and purposelessness in her heart. In time, she chose to go deeper into her spirituality to celebrate and understand this grace that was happening to her. Her participation in small groups provided her with intimates and mentors, and it deepened her sense of connection with God. She uncovered spiritual gifts she never knew she had. She became involved in the Model Railroad Ministry to youth and experienced the satisfaction of giving life to others.

As time went by, she began more intensively to listen for God's call to her to use her gifts in specific and practical ways. Her own life experience with her mother's death, and her father's illness, began to reveal a calling to minister to people with Alzheimer's disease. Her church began to equip her for ministry among such people. As Sally's vision grew and became concrete regarding the ambitious project of a church-sponsored elder day-care center for Alzheimer's victims, the church helped her find others who shared her vision. They subsidized her training at the community college, and helped her gain experience with various related social services in the community.

It took several years, but the church helped place her vision before the congregation and community. Contributions from motivated givers began to build. Sally developed partnerships with the municipality to assist in the funding. She began training the emerging gifted and called church people who would become the core staff of the elder-care center. Finally, after several years of quality preparation, the center was launched and became a core ministry of the church. Sally dreams that one day it will become her full-time occupation.

During all this time, Sally was highly motivated for her calling. There were many setbacks and worries, but she overcame them. She was always linked to a small group who shared her vision. She always attended worship, and continued to sense the transforming power of God changing her life. She regularly received the help of the church to upgrade her skills. At the same time, never once did the church say to Sally:

"We never did it this way before."
"We can't afford it."
"We need you to serve on a committee."
"We don't think your calling is legitimate." Or
"We need to see long reports and approve each step of the project."

Always, always the church said to Sally, "Go for it. We will help motivate you, support you, and equip you. We will help you refine, share, and build your vision. If ever you worry about stepping beyond the perimeters of our basic congregational beliefs, values, and vision, we will help you clarify your direction. If you fail, we will love you anyway and help you learn from the experience to find another way to exercise your gifts. If you succeed, we will praise God together."

Many times people beyond the church would ask Sally why she was spending so much time with this daunting task. One day, for example, another young woman with a parent in the elder-care center approached Sally. "Sally," she said, "why do you do this? Why are you here?" Sally did NOT simply say, "I am here because it is a good thing to do." She said, "I am here because Jesus Christ calls me to do this." She described her own journey of being changed, gifted, called, equipped, and sent. She confessed that her ministry was not a sacrifice of her time, but a fulfillment of herself. Her questioner considered the answer. She said that she, too, would like to escape her addictions. She, too, would like to know her gifts and callings. She, too, would like to be trained to do valuable things and be given the freedom to do them creatively. Sally replied: "Great! I will introduce you to the place and the people where that happened to me. I'll pick you up tomorrow, and you can come to worship with me."

The thriving church grows because growth is never its primary purpose. Mission is its primary purpose. Increasing participation and membership is a side effect—but it is an inevitable side effect. In the universal yearning for self-worth, inner meaning, and a noble destiny, people always discover that it is far more meaningful actively to give life away to the world, than passively to preserve life within the institution. The fulfillment of the healing touch of Christ will always be the touch of healing toward others. When Sally is asked to describe her life in the church, she does not list the offices she has served. She never served any! Instead, she reflects on her experience of the whole system of transformation. She says simply, "I feel like I have become the fingertip of Jesus."

Chapter 4

Comparing the Two Systems

Occasionally with friends, Bob and Sally Public reflect on their very different experiences with St. Friendly-on-the-Hill Church and New Hope-in-the-Heart Church. They are not quite sure why these two churches are so different. Many specific things come to mind. St. Friendly's uses a long printed bulletin in worship, does everything through meetings, recruits as many people as possible into offices, and is always worried about money. New Hope prints newsletters and produces videos, does everything through small spirituality cell groups, encourages people to discern their spiritual gifts, and is always thinking about new ministries.

Bob and Sally are aware, however, that these specific contrasts do not explain the core of the difference. There is simply a different "spirit" about the two churches.

Bob and Sally remember vividly two parallel conversations they had with the pastoral leaders of these churches. Some years ago, St. Friendly-on-the-Hill Church received a new ordained minister. Bob and Sally asked him one day if he had found it difficult to enter into the life of a new church. His response was as follows:

"No, Bob," he said. "It's true that St. Friendly's is unique in many ways. The sanctuary is more beautiful than many in which I have led worship, and the organ is the best I've ever heard. And it's true that there is a harmony here that many churches have yet to achieve. I'm glad I came here. The fact is, however, that every church I have served is basically the same. They all seem to have the same group of unusual personalities. They all have trouble keeping the youth involved. An annual deficit is always a burden, and the basic categories of church programs look pretty much alike. Walk into any church of our denomination, and you will feel at home. I guess it's part of our church 'ethos.'"

In contrast to this conversation, Bob and Sally remembered talking to the pastoral leader of New Hope-in-the-Heart Church. He was sharing his experience of his first years with the congregation.

*"Sally," he said, "it was tough. Within weeks I realized that New Hope-in-the-Heart Church was unlike anything I had experienced in past congregations. It wasn't just that people had different names for programs, or that the sanctuary didn't have a pulpit. People just behaved in ways I didn't expect. Routine things I used to do, that were quite effective, didn't work here. On the other hand, some things I did by chance, or by simple intuition, seemed to succeed beyond expectation. The truth is that my seminary never equipped me for **this** kind of church, and I had a lot of learning to do. When my colleagues visit here, they know it's a whole new 'ball game'!"*

*Call it a "new ball game." Call it a "different spirit." Call it a return to "first-century" church experience. Bob and Sally have trouble putting their finger on the essential difference. They just know it is a different **system** of church life.*

A system is a unity of movement. Although the system may be very complex, and include a variety of stages and activities, it will have a single "flow" of purpose and meaning. Fundamental patterns of behavior will be repeated over and over again, in order to attain desired results. When one moves to a different system, one will experience an entirely different "flow" of purpose and meaning. The various stages and activities may resemble those of the former system, or they may not. Some aspects of the new system may be the same, or only superficially alike. Yet one's movement through these activities will feel very different. The fundamental patterns of behavior that are repeated over and over again in the new system are different from those of the old system.

This is why systemic change is far more stressful than programmatic change. In programmatic change, the same basic system is simply experimenting with a new curriculum, a new committee, an alternative program, or a renovation in church life. In systemic change, the fundamental patterns of behavior which previously undergirded all activities (big and small, old and new) are changing. Nothing works as it did before. Until one becomes accustomed to the new system, there is very little predictability. Later, once we have examined the organizations that lie behind the systems, I will offer a plan for systemic change that attempts to "manage" the stress.

The pastoral leader of New Hope-in-the-Heart Church called the transition "a whole new ball game." Sports metaphors come naturally when referring to systemic change, because a sport typifies the "unity of movement" or "single-minded flow of purpose" that is essential to understanding a system. Two sports metaphors come to mind in comparing the two systems of church life.

The Declining Church System is like a game of "croquet." The chart illustrates the "flow" of movement through the system.

First, movement is "managed" throughout church life. Not only will the ushers conduct Bob and Sally to their designated seat in worship, but every step along the way will require the approval and initiative of the institution. The institution must initiate them into membership—before they proceed through the next "hoop" of church life. Similarly, they will be recruited into church office, and each decision will need to be verified and affirmed by the institution before it can be implemented. Not only must Bob and Sally go through the standardized "hoops" to advance in church life, they must also go through the hoops *in the right way.* In croquet, the ball must pass through the hoop in the proper direction. In the church, any idea or proposal must be forwarded through the proper committees with the correct procedure.

Second, movement is "controlled" throughout church life. In addition to going through the hoops, in the right order and in the right way, croquet allows the most skilled players to make contact with the ball of another player, and then "send" that player to the fringes of the playing field. The Declining Church System provides the same power to the most skilled church "insiders." They can prevent access to a hoop and "send" other church members in directions different from those originally intended. Access to hoops can be blocked. People can be exiled to the fringes of church life. Note that the progress of croquet is deliberately *slow.* Every shot must be carefully considered, just as every decision of the church must be carefully scrutinized. There is always the risk that if the rules of process are broken, or if the wrong people or ideas get forwarded through the hoops, then the unique "ethos" or "identity" of church life will be lost.

Third, all movement must pass through meetings. The central hoop in croquet is the key to the game. Going or coming, everything must go through that hoop—one at a time. Meetings for the church function like central hoops in croquet. Nothing can happen, no progress can be made, in any direction, without them. In fact, ideas and proposals must "line up" to pass through the hoops of the meetings one at a time. Agendas will be prioritized according to the mission plan of the institution, and everyone must await a

DECLINING CHURCH SYSTEM

turn. For this reason, the Declining Church System can rarely forward more than two or three serious outreach programs in any given year.

Fourth, all movement is subtle and self-contained. Aside from a few dramatic moments when a skilled player "sends" another player's ball to the fringes of the playing field, most of the action is concentrated in a small area. Players seek to finesse their balls through the hoops and avoid confrontation with other players' balls. In the same way, church life in the Declining Church System is remarkably self-absorbed. Everything of real importance is happening within the limited boundaries of the institutional playing field. That is where the issues of "belonging" are really at stake. Members seek to finesse their ideas through meetings, and avoid confrontation with the most powerful board members at all costs.

For those who play the game *well,* croquet is a great game! And for those who are really skilled in the subtleties of declining church life, the Declining Church System is a great system! As you can tell from the picture, however, many people who are not skilled at the game find it very boring. It is tedious. Only one player can play at any given time, and if, when your turn finally comes, you *fail* to make progress, frustration runs very high. *In the Declining Church System, everybody holds a mallet, but most people spend most of the time leaning on it, instead of using it!*

In contrast, *the Thriving Church System is like a game of "jai alai."* The game of jai alai is not an indigenous North American game. Many North Americans do not know it. It is imported from Spanish and Central American cultures. In a parallel way, the Thriving Church System is influenced by the church life of non–North American mission partners. Immigrants to North America, who cannot understand or feel comfortable with the Declining Church System, quickly recognize and celebrate the Thriving Church System. The chart illustrates the "flow" of the system.

Jai alai is an extraordinarily fast-paced game in which a speeding ball is caught by a player with a curved racket. Like a windmill, the player rotates his or her arm, and the ball accelerates by centrifugal force through the racket. The ball is fired out of the racket, this time with a new speed and direction. It hits the wall of the arena, and ricochets back to another player, who repeats the effort. It is this constant movement of reaching out to catch the speeding ball, accelerating it through the racket, and firing it back again with new speed and direction, that is the "unity of movement" which symbolizes the Thriving Church System.

THRIVING CHURCH SYSTEM

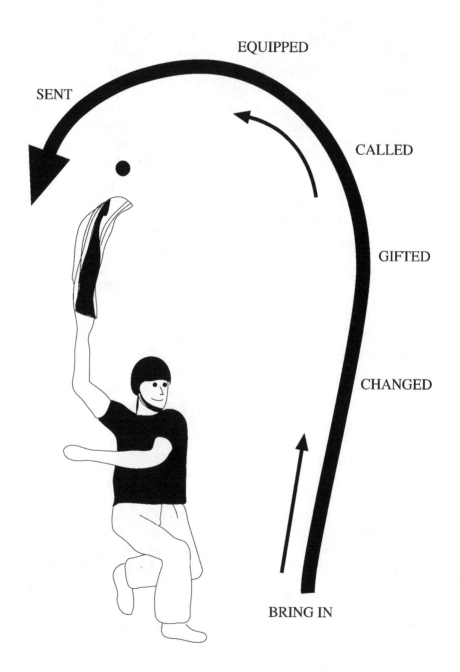

EQUIPPED

SENT

CALLED

GIFTED

CHANGED

BRING IN

Imagine the speeding ball to be Bob or Sally Public. He or she is already speeding through life on a spiritual journey, with a spiritual yearning. The church is definitively *not* playing croquet. Therefore, they do not simply wait for the speeding "ball" of Bob or Sally to slow down, sedately enter the croquet playing field, and begin regulation play in a civilized manner. Instead, like the jai alai player, the church reaches out to catch the speeding ball, heedless of where the ball is going or where it came from. They do not evaluate who that speeding person is on his or her spiritual journey, nor do they wonder what skills that speeding person might contribute to the institutional church. In fact, there is no cumbersome machinery that the church really needs that speeding person to maintain. The church is a lean, streamlined, focused athlete, whose sole and entire reason for being is to catch speeding persons who travel from afar.

Next, the church scoops Bob or Sally Public into an *experience of God's transforming power.* It is not so much a thoughtful progress through an educational process, but an exhilarating and disturbing ride through a whirlwind. It involves Bob or Sally Public in every dimension of their being. The "racket" the church uses to "scoop up" Bob or Sally as they "speed by" may be elaborate or simple. Some jai alai rackets are technologically designed and very ornate; others are just a simple wicker basket. In the same way, some churches will have big and fancy buildings, and some will have small and simple facilities. It doesn't matter. What matters is that Bob and Sally Public are scooped by the church into a whirlwind of movement. In that movement, they are changed, gifted, and called.

The church accelerates the speeding Bobs and Sallys through a process that increases their awareness of their own spiritual gifts and of God's call to ministry. They become intense, focused, and clear about their developing values and beliefs. However, lest they become merely dizzy by this movement through the whirlwind, the church accelerates them into a process that trains and equips them to pass on the life they have received to other people.

Finally, then, the church fires Bob and Sally back out into society. The church does not try to keep Bob and Sally within the matrix of church life. The whole point is to send them out of it. When Bob and Sally emerge from the "jai alai racket" of the church, they are traveling faster. They speed into life with more intensity and dynamism than ever before. They have more positive motivation, and more willpower to achieve positive things, than ever before. More than this, they speed into life in a new direction. They have a purpose to pursue and a goal to achieve. They have growing clarity regarding their gifts, their calling, and the manner in which both will be fulfilled. They have a sense of destiny. That destiny is their mission, their responsibility, and their work. They do not serve a bureaucracy, but move freely within the basic perimeters of vision, beliefs, and values of the church. Their real accountability does not lie with a committee, a treasurer, or an entitled officeholder, but with their spirituality cell group, their conscience, and God.

As Bob or Sally Public fly from the "jai alai racket" of the church, the church no longer tries to control them. The church lets go. Bob or Sally Public fly back into society motivated and equipped to do whatever it is they are gifted and called to do. They do it. They have an impact on society, as the jai alai ball has an impact on the wall of the arena. Perhaps that impact is painful for them. Perhaps that impact is joyful for them. Perhaps it is both. Most likely, Bob and Sally discover that, in order to really make a dent in the wall, they need to continue deepening their spirituality and upgrading their skills. Bob or Sally rebound off society, flying back again through the air. The church catches them again. Perhaps it will be the same thriving church, or perhaps it will be another thriving church. Perhaps they will be scooped into the same small groups, with the same mentors; or perhaps they will become involved in another small group, with different mentors. Nevertheless, the church scoops them again, accelerates them again, and sends them again. They are perpetually changed, gifted, called, equipped, and sent.

In the croquet game of the Declining Church System, all that really matters is that you make it through all the hoops to come "home." In the jai alai game of the Thriving Church System, all that really matters is that you have an impact on the world, in fulfillment of your destiny, in the name of Jesus Christ.

For those who play croquet well, it seems like the only game there is. People addicted to the Declining Church System cannot even imagine another game. If another game is described to them, they are likely to say, "Oh, that comes from another country. *We* couldn't play that game. It's not part of *our ethos.*" The first step in church transformation is to *dare to compare!*

DARE TO COMPARE

PAST	FUTURE
ENROLLED	CHANGED
↓	↓
INFORMED	GIFTED
↓	↓
NOMINATED	CALLED
↓	↓
SUPERVISED	EQUIPPED
↓	↓
KEPT	SENT

Part 2

THE ORGANIZATION BEHIND THE SYSTEM

The System and the Organization

Bob and Sally Public have been involved in New Hope-in-the-Heart Church for long enough to know that it is different from most other churches they know in the area. The Protestant evangelical churches are perplexed that New Hope-in-the-Heart Church celebrates transforming personal experiences with God, and yet does not impose an extensive doctrinal agenda with which people must agree. The folks at New Hope-in-the-Heart Church seem to have an unsettling freedom to discover and define their faith for themselves. The Protestant "mainstream" churches are perplexed that New Hope-in-the-Heart Church releases so much energy into the community for social reform and charitable outreach, and yet as a body takes relatively few public ideological stands.

One day Bob and Sally happen to be with a group from the local community "ministry association," which is trying to build mutual understanding among the religious groups of the area. People are asked to draw a picture of how their churches operate.

Most people draw structural diagrams with solid or dotted straight lines, and large or small boxes. All of the committees, groups, and offices are depicted; many lines of accountability and communication are clearly defined. It looks very efficient. It does not seem to work. Everyone is doing "restructuring." Bob and Sally Public overhear the tales of woe:

"We tried inverting the triangle," says one church, "so that real authority in the church lies with a consensus of the people, rather than with the minister and a few board members."

"We've been amalgamating committees," says another church, "since we can't find enough people to serve them anyway."

"But we've been multiplying committees," replies a third church. "We want to get as many people involved in decision making as possible."

"We took a whole year to rewrite our mission statement, and another year to rewrite our church constitution," says a fourth church. "We've decreased the number of years anyone can serve in office, and added congregational meetings in the year."

"We tried that," says a fifth church leader. "We rewrote our mission statement and constitution to build more continuity with the past. Our officers now serve more years, and the congregation only meets every other year."

On and on, the restructuring discussion continues. It becomes apparent to Bob and Sally that nothing seems to work. No matter how they deal the cards, the game is always the same. Despite all the structural tinkering, and the years of writing new mission statements and constitutions, nothing has really changed.

Finally, Bob and Sally are asked to describe how their church works. Given the context of the conversation, this isn't easy. Where others draw straight lines, Bob and Sally seem only to draw curved lines. Where others draw boxes, they draw circles. Where others have a diagram in which everything is linked to everything else at least twice, Bob and Sally have a diagram in which some things don't seem to be linked to anything at all! The other diagrams all look so neat, tidy, and complete. Bob's and Sally's diagram looks messy, untidy, and incomplete. Reactions from both "evangelical" and "mainline" church partners are unanimous.

"This looks like anarchy!" some say. "This is chaos! People are allowed to go all over the place. Where is the accountability? How can you make sure nobody does something stupid or downright immoral?"

"This looks like dictatorship!" others say. "The ordained minister and a few lay leaders will control everything. How can you make sure that your leadership will not do something stupid or immoral?"

"Where is the group identity?" still others protest. "The diversity is so great that there is nothing—no clear convictions, no firm Christian stand on the issues—to hold people together with a common cause!"

Bob and Sally do their best to explain. It is not anarchy, but there is an incredible ferment of activity. It is not dictatorship, but the leaders of the church are powerful motivators and visionaries. The people are, indeed, incredibly diverse, but the fact that they all agree about almost nothing doesn't matter.

Although Bob and Sally are not very good at explaining it, especially with the terminology and conceptual framework assumed by the local ministry association, they do have one telling argument: "It works." Somehow New

Hope-in-the-Heart Church avoids anarchy and dictatorship, does not seem to do anything overwhelmingly stupid or immoral, and manages to celebrate amazing harmony among many really different people. Perhaps to understand how this is possible, the ministry association will have to step beyond its conceptual assumptions—or simply confront some of its addictions!

A system will produce exactly what it is designed to produce—and nothing else. The organization that lies behind the system is the engine that achieves the purposes of the system. Even if the organization is not purposely designed to match the system, the system itself will slowly mold any organizational structure to fulfill the purposes of the system. So long as the system remains the same, it will not matter how radical a congregation might attempt to be in restructuring the board, or rewriting the mission statement, or redesigning the constitution. In the end, the system will mold the organization to match its own purposes. This is why many congregations devote enormous time and energy to restructuring and remissioning, only to discover several years later that *nothing has changed!* The church looks, behaves, and declines as it has done in previous years.

On the other hand, once the system changes, a radically new organization will inevitably emerge. Sometimes the new organization will be designed to match the purposes of the new system. Most often the system itself will slowly mold and shape an organization that is appropriate to the new system. If the new system is like the one described here, the resulting organization will itself be perpetually changing and adapting to new circumstances. It will not be a *rigid* organization, nor can it be legitimately called an organizational *structure*. It will be more akin to magnetic waves, in which the powers of attraction and repulsion guide the many dynamic atoms of the complex molecule.

Systemic change is *not* achieved through organizational change. It happens as bits and pieces of congregational life begin to behave differently, and then network with an ever-increasing number of other bits and pieces of congregational life to jointly behave differently. From the point of view of the existing organization, things are "getting out of control." There is often friction and conflict. The controllers may describe the situation as "chaos" or "anarchy," and seek to "clamp down" and be "authoritative." From the point of view of the participants, however, life in the church is becoming "creative" and "interesting." Eventually the old organization does collapse, but it is not necessarily replaced by chaos. It is replaced by a very different organization appropriate to the new system that is emerging.

Although systemic change never *begins* with organizational change, it inevitably *results* in a new organization. The system requires an organization to drive or guide its activity. What the new organization will look like can only be a mystery during the transition from system to system.

A system will produce exactly what it is designed to produce—and nothing else. This statement may seem obvious, but its truth is consistently ignored by countless declining churches. In the panic of church decline, these congregations lament falling worship attendance, reduced revenues, and aging membership—and at the same time they praise the close "family" bonds shared by the remaining members. They can't understand it! "How come people don't want to come to this family-oriented church?"

They blame the inadequate parking lot, but paving it does not reverse the decline. They blame the Sunday school curriculum, but buying a new resource does not reverse the decline. They blame the absence of a youth group, but cannot seem to attract youth. They blame the pastoral leadership, but can never find the right "messiah" who will rescue them from decline. They tinker with the organizational structure, rewrite the mission statement, and repair the organ, all under the banner of "church renewal." Nothing changes. They blame everything except the one thing that is really wrong: *the system!*

The "church renewal" efforts of the last twenty years have largely been a failure, because these efforts merely tried to make the old system work better. Congregations sought to improve the organization through restructuring, believing that a more efficient hierarchy would enable the old system to regain vitality. Some denominations, for example, urged congregations to move from traditional "Official Boards" composed of session and stewards, to "Unified Boards" composed of executive and multiple standing committees. The truth is, however, that it does not matter which board structure a congregation uses—*they still decline.*

The "church transformation" movement on the edge of the twenty-first century is succeeding because it addresses systemic change. Congregations in this movement realize that significant change will never happen hierarchically. That is, they understand that the organizational "top" of the system is ultimately powerless to change the system itself. Change will only happen as the bits and pieces of congregational life that lie dispersed at the "bottom" of the system, begin to network together with a common vision. Chaotic systemic change will ultimately transform the organization.

Although there is certainly an experience of chaos in this transition, it is possible to observe trends and patterns sufficiently to devise a broad strategic plan for change. The plan will constantly be redeveloped or reworked, as the networking process among the bits and pieces of congregational life refines the emerging common vision. Indeed, if the organization is willing to cooperate with change, rather than simply try to control change, it is possible simultaneously to deconstruct and reconstruct the organization in ways that keep the stress level of the participants manageable. The vision, however, always comes systemically from "below," rather than from "above," in the congregational life. To say it another way, the vision always comes from the discontented fringes of congregational life, rather than from the contented center of church membership.

Chapter 5

The Declining Church Organization

The declining church system is all about "belonging." It assumes that belonging to an institution will provide people with meaning in life. It seeks to recruit and initiate people into a group membership parallel to a "family" identity. It educates people with all the appropriate information they need to understand the system and to adapt themselves to life within the system. It seeks to preserve a heritage and concentrates on passing that heritage on to children and youth. It draws people toward the unity of a central control for church life, so that the intensity of one's "belonging" matches the degree to which one holds power. It seeks to raise money to pay for others to do ministry. It seeks to supervise those who do ministry and to manage that ministry, so that it never inadvertently contradicts the ethos, heritage, or identity of the group. This is a system in which keeping people is more important than welcoming people; and in which preserving the system is more important than addressing public needs. Mission results from whatever surplus energy and resources remain after maintaining the organization.

Such a system is best served by a hierarchical official board structure, such as the one illustrated on page 106. Congregational mission is divided into administrative units, each with a standing committee. The full council has an executive, a separate board of trustees, various large groups represented by their own officers, and an assorted number of ad hoc committees. Those who do any activity in the church are accountable to a standing committee or large group, who in turn are accountable to an executive of the board, who in turn are accountable to the full council, who are ultimately accountable to the annual meeting of the membership. Annual meetings are essentially business meetings, which review the reports of all the committees and groups, and grant permission for the agenda of the coming year.

DECLINING CHURCH ORGANIZATION
Structures, Committees, and Programs

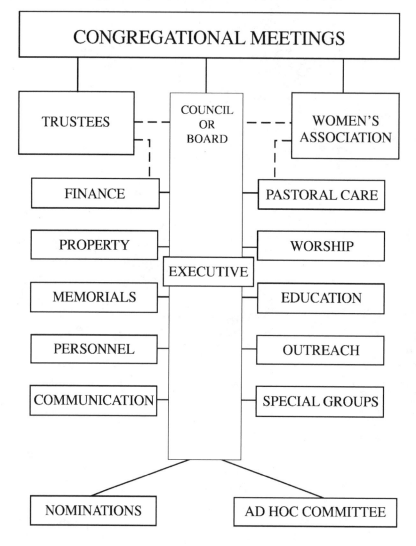

AVERAGE CHURCH PROFILE:

Members: 250
Volunteer Vacancies: 50-60
% on Committees: 20-25%
Volunteer Hrs/Mo: 60-100
Outreach Programs: 3-5

Three features of this management model are fundamental to fulfilling the goals of the system.

1. *Central control and coordination.* Each committee or group has a detailed mandate that defines everything it can or must do. The management theorist, John Carver, describes this model as "prescriptive" in that it "prescribes" or lists all the activities the group or committee has permission to undertake. The official board identifies everything on the institutional agenda that needs to be done, divides the work among the various committees, and then recruits volunteers to serve the committees, which meet the needs of the institutional agenda.

Occasionally, a request for action does not easily fit the prescribed mandate of any committee or group. The central council or executive will then appoint an ad hoc committee to either deal with the matter, or determine to which group or committee the matter should be referred.

2. *Bureaucratic consensus decision making.* Even when committees and groups act within their mandates, every decision can be appealed to the next rank of bureaucracy. Potential controversy that might disrupt the harmony of the congregation is usually avoided, since in principle even the smallest decision requires the nearly unanimous consent of the congregation. Individual actions must occur within the context of a standing committee or group, and their permission can in turn be reviewed, modified, or overturned by the executive, full council, or a congregational meeting. Every level of government must concur before any action can be taken.

Therefore, this management model is as concerned about the *process* through which possible actions are considered, as it is about the *content* of the action itself. It must be considered by the appropriate offices or structural units, and in the appropriate order, before any action is taken. Consensus is crucial.

3. *Unity through agreement.* Control, coordination, and decision making all aim at achieving a common agreement. Such agreement forms the basis of their unity. Newcomers must be initiated into concurrence, and all activities of the church must reflect that concurrence. The more detailed that concurrence can be, the more united the congregation can become—and the more aggressive the church can be in positioning itself in the spectrum of opinions held in the community. Agreement may be doctrinal, ideological, or cultural.

Therefore, this management model both assumes, and builds, homogeneity. Although diversity is acceptable, dissent around the core "agreement" of church life is not welcome. The church "family" must share the same fundamental point of view. Or, to say it another way, advancement in the system of church life depends on one's loyalty to "the party line."

These features will bind individuals to the congregation, and congregations to the denomination, so that they always confront society with a "united front" or majority perspective. Such a model requires widespread and energetic participation in the governance of the church. For example, in the typical congregation of 250 members, a total of 50 to 60 volunteer vacancies must be filled in the governance structure each year. As many as 20 percent to 25 percent of the members must serve on committees or hold offices, and together they will spend 60 to 100 total hours *every month* simply attending meetings to manage the church and participate in the bureaucratic consensus decision making. If things don't go smoothly and disagreements are not easily reconciled, the percent of the congregation required for governance will rise sharply, and so also the hours each month devoted to meetings. One denominational publishing house reports that their single, best-selling product to congregations is the "Notice of Meeting" postcard! Meanwhile, the despairing complaint in every congregational consultation is that "there are just too many meetings!"

The point is that this is exactly the organizational model which best meets the goals of the declining church system. Consensus decision making ensures that the ethos, identity, and heritage of the church will not change dramatically. The central body that sets the agenda of church activity, also divides the work, monitors the committees, and sets the pace and process of decision making. Participation in that body is carefully screened, and there is a recognition that nominees must wholeheartedly uphold the traditions of the church. If, by accident or token gesture, someone who is more radical joins the board, the radical tendencies can be neutralized by the overlapping levels of bureaucracy that are required to give permission to all things.

In this system, lay leadership manages the church. Therefore, this organizational model quite rightly multiplies opportunities to manage. The system requires newcomers to assimilate vast quantities of institutional information, for which the organization provides an endless number of meetings. The system assumes that people find meaning in life through belonging. Therefore, the organization emphasizes the holding of offices and participation in committees and large groups as the visible signs of a meaningful life. "Confirmations," "initiations," and "installations" mark the successful progress of one's participation in the church. In fact, the larger the board, the more successful the organizational model is in fulfilling the goals of the system. Since the system values membership, the organization values "input." That is to say, the organization cares less about the actual decisions made, and cares more about how many people participated in making the decisions.

In this system, keeping the members and caring for their needs is central. Therefore, this organizational model quite rightly has large pastoral care committees and devotes enormous energy to one-on-one visitation. They maintain "active" and "inactive" membership roles, and rarely remove anyone from the roles unless by request. Evangelism committees are small and oriented toward membership recruitment. The organization enables the *assimilation* of newcomers, but disables the *initiative* of newcomers. The system gives priority to the needs of the members over the needs of the guests who visit or who are sought. Thus, again, the organization refers the mission of the church to experts and professionals, and gives energy to maintaining the institution that funds and supervises the mission.

St. Friendly-on-the-Hill Church operates with this management model. Despite the fact that they are declining, they believe the top virtue of their congregational life is that they are "friendly." They refer to themselves as a "church family" and are rather hurt when Bob and Sally Public do not actively participate. Recently, uneasy about their aging membership and declining attendance, they sent a long survey *to all the people inside the church* asking them for advice to set priorities for long-range planning. The top four responses were to (1) plan more potluck suppers, (2) repair or replace the organ, (3) start a youth group, and (4) maintain the beauty of the property. St. Friendly-on-the-Hill Church has been through several restructuring initiatives and five years ago wrote a new mission statement. Nevertheless, if one asks youth or young adults, inactive or fringe people, to the congregation, they will say that nothing has really changed. Why?

The following diagram explains the answer, by tracing the journey of a creative idea through the organization of St. Friendly-on-the-Hill Church: Someone has a creative idea. Perhaps a new style of worship. Perhaps a vision for a Hispanic ministry given changes in the region. It does not matter. As is the case with all authentic visions, it causes this person literally to jump up and down with excitement. Such people have seen a burning bush, been blinded by a light, or heard a still, small voice, and they literally cannot rest until they have told someone about it. The creative idea may be large and complex, or it may be quite small. It may imply a significant expense or no financial risk whatsoever. Whatever the creative idea is, the system requires that the originator obtain permission to act upon the vision. The first group of people to hear about the exciting idea is a standing committee.

"WHY DOESN'T OUR CHURCH CHANGE?"
The Journey of a Creative Idea in the Program Church

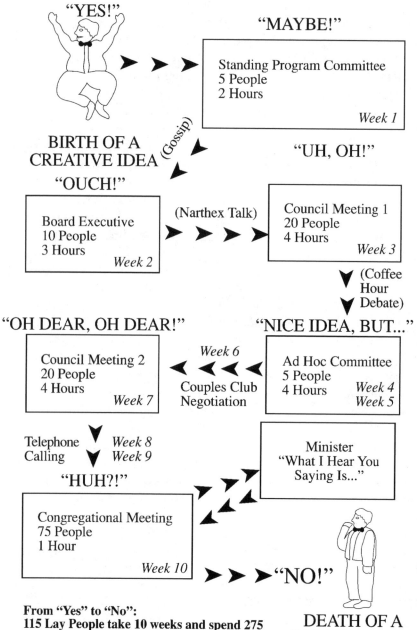

From "Yes" to "No":
115 Lay People take 10 weeks and spend 275 hours in order to say "NO"

The standing program committee meets once a month and listens to the creative idea with mixed emotions. Some get excited too, while others are more cautious. They function within a "prescriptive" model of management, which means that they have a long mandate that lists everything they can or must do. They compare the creative idea with the long list of everything they can do. Is it there? No. Therefore, they cannot take action, and they refer the matter to the executive of their board. People begin to gossip about the strange, new idea and its originator.

The next week the idea comes to the board executive. The executive committee experiences a collective "Ouch!" because they realize the idea does not appear in any of the prescriptive mandates of any committee. Indeed, it seems to involve more than one committee mandate, and they become anxious that some lay leaders will become hostile to an apparent invasion of their topical "turf." Since someone might become upset by the implementation of the creative idea, the executive decides they need a larger consensus. Now the idea is being discussed in whispered conversations in the narthex before and after the Sunday service.

The following week the full council meets, and the idea is presented. They ponder the implications of the creative idea for their identity and heritage as a church, and worry that someone might complain, lower giving, or even withdraw membership. If it costs more than $100, the finance committee casts doubt on its financial feasibility. The very fact that the full council spends an hour on the subject, and still cannot achieve a unanimous decision, increases everyone's anxiety. They refer the matter to an ad hoc committee. By this time people are beginning to debate the merits of the idea during coffee hour following the Sunday service.

The ad hoc committee includes veteran members of the church, key officers of the board, perhaps one representative of the standing committee that originally heard the idea, and rarely includes the originator of the idea. They have two meetings, and create a compromise that sounds like this: "It is a great idea, and the originator of the idea should be praised and perhaps considered for nomination to the official board next year . . . but there are several reasons why we cannot implement the creative idea." Their list of objections will include:

"We tried it once and it didn't work."
"We don't do that sort of thing."
"Someone will be upset."

"It is too expensive."

"No one knows how to do it, and we can't afford a professional."

Now debate is occurring among the "younger" and "older" couples' clubs, and women's and men's groups.

Seven weeks after the originator of the creative idea first jumped up and down, the ad hoc committee brings its recommendation back to the council. Unfortunately, the compromise fails to resolve the matter. There are still advocates of the idea who will not back down, and opposition to the idea is now becoming clearly identifiable. The majority of the council make a clear decision, a vocal minority doesn't like it, and an irritated majority feel angry that the minority will not simply accept the majority decision and keep quiet. There is no alternative. They must call a congregational meeting. During the required three weeks of waiting prior to the congregational meeting, the telephones begin ringing as advocates pro and con enlist support.

The idea is once again debated in the congregational meeting. Many of the participants in the meeting have no idea what is going on, because they are not members of the council. In fact, a number of the participants in the congregational meeting do not even attend church services regularly and have not heard the narthex gossip. As the meeting progresses without an easy consensus, the congregation asks the minister for guidance. However, the system of their church life has provided them with an enabling minister who understands himself or herself to be a servant of the people as a unified group, not a directive leader. She or he can only help them identify and resolve their feelings toward one another, and is already preparing an intensive person-to-person healing ministry following the congregational meeting. By the time the meeting ends, the congregation has made a decision. It has taken 115 laypeople approximately ten weeks and 275 total volunteer hours to say "NO!"

The originator of the creative idea is left wondering what happened. This person's vision did not seem to be accorded any merit. The excitement and energy begin to fade. The subsequent invitation to be nominated to the official board is received with mixed emotions. If such people accept the nomination, they are fearful that the system will not permit them to do much anyway, and that they will always be in the minority. If they do not accept the nomination, the church will conclude that they do not want to move closer to the center of the church family and are not prepared to be "one of us." In the 1970s and 1980s, such a person probably would have accepted the nomination to the board and given it a try. In the 1990s and beyond, that person will likely give up and go somewhere else.

The people of St. Friendly-on-the-Hill Church may themselves feel frustrated by the organization of their church. Yet there is a tremendous power and subtlety about the systems in which congregations live.

They assume that the absence of central control over all aspects of church life and mission *must necessarily* lead to chaos and discontinuity with the past. They assume that the absence of bureaucratic consensus decision making *must necessarily* lead to dictatorial leadership and disunity. They assume that healthful change *can only happen* in the church when it is initiated and controlled by the people at the "center" or the "top" of church governance.

The system itself is rarely raised to consciousness, and yet it pervades all activity and thought. The most well-meaning, generous, and thoughtful leaders cannot even imagine an organizational alternative. Indeed, if they try to do so, the system itself will block change and slowly draw the organization back to the model which best fulfills the goals of the system.

In the 1970s and 1980s, it was at least possible to stabilize church decline using this organizational model. Congregations could recognize their declining attendance, declining financial support, and aging leadership, and still take action that would slow or temporarily halt advancing crisis. Better advertising, more aggressive fund-raising, additional expert staff, and property improvements could stabilize the church. "Church renewal" helped the organization become more effective.

On the brink of the twenty-first century, however, the spiritual yearning of the public has changed so significantly, and the institutional addictions of the church have deepened so dramatically, that church decline rapidly accelerates out of control. We are entering the phase of the "Tornado of Church Decline."

One autumn, for example, a congregation not unlike St. Friendly-on-the-Hill awakens with a sense of panic to its decline. The beneficial impact of recent aggressive fund-raising, membership recruitment, and property renovations has peaked. A drop in leadership energy becomes all too apparent. A vicious downward spiral gathers destructive force.

First, they do what the organization does best. They look inward. They survey the membership of the church looking for new talent and new financial support. They ask their own constituency for the answers to what is wrong. They may send their board on retreat, so that they will bring back a new vision or discover a creative new idea to rescue the church. It is not unlike an alcoholic asking for advice from his buddies at the bar.

THE TORNADO OF CHURCH DECLINE

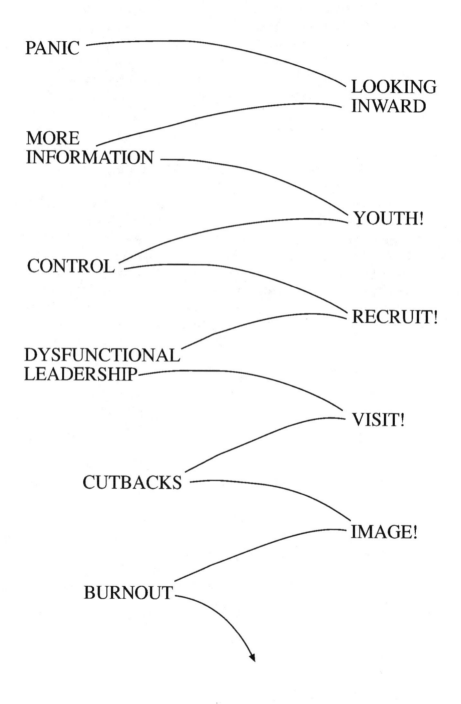

Usually, the board returns from retreat, or the surveys returned from the congregation identify a strategic plan that is much the same as the plan they used in previous years. The issue becomes communication. They believe that the reason people do not support the church is that they do not understand the church. Therefore, newsletters, personal visits, and special appeals multiply. There are more meetings, which people are vigorously encouraged to attend. The bulletin contains more and more data regarding the financial deficit, offerings, membership, and organizational events.

Next, the congregation becomes obsessed with the loss of "the youth." A successful youth program is imagined to be the salvation of the congregation. They may renovate a new "youth room," encourage teenagers to participate in worship services, and even hire a youth worker. If they are experiencing a pastoral relations change, the biggest question for prospective candidates will be, How would you reach the youth?

As efforts to recruit youth into the institutional life of the church fail, the board becomes more and more concerned with control issues. They scrutinize every line in the budget, and place "governors" on the telephones and photocopiers. They become increasingly unforgiving about mistakes, and meddle with every committee and staff position to ensure that they are doing enough work. Like people going downhill on a bicycle, they clutch the handlebars more tightly.

The church becomes preoccupied with recruitment. They "fast-forward" newcomers toward membership and office holding. They form "evangelism committees" whose chief task is to invite people to come to church and encourage their institutional support. These recruits usually bear a remarkable resemblance to the cultural, racial, linguistic, educational, and economic identities of the people already inside the institution, and are welcomed into the church specifically for the skills they bring that might support the institution. Weddings and funerals become opportunities to inform people about the benefits of church membership.

The church begins to experience "nominations nightmares." They have increasing difficulty filling all the vacant offices. Core lay leaders take on more and more tasks, accelerating their own exhaustion. Individuals are appointed to leadership without concern for their gifts, calling, or motivation. As the best lay leaders become tired, and ill-equipped or poorly motivated people fill the growing power vacuum in the church, leadership becomes dysfunctional. Some leaders become more interested in holding power over others than in empowering ministry.

Part of the scrutiny of pastoral leadership is the belief that the minister needs to visit more people, more often. If only the minister would visit all the people on the inactive list, surely they would all come back! If only the minister would visit the faithful, additional talent and energy would be revealed! The old division of labor in which the clergy do ministry and the laity do management, is transformed by dysfunctional leadership into a system in which the clergy do ministry and the board members tell them what to do and whom to see.

The finance committee becomes the key force in the church. Financial cutbacks are initiated. Salaries are frozen, support staff time is cut—and that "unproductive" youth worker hired earlier in the tornado of church decline is given notice. Program budgets are slashed. Fund-raisers concentrate less on envelope offerings and seek out memorial gifts.

As the tornado of decline reaches its final crisis, "image" becomes everything. The congregation becomes jealous of its "standing" in the community. Increasing energy is given to property maintenance, symbolism, and ceremony. Service to the organization is exaggerated in significance, as retirees are honored and nominees are initiated. They are a "proud heritage" surviving in "evil days." They strike a noble pose in community life but have little involvement in community affairs.

The actual end of the tornado of church decline can be remarkably peaceful. At the risk of confusing tornadoes and hurricanes, we notice that churches finally enter a very calm "eye" of the storm. The remaining groups and clubs meet with great affection. The small worshiping congregation lingers after services for amiable conversation. Dysfunctional leadership that enjoys power has departed, since there is now little of substance over which to have power; and the traditional leaders reclaim their central role of friendship in church life. Nevertheless, the trust funds are gradually depleted, and, in a spirit of contentment from many years of sacrificial service, the church retires toward amalgamation or closure.

Is it all inevitable? No. The spiritual yearning of the public is in a ferment of longing. The addictions of church life can be faced and overcome. The *system* of church life can be different. The organization behind the system can be changed. There is another way.

Chapter 6

The Thriving Church Organization

The thriving church system is all about "changing." It assumes that doing high-quality ministry, which flows from one's own experience of God's grace, will provide people with meaning in life. The combination of motivated action and faith-sharing, draws people into an accelerating experience of personal transformation. The system helps people feel the healing touch of God that frees them from destructive addictions and empowers them to "stand outside" themselves to become new creatures. It helps them go deeper into spirituality and faith through the close intimacy of mutual support. The thriving church helps them to discern and use their spiritual gifts in surprising and unexpected ways. It assists them to explore their relationship with Christ, and to discover a personal and practical destiny, or calling, the fulfillment of which lies beyond the church among the public. The system then equips them to do mission and ministry with excellence, and stands aside to release them into the world to bring the hope of transformation to individuals and society.

Such a system is best served, not by a "structure" of governance that guides an institution, but by an ever-changing magnetic field that surrounds and binds together a complex organism. The energy waves of attraction and repulsion keep an organism from flying apart in a thousand directions, and yet at the same time animate all the many atoms and molecules of the organism to grow and develop in a million-and-one unique ways. It is not a "timeless" structure that endures despite the changes in society around it, but a "timely" organism that changes shape in constant response to the changes around it.

The thriving church organization diagram is imperfect due to the limitations of the printed page. The organization that best serves the thriving church system is, in fact, *four-dimensional*. It will look different over time. It has a "cinematographic," rather than a "photographic," character. Think of the picture here as but a "freeze-frame" of a much longer movie.

THRIVING CHURCH ORGANIZATION

Energy Field, Small Groups, and Missions

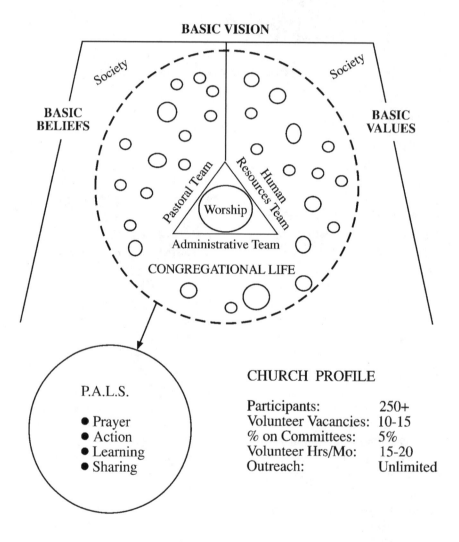

BASIC VISION

Society

Society

BASIC BELIEFS

BASIC VALUES

Pastoral Team

Human Resources Team

Worship

Administrative Team

CONGREGATIONAL LIFE

P.A.L.S.

- Prayer
- Action
- Learning
- Sharing

CHURCH PROFILE

Participants:	250+
Volunteer Vacancies:	10-15
% on Committees:	5%
Volunteer Hrs/Mo:	15-20
Outreach:	Unlimited

The thriving church system is best served by an organization that encourages individual initiative, self-discovery, and deep spirituality. It will be an organization that nurtures the multiplication of small groups, even as "cells" multiply in the organic body. It will be an organization with an overarching sense of identity and purpose, but which allows the many parts of the organism absolute freedom to do what they were created to do. Such an organization will concentrate on motivating, communicating, and training, rather than controlling, coordinating, and initiating. The organization will serve the individual participants, rather than insist that the participants serve the organization. Such an organization will not see itself in constant confrontation with the world, but rather in constant conversation with the world. It equips people for profound interaction with the public. Finally, and most important, such an organization will give priority to experience over mere understanding. It will be open to the inbreaking of the "Holy." It will be unafraid of the irrational.

Three features of this organizational model are fundamental to fulfilling the goals of the system.

1. *Decentralized control and multiplying, self-guided mission units.* Responsibility for the design and implementation of ministry is given to groups (large and small), and even given to individuals as they discern their gifts and hear their callings. The management model is proscriptive rather than prescriptive.

The church does not list everything that can or must be done, but simply names that which *cannot* be done. This means that the agenda for mission is not determined by an official board, or even by an annual meeting, but emerges from the groups and individuals as they are motivated to use the unique gifts they have discovered.

2. *Streamlined administration by the trusted, gifted few.* The day-to-day maintenance, financial management, and administration of the church is entrusted to a small group who are spiritually gifted, called, and trained. Their mission is administration. Their purpose is not to give permission for work, but to enable the work to be done with excellence. Administrative decisions are made quickly and efficiently. Rarely, a potential activity may test the perimeters of the basic values, beliefs, and vision of the church, and the administration team will consult with the staff to make a decision regarding implementation.

Even more rarely, a proposed complex project may be brought before a congregational meeting. However, congregational meetings are reserved for celebration and visioning, not reporting and accountability.

3. *Unity through experience.* The church is radically diverse, and bursting with any number of activities or missions, involving all ages, cultures, languages, and races. Disagreement is acceptable, and diversity in doctrinal and ideological perspective is expected. The unity of the church lies in the continuing shared experience of the transforming power of God.

Aside from its basic beliefs, values, and vision, the church as an organism rarely seeks to take public positions on issues. Indeed, small groups within the church may passionately disagree about political, social, ethical, or doctrinal issues. Unity is "of the heart," rather than "of the mind." Mutual respect is built through the spirituality of church life, rather than the consensus of church bureaucracy.

Such a model requires widespread and energetic participation in the *spirituality* of church life, but not the *governance* of church life. There are only two management teams, and only ten to fifteen volunteer vacancies that must be filled in order to manage the church. If the congregation has about 250 participants, only 5 percent of the congregation must serve the organization. Indeed, *the larger* the congregation becomes, *the smaller* the portion of the congregation required for governance. This is exactly the reverse of the declining church organizational model, which must proportionately increase the administrative structure as the congregation grows. In the thriving church model, the staff spend very little time with administrative matters, and even the volunteers need to spend only 15 to 20 total hours a month attending team meetings.

Once again, this is exactly the kind of organizational model which best meets the goals of the thriving church system. Streamlined decision making ensures that people are liberated to deepen their spirituality, explore their continuing experiences of God's transforming power, and actively *do* ministry. The combination of motivational worship, small group sharing, and quality training addresses the spiritual yearning of the public for ecstasy, intimacy, and destiny. The entire energy of the church is shifted *outward* to interact with the world.

In the thriving church system, lay leadership does ministry. Therefore, the organizational model minimizes management and frees individuals to take immediate action in response to the passion of their callings. Since the system assumes that meaning in life results from active giving, rather than passive belonging, the organizational model aims at mission rather than maintenance. Since the system gives priority to the needs of the public over the needs of the membership, the organization equips people to use their spiritual gifts to engage the public and expects them to do so. There is no such thing as an "inactive member" in this organization. Membership *means* a covenant to go deeper into faith and mission. Indeed, if a "member" is not engaged consistently in purposeful faith development and action, that person is not a "member." Membership may even become a commitment that is annually renewable on the part of both the individual and the church.

Step-by-step, we can use the diagram to better understand the emerging organizational model of the thriving church system.

Note at the very beginning that the diagram is not a pyramid shape, pointed up, down, or sideways. Standing a hierarchical pyramid upside down to give the illusion that control of the organization has been transferred to the "grassroots" membership is merely tinkering with the same old paradigm. Thriving churches are moving to a whole new system, and to a whole new organizational model. Solid vertical lines of accountability and carefully defined boxes for mandated committees are missing from the new organizational model. Within the limitations of a printed page, the diagram describes a dynamic organization.

Thriving church organization is NOT a structure. It is a magnetic field that shapes and reshapes itself in response to the changing context of community need and emerging mission.

Thriving church organization is NOT three-dimensional. It is four-dimensional. It expects and desires to change over time. Stress in the organization does not result from a fixed structure forced to adapt to changing circumstances, but results whenever an ever-changing magnetic field is in danger of becoming fixed.

The dynamic organization is not primarily interested in *control,* nor is it preoccupied with survival. It is interested in *motivation,* and is eager to transform itself into whatever form is required to deliver mission to the point of human need.

The old organizational model might perhaps be pictured as a system of rigid pipes and conduits through which energy is conducted to prearranged destinations. As the pipes and conduits multiply or age, the energy conducted through them diminishes. In the end, every conceivable destination is linked by organizational "conduits," but there is little energy left over to be delivered to the destination of human need.

The new organizational model might perhaps be pictured as an "electromagnetic field" in which energy is accelerated and then released to unknown destinations. The magnetic polarities embodied in the basic beliefs, values, and vision of the organization activate and accelerate the flying "electrons" of individual participation, even as the heat of the Holy Spirit causes the "atoms" of small group life to interact vigorously. Energy radiates from the electromagnetic field in any number of directions simultaneously. However, the energy particles are not conducted to prearranged destinations, but are self-guided to deliver greatest impact at the point of human need.

The thriving church system is a high-speed, intense experience. The organizational model, therefore, is designed to be explosive. However, if properly handled, the impact on congregational life, witness, and mission is enormous.

The Energy Field of Church Life

The congregation must determine the basic, fundamental, or essential vision, beliefs, and values of church life. This defines the essential identity of the church as it exists for the participants today. It is not a repetition of the heritage of the church, or an articulation of the beliefs and values of past founders of the church. It is today's answer to the key question, *What is it about our experience of Jesus Christ that this community cannot live without?*

Although it is true that there must be broad consensus about the basic vision, beliefs, and values of church life, this consensus is not achieved by bureaucracy. Committees do not simply go away on retreat and return to deliver a printed summary that is as inclusive as possible. Consensus is achieved through an intense discipline of spiritual "waiting" and "searching," as the Holy Spirit works among the individuals of the church. The consensus that emerges is not an assent to a list of propositions, but a "team ownership" of a particular orientation to God. Its power and authenticity are verified by the fact that *some people will leave the church!* There are various possible orientations to God, with equal respectability, and some people will decide that this particular orientation to God is not for them. Or, some people may decide that they are simply not ready or willing to commit themselves to the covenant shared by the emerging "team."

The thriving church system is not concerned with keeping people but with welcoming people. Even so, the organizational model will define the perimeters of church life beyond which one cannot go without leaving the identity of the church. These basic perimeters function like magnetic polarities of "attraction" and "repulsion." They must be basic enough that they define only the essentials within which many different interpretations and perspectives are possible. They draw an enormous diversity of people into the life of the church who wish to explore life's meaning within a rather large arena for experience and understanding of the divine. At the same time, they must be specific and clear enough to mark the boundaries that separate *this* religious experience from others which may have equal legitimacy in the eyes of the world.

A. THE "ELECTROMAGNETIC FIELD"

OUR BASIC VISION:
OUR "SONG IN THE HEART,"
"MOTIVATING POWER," OR "REASON TO LIVE"

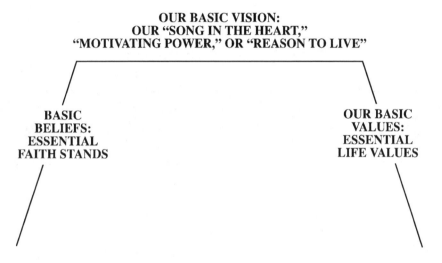

BASIC	OUR BASIC
BELIEFS:	VALUES:
ESSENTIAL	ESSENTIAL
FAITH STANDS	LIFE VALUES

The *basic vision* of the church is the "electricity" that links and energizes the magnetic fields of beliefs and values. It is not a "mission statement," but a "song in the heart." It is not prose, but poetry. It is the key vision (image, metaphor, song, picture, symbol, etc.) which makes the heart of every participant beat faster. It is not a rational or intellectual matter, but an emotional or heartfelt point of association. Indeed, if the vision can be expressed fully in words, it is not an authentic vision. No two persons of the church will describe the vision exactly the same way, but when they see it they will both embrace each other in team jubilation.

For example, in one church the vision was revealed through a song entitled "From the Slave Pens of the Delta." The song had a rhythm and beat, a melody, and poetic phrases that evoked a heart-pounding and enthusiastic response from all who shared the vision. Whenever they sang it (and they sang it frequently), people would stand and clap and sway and smile and laugh, and generally get thoroughly *excited*. When they left the church they were possessed by an inner compulsion to stop in the coffee shop and tell complete strangers about their vision. They felt an urgency to *do something—now!* The vision led them to tear down their huge, old, drafty, beautiful Gothic church building, and construct an eleven-story apartment building for newly arrived immigrants, with the church sanctuary on the first floor.

Visions come only to individuals, usually after an unpredictable amount of time of waiting and prayer, but sometimes right "out of the blue" to someone who never sought them. Visions are often frightening, always powerful, and transform the lives of people who experience them. Consider Jacob's vision of the ladder into heaven; or Moses' encounter with the burning bush; or Isaiah's visitation by the seraphim in the Temple; or Peter's dream of inclusivity that led to the conversion of Cornelius. Consider Saul's transformation on the Damascus road, or the Philippian jailer's experience of an earthquake. All these are visions, and they happen to ordinary people.

Visions only survive, however, as team visions. Individuals experience visions, and share them with others. Together the vision is refined, clarified, and tested to make sure it is not a lingering addiction. The very urgency with which visions are experienced makes the vision a public proclamation. The interaction of the vision and the public tests its authenticity and power. If it meets public needs and is greeted with celebration, the vision may be authentic. If the vision has no inner urgency to move beyond the church, or if it meets only institutional needs and is greeted with public indifference, it is likely an addiction.

The emerging basic vision may be elaborated as a mission statement, but the statement cannot take the place of the vision. A mission statement can only place an individual in an organization, but an authentic vision that is foundational to the church will make participants feel that they are a part of a great destiny. They are the "nobility" or the "royalty" to which Scripture refers: "But you are a chosen race, a royal priesthood, a holy nation, God's own people, in order that you may proclaim the mighty acts of him who called you out of darkness into his marvelous light" (1 Pet. 2:9). In the end, all authentic visions will be visions of Jesus Christ. That is to say, they will be visions not merely of creative growth or wilderness journeys, but of the transforming power of God that frees people from addictions to new life.

Once the basic vision becomes clear, the congregation must articulate its essential or *basic beliefs*. There is a sense in which basic beliefs might simply be summarized by the conviction of God's transforming power revealed through Jesus Christ. The summary of basic beliefs will likely say more, however. Perhaps it will include some reference to the sources of Christian truth, the nature and destiny of creation, or the experience of God as Creator, Sustainer, and Redeemer. Whatever is included, the summary of basic beliefs will be relatively brief and abundantly clear, and it will be given in current and easily understood language.

The summary of basic beliefs is not a catechism, nor is it a long or detailed list of dogmas and doctrines. It is intended as a summary of the essential beliefs that are normative for a specific church, and which shape their congregation's identity. It never attempts to say everything about faith, pursue every doctrinal option, or clarify every nuance of dogma for universal agreement. It is a basic summary that invites and welcomes further dialogue and continuing discussion.

Similarly, the summary of basic beliefs is not a repetition or a revision of a historical creed or a denominational affirmation. It is the fresh summary of the normative beliefs of a specific group of people, expressed in their own words and out of their own experience. A "team ownership" of the basic beliefs is formed, not because it has been handed down by former generations in books of law, and not because it has been written by theological experts, but because every person can say, "Yes! This is how I myself have come to understand the transforming power of God that I, myself, have experienced."

Some people have found a modern language version of the Statement of Faith from the United Church of Canada a helpful guide as they ponder their basic beliefs. This is because it was written purposely for evangelical conversation with the public. The preamble declares: "But Christians of each new generation are called to state [the Church's faith] afresh in terms of thought of their own age, and with the emphasis their age needs." This statement of faith then tries to describe, briefly and clearly, what they mean by God, Jesus Christ, the Holy Spirit, the church, church leadership, Scripture, and the final purposes of God for the world.

Such statements of faith can only be guides. The summary of basic beliefs must be generated afresh by the specific congregation. Just as the basic vision may be different from church to church, so also the summary of basic beliefs may be different. For example, one church may consider certain sacraments (signs of God's grace) essential to its beliefs, while others may not. Some churches may consider certain interpretations of the role of the clergy as essential, while others may not. Some churches may conscientiously use trinitarian formulas, while others may not. The important thing is to make the basic beliefs a summary of what is truly essential to the congregation.

Congregations must cross-examine themselves, challenge themselves, and search themselves. What is truly *essential?* And what is important to many, but not truly essential to all? And what is merely the passion of a highly visible small group or a particularly vocal individual? Are certain beliefs about sacraments, the clergy, or Christian life and duty truly essential to the identity of this specific church? For example, some may believe the virgin birth central to their faith, while others do not test their mission and ministry by assent to that dogma. Some may believe Scripture can be interpreted literally, while others will interpret Scripture more broadly. The process of determining what is essential for a specific church is to answer this question: *On what basis can people hold different, and even contradictory views, about a specific doctrine or dogma, and still live together in mutual respect in this church?*

The congregation must articulate its *basic values* in much the same way. These are the behavioral principles or guidelines which will shape the quality of life within the church, set the standard for personal relationships, and establish the moral identity of the church in the community. A simple statement of the Golden Rule is not sufficient. The congregation must list and name its values in a way that invites concrete evaluation and commands the respect of the public.

The summary of basic values is not an ideology. It is not intended to convey a specific social, political, or economic agenda. It should name expectations of the church for healthy and responsible interpersonal behavior regardless of social, political, or economic point of view. It does not use vague jargon, or make broad claims to being in "solidarity" with specific groups of people. It should specify how newcomers, visitors, observers, and even antagonists of the church will be treated. It does not impose a mission agenda on the church. It should describe how members of the church will behave in any and all activities of the church, from the simplest to the most complex task.

Similarly, the summary of basic values is not a book of manners. It does not try to define social skills, restrict spontaneous self-expression, or classify mannerisms as "appropriate" or "inappropriate." It should not force people to pretend they have a certain type of personality when they do not. Keeping silence in the sanctuary, avoiding profanity, and observing dress codes are all examples of nonessential matters of etiquette. The summary of basic values should describe the fundamental attitudes that should motivate all behavior, whether loud or quiet, cultivated or socially inept.

Many municipal governments, boards of education, charities, and businesses have begun naming their basic values. Consideration of human rights charters will also help the congregation define its own position. The summary of basic values may include reference to gender equality, inclusion of children, equal respect for single or married people, guidelines to avoid sexual harassment, protection against coercion or manipulation, and so on. Once again, the important thing is that the summary be truly *basic* to the credibility of the church. The basic values have team ownership, not because an outside authority has named them, but because each individual within the church can say, "Yes! These are the values to which I aspire, because they are grounded in my own experience of the transforming power of God."

Congregations will need to challenge themselves profoundly to determine what is truly *essential* to their basic values. There must be a clear and conscious continuity between the way members speak and behave when they are within the church, and when they are at leisure or in the workplace. The extent to which members are willing to risk specific actions in the public arena is the true indication of what is really "essential" in the basic values of their church. Here is the key question for formulating basic values: *On what basis can people behave very differently in public, "get on each other's nerves," and even quarrel with one another at home and at work, and still live together with mutual respect within the church?*

The Circle of Church Life

Within the energy field of basic vision, beliefs, and values, there is a ferment of church life. The basic vision, beliefs, and values of the church define the perimeters beyond which church participants cannot go—but within which they are completely free to do whatever they are called to do. They do not have to ask permission. They do not have to wait for a bureaucracy. They do not have to have the consensus of the whole church. They can take initiative instantly, designing and implementing mission in any direction they wish. No matter how crazy the idea may seem, or how complex and challenging the activity may be, people are free to try it. The church will help them do it with excellence.

B. THE "CIRCLE OF CHURCH LIFE"

BASIC VISION

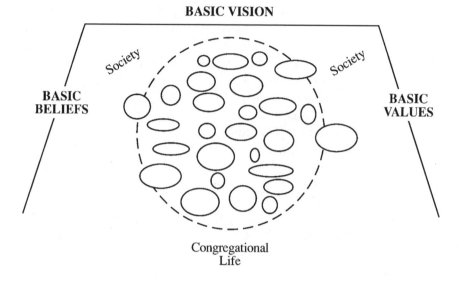

Congregational
Life

It is important to note that while much of society may be outside the energy field, with significantly different visions, beliefs, and values, there will be many others in the community who are sympathetic in a variety of ways with such perimeters for meaningful living. They represent the primary source of partnership and dialogue for the church in the community, and the group most likely to be drawn into the spirituality and mission of the church.

Unlike the old organizational model of church life, there is no clear boundary line between the "insiders" and "outsiders" of church life. Membership represents a commitment to spirituality, not a status in an organization. In the new model, the church is composed of "participants," and if that seems ambiguous, so be it. If someone is not participating in some way, that person is not really part of the church—regardless of official membership "status." On the other hand, if someone is participating in some way with the church, that person is a part of the church—regardless of institutional allegiance. In the old model, it was possible to declare on statistical forms an exact membership total. In the new model, not only is it difficult to declare exactly how many people are members of the church, but the church itself believes that that is not a particularly important statistic!

Notice that the boundary line between the church and the surrounding society is *porous*. Points of entry into church life are everywhere.

The public is coming and going, exploring and experimenting with church life all the time. One does not have to start with a visitor's card in the church service, and proceed through specified membership training classes, in order to be wholeheartedly in the church. Instead, there are a million-and-one interactive ways in which the public can penetrate into the heart of church experience, and, if suddenly hesitant or overwhelmed, they can back away again. *It is the public that controls the manner and pace of its involvement with the church—not the institution.* The church is like "Velcro," with a million-and-one "hooks" with which people can connect some aspect of their lives with the mission of the church.

Not only is the public coming and going vis-à-vis the church, but all the participants in the church are going and coming vis-à-vis society! There is no committee charged with "outreach" into the community, nor is there some designated group responsible for the "recruitment" of new members. Instead, all in the church are purposely interacting with the public, communicating the degree of joy authentic to their individual discovery of faith, and exercising their spiritual gifts as they have come to understand them so far. *It is the individual participant who controls the manner and pace of action and witness with the community—not the institution.* The church is like "radiation," sending off a million-and-one glowing, uniquely different particles that affect the world in large and small ways.

Remember Bob—whose experience with the thriving church system— led him to discover gifts of mentoring and callings with addicted youth? Bob radiates into society as one who is changed, gifted, called, equipped, and sent. Along the way, he gets to know his neighbor, Fred. It would be hard to describe Fred as a "seeker," because he is relatively content with his life and not particularly motivated to explore matters of faith more deeply than he did when he was in college. Moreover, Fred is institutionally disenchanted, and has little enthusiasm for attending church except on Christmas Eve. However, Fred does share many of the basic values Bob celebrates, and some of the basic beliefs Bob advocates. Most important of all, Fred has a teenager.

Fred and Bob get to know each other and talk. They talk Saturday morning when they set the trash by the curbside. They talk over a beer after work. They discover a mutual motivating point, which is related to teenagers and temptations. Fred becomes quite interested in Bob's volunteer work with kids. Bob invites Fred to be part of their small group, from which the mission originates. Fred never comes to worship, he is allowed to be skeptical of their process of discernment of spiritual gifts, and he never speaks a word in prayer—but he does get involved in working with teens. He becomes a part of the church.

Remember Sally—whose experience with the thriving church system led her to discover gifts in administration and callings with elder day-care? Sally radiates into society as one who is changed, gifted, called, equipped, and sent. She never *plans* to share her faith. It just happens, because the touch of God that changed her, and the meaningful life God has opened for her, are things worth talking about. Sonja, another student in her community college class, shares her interest, but cannot understand her motivation. They talk—during coffee breaks, at the supermarket, on the telephone—and it becomes clear that Sonja carries lots of griefs, hurts, and anxieties that have given her great compassion for others, but which also give periodic fits of deep depression. She longs for a vision that can really sustain her compassion. She would like to be free . . . changed . . . different.

Sally invites Sonja to come to worship with her. Sally picks her up, sits with her, and talks with her about it during the week. Sonja fears the intimacy of a small group, is openly doubtful about some of the things that are said in the mentoring message of the service, and never reads the Bible. That's O.K. with Sally. Sally never pressures Sonja, even when Sonja becomes too uneasy in worship and stays away for a few weeks. What attracts Sonja is the perception of authentic life changes happening in the lives of worship participants—and her own longing to be different. More often than not, she is there with Sally in worship. She becomes part of the church.

Within that porous, ambiguous circle that defines the church in society, much of the ferment of self-discovery and mission happens in the context of small groups. Unlike the old model, there are no program committees planning and implementing the mission agenda of the institution. Instead, there are increasing numbers of spirituality cell groups, which generate and implement their own mission agenda. These are the many small circles that are pictured in the diagram. They are the multifaceted nuggets of supreme worth in the system, because that is where the maturing process of authentic faith happens. They are the shining gems that reflect the joy of the worship service back into the world in innumerable, surprising, and concrete ways.

The small groups are so diverse in participation, organization, and topical interest, that it is difficult to describe them collectively. They are not all stamped from an institutional "cookie cutter," because the participants design each group themselves in a manner that best suits their time, topic, and personalities. There is not even a single pattern to their creation. Initially, two or three persons may come together around a shared interest. The interest may be a topic, task, hobby, activity, life experience, social issue, or anything else that brings people together in intense conversation. As these few people meet others who share their interest (within or beyond the church), new enthusiasts are invited to join the group.

For example, Bob and Sally joined a group whose interest was model railroading. They were invited to join through an encounter with a new friend within the church during a fellowship dinner. Later, Bob moved on to a group related to youth work, and he brought Fred to the group through his neighborhood associations. Other groups may include people who build and renovate homes for the poor, people who study the great religious texts of the world, people who love performing rock music, people who play handbells, people who pray, people who care for the terminally ill, people who promote environmentally friendly household products, people who play contract bridge, people who repair automobiles, people who fight child pornography, people who resist alcohol abuse, and so on. Some people will join a topical small group, and, as self-awareness and trust grow, move on to a group oriented around a deeper personal issue or social task. Others will leap into a support group motivated by a deep personal need.

New-Hope-in-the-Heart Church calls these diverse associations of people "P.A.L.S. Groups" (short for Prayer, Action, Learning, Sharing). In addition to their topical conversation or activity, they all do the following four things:

1. *Prayer.* Whenever the group meets together, participants pray for others. Prayer may be sophisticated or simple, long or brief, liturgical or spontaneous, or offered in silence or spoken words. However it is done, each group will take time to focus on a personal connection with God that is also oriented toward the well-being of others.

2. *Action.* Whenever the group meets, participants do what they love to do. It is a "hands-on" and personally involving time. As the group deepens in trust and faith, the activity evolves into a *mission* activity. That is, they do what they love to do in a manner that benefits somebody else.

3. *Learning.* Whenever the group meets, participants read and talk about the Bible in relation to their daily lives. This is more of a "Bible conversation" than a "Bible study." They simply read a "chunk" of Scripture and talk

about it. They may read their local newspaper, too, but the point is that they discuss how the Bible is or is not relevant to their lives.

4. *Sharing.* Whenever the group meets, participants build a trust that leads to intimate sharing. Not only do they talk about their interest, but they begin talking about their personal struggles and joys, worries and hopes. They support and mentor one another, building profound friendships.

The proportion of time spent on these four things will vary from time to time, and from group to group. Gradually, however, as honesty and caring grow, the joy of their interest also grows. As spirituality deepens, the joy of their interest is carried over into positive activities for others. Throughout the twin processes of relationship-building and faith-building, individuals become increasingly aware of their spiritual gifts and begin listening for their spiritual callings.

The church lets the small groups develop as the participants wish, but it does nurture every group with the following strategy:

1. *Trained leaders.* Every group will have a leader who is gifted and called to that ministry. This is the "eldership" of the church. These leaders are the "pastors," "shepherds," and "mentors" of the group. They not only share enthusiasm for the group's mutual interest, but they are trained in prayer, Scripture, and counseling. Beyond the content of group life, they are trained in group process and communication skills, so that they can help the group build the trust and intimacy that overcome inevitable personality conflicts. Such leaders meet periodically together with the staff, mutually supporting one another to overcome emerging problems, and upgrading their skills. They will become the caregivers who will be the first contacts for group members in times of crisis.

2. *Weekday home gatherings.* Most groups will meet outside the church building, usually in the homes of the participants. The nature of the group may lead them to meet in other public places, but it will always be in the surroundings of daily life. Groups will usually meet weekly, although the exact times will also vary according to the nature of the group.

3. *Time-limited commitments.* Participation in the group is not "forever," but for a specific period of time (often nine months to a year). The mission activity of a group may further define the time unit of commitment for a participant in smaller, workable portions. If the task of the group is complex, they will form partnerships with other P.A.L.S. groups in a cluster of overlapping efforts. If the task of the group is intended to have a long life,

the group itself will strategize how to pass its work on to others. The message is clear: "It is important to start, great to be involved, and O.K. to stop!"

4. *Intentional multiplication*. The small groups never exceed ten to twelve persons, in order to preserve the intimacy of the group. If more people become involved, the group divides to form two or more groups. Even without new people, the personal and spiritual growth of the group should lead participants in new directions. Therefore, the norm of small group life will be for a group to divide and multiply every nine to twelve months. This adds incentive for personal growth and proactively welcoming newcomers. New group leaders will emerge either from within the group (as the current leader identifies and mentors someone with the gifts and calling), or from beyond the group (as the church enables individuals with the gifts and calling to be equipped to start a new group).

The important thing to note here is that in this organizational model, all of the "program," "ministry," or "mission" work of the church happens through such groups. It does not happen by committee. Mission emerges out of the intentional spirituality and intimacy of small groups. The small groups set the agenda for mission—not the institution. The church trains and nurtures the small groups to function in a certain way, but does not dictate the content or direction of small group life.

Although the multiplying small groups are the primary vehicle of mission and ministry for the church, there is still more to the ferment of ministry that lies in the circle of church life. Each changed, gifted, called, equipped, and sent layperson becomes a mentor or midwife for others.

Remember Sonja—the person Sally befriended from her community college class, who is searching for healing and personal change, and who attends worship periodically? Sonja is very uncomfortable in small groups. There are, however, a number of topical large groups within the church which Sonja can attend in relative anonymity. There is an in-depth Bible study class, for example, that includes about thirty persons in four intensive sessions. Sonja finds that class helpful in answering some of her questions left over from the mentoring message of the worship service. Also, there is a continuing Sunday school support network that interests Sonja. She is a single parent, and finds this loose network of Sunday school workers a nonthreatening way to do helpful tasks that keep her near her young son. Both these large groups require minimum commitment from Sonja, and plenty of opportunity to ponder any future steps. More than this, she is able to meet a variety of other people at various stages of searching and spiritual growth.

Remember Fred—the person Bob has invited to be a part of the small group involved with teenagers? Fred still has no interest in the worship service, or in the church as a whole, but his small group experience is beginning to open his eyes to some new possibilities and questions. For one thing, Fred is motivated to get more serious about joining Bob in community youth work. Therefore, when the opportunity came to take a special class at the church training youth workers, he jumped at the chance. Of course, the fact that Bob was one of the resource people for the event helped! For another thing, the small group experience piqued Fred's curiosity about the Bible. When the class was offered to do deeper Bible study, he attended a few sessions that touched on issues of particular interest.

(Curiously enough, Sonja and Fred met for the first time in the Bible study class. Fred thought Sonja was weird and too concerned with speculative imaginings about the Bible that were rather bizarre. Sonja thought Fred was boring and overconcerned with scientific fact-finding that was largely irrelevant. Although they really couldn't tolerate each other for long, they were both a little amazed that they each gleaned something valuable from Bible study.)

Generally speaking, in New Hope-in-the-Heart Church there are five categories of faith development opportunities beyond the small groups:

1. *Large fellowship and learning groups.* These are groups of twenty or thirty persons who gather periodically through the year for fellowship or parties, or for detailed Bible study or topical presentations. Such groups are always time-specific for a stated number of sessions, a weekend retreat, a day or an evening, or a specific workshop. They may target a particular demographic group: age, gender, language, and so on.

2. *Large support networks.* These are informal volunteer networks related to various support, maintenance, or educational tasks. Participants attend no regular gatherings, but they have an interest in a task and are willing to be "on call" to help with a specific project. People who do crafts, carpentry, telephone calling, cooking, and so on, may form such informal networks.

3. *Child care and Sunday school.* These are the trained, volunteer staff who teach Sunday school classes or lead the nursery. They usually work directly with a pastoral leader on staff with the church, and design and implement curriculum and learning activities for children. They function as a P.A.L.S. Group.

4. *Spiritual gifts discernment and counseling.* These groups combine classes using spiritual gifts and personality inventories, with confidential counseling to assist individuals in the discernment process. Such groups may meet several evenings or for a weekend retreat, and may convene over and over again through the year for people who are motivated by the worship services or small groups to go deeper in search of their callings.

5. *Specialized training.* These training classes may be short-term or long-term, involving many people or just one person. They are specifically created to equip people with special skills to fulfill any calling with excellence. They do not include the merely curious, but include motivated, gifted participants who are serious about doing a specific ministry.

These large groups and networks almost all rise out of the small groups of the church. That is, behind every large group or faith development network, there will almost always be a small group of people who provide the leadership and development of the program. The large group emerges as a mission of a small group. If a fellowship or educational event is planned, there will always be a small group behind it. If spiritual gifts discernment or specialized training courses are offered to the church, there will always be a small group of covenanted laypeople who provide the expertise and motivation for it. Even the Sunday school and nursery are organized and operated by multiple small groups. Indeed, different small groups may offer parents choices of different styles and methods of Christian education in which their children can be enrolled. Once again, nothing happens by committee. Everything happens as it arises from the spirituality of a small group that is gifted, called, and equipped to do ministry.

In New Hope-in-the-Heart Church, Sonja participated in a support network for Christian education for children. She would come as needed to help children with crafts. In the process, Sonja discovered that she didn't like the basic Sunday school program for her children. Then she heard that another small group was organizing an alternative Christian education experience for children based on Montessori principles. For the first time, Sonja felt motivated to join a small group!

The Stability of Church Life

From the point of view of the old organizational model, New Hope-in-the-Heart Church should be on the brink of anarchy. Individuals and small groups have been freed to design and implement any activity they wish, without central control. The mission agenda is not fixed by a central board (which then recruits the required talent), but emerges from the participants (who expect to be trained in creative ways). The coming and going of the public through church life, and of the church participants into the public arena, is happening so fast, and in so many ways, that no one can really keep track of it. Surely the church is in danger of losing its identity, and exploding itself into a thousand fragments! What keeps the church together?

C. THE STABILITY TRIANGLE

BASIC VISION

BASIC BELIEFS

Pastoral Leadership Team

Human Resources Team

Administration Team

BASIC VALUES

Stability comes in two ways. The first way has already been mentioned, namely, the perimeters of basic vision, beliefs, and values which form the "electromagnetic field" within which the ferment of church life occurs. Although anything can happen within the perimeters, those perimeters provide a continuity of church ethos that stabilizes congregational life. Individuals and groups cannot go beyond the perimeters.

The second source of stability for church life comes from the triangle in the center of the diagram. The three connecting legs of the triangle which coordinate, manage, and monitor church life are the pastoral leadership team, the administration team, and the human resources team. Each has its separate function, which will be described shortly, but together they maintain the energy field of basic vision, beliefs, and values. On those rare occasions when the perimeters seem to be tested by an unusually creative or bizarre idea, these are the people who will determine whether or not the idea is beyond consideration.

For example, imagine for a moment that a small group of people in New Hope-in-the-Heart Church come to the pastoral leadership team, and say, "We believe Jesus Christ has called us to start a 'white supremacy' political organization within our church." It will not take long for the pastoral staff and administration teams to respond, "We're sorry, but the idea of a 'white supremacy' group within our church contradicts our basic value of racial equality. It can't be done." Those within the "stability triangle" of leadership will then cross-examine themselves. Have they somehow erred in clarifying or communicating the basic values of church life? Has the leader of that small group guided them in a wrong direction? Does the leader of the small group need additional training? Is there something wrong with the spirituality of the group? The staff always asks, "What could we do better to make sure people understand the basic vision, beliefs, and values of church life?"

It does, of course, happen that people will leave New Hope-in-the-Heart Church because they cannot live even within the broad perimeters of basic vision, beliefs and values. Some people have rejected New Hope-in-the-Heart Church because they believe deeply in male superiority over women and cannot abide the basic value of gender equality in the church, which brings many women to leadership. Others have rejected New Hope-in-the-Heart Church because they do not insist on a particular doctrinal position or advocate a particular ideological point of view.

However, the most common, deeper reason people leave or reject New Hope-in-the-Heart Church is that it refuses to control people. New Hope-in-the-Heart Church insists on being incredibly diverse. They do not censor anyone's thoughts, or limit anyone's exploration of God, chide and judge anyone's behavior, or instruct anyone how to vote in political elections. Those who are extreme (liberal or conservative) often accuse New Hope-in-the-Heart Church of being "wishy-washy" or "soft" on various doctrinal or political issues. They believe the central control of a church should confront, push, and cajole people to think and behave a certain way. *People who want to have power over other people do not stay long in New Hope-in-the-Heart Church.* They prefer bureaucracy.

For example, a small group comes to the pastoral leadership staff team and says, "We believe Jesus Christ is calling us to ministries that criticize 'abortion-on-demand,' which counsel women to find creative ways to maintain even unwanted pregnancies, and which advocate the rights of the unborn for life." Sally, herself, along with a number of her friends, is sympathetic to this vision. The group wonders if such a position tests the limits of the basic vision, beliefs and values of the church. The leadership considers it. "Does it contradict, or move beyond, the perimeters of church life? No. Then how can we help you do it?" Simultaneously, another group approaches the pastoral leadership team and says, "We believe Jesus Christ is calling *us* to ministries that advocate freedom of choice for women with unwanted pregnancies, which counsel women to make wise choices for their own health and future happiness." Sally's friend Sonja, along with Fred's wife, Estelle, are sympathetic to this vision. Again the leadership considers it. "Does *this* contradict the basic perimeters of church life? *No. Then how can we help you do it!*" In the end, two gifted, called, and equipped groups work within the church with equal recognition. More often than not, they disagree with each other. That does not matter. Agreement is not what binds the church together.

Stability for the church is encouraged by the basic vision, beliefs, and values of the system—and by the triangle of church leaders who maintain the energy field. They constantly proclaim, model, describe, and celebrate the basics of church life. Occasionally they must make a decision, but rarely do they have to say no. Notice that all this happens without the consensus of the multiple layers of bureaucracy. Their decisions are not appealed to higher courts, or to the far corners of church membership. They are trusted.

There will be annual congregational gatherings, but, since the church is growing larger and ever more diverse, no one expects such gatherings to be "accountability meetings" in which consensus can realistically be achieved. Such congregational meetings do not review decisions, with an eye to confirming or overturning the work of the pastoral leadership team. Annual congregational gatherings focus on the basic perimeters: defining, refining, and celebrating their vision, beliefs, and values. In this context, occasional large or complex projects, with extensive legal or financial implications, might be considered by everyone. Sally's project involving the creation of an elder day-care center for Alzheimer's patients, for example, was pondered by such a congregational meeting. The question they considered, however, was not, *Will we do it?* but rather, *Will it carry us more deeply into our basic vision, or will it divert us from our basic vision?*

Now let's take a closer look at the three fundamental "legs" of the Stability Triangle in the organization of the thriving church.

Pastoral Leadership Team

Members of the team may be salaried or volunteer, one person or several, depending on the size of the church. They do not "do" ministry. That is to say, the people of New Hope-in-the-Heart Church do not raise money in order to pay these experts to do various ministries in their name. Nor do the people of this church expect the staff to exhaust their energies "taking care" of each individual member of the "flock." They do not do the ministries of the church. Instead, they *envision, train,* and *motivate* ministry.

The pastoral leader, once called "the Minister," is a *visionary* and *not* an administrator. She, he, or they do not spend much time attending meetings, writing reports, or interpreting the structures of the church to newcomers. They spend far more time out among the public—in coffee shops, sports arenas, shopping malls, and any public place—listening for the changing spiritual yearnings and personal needs of people. They engage anyone and everyone in conversation, not to convert them or judge them, but to hear what they have to say. These leaders couple such dialogue with an intense, and intentional, spiritual discipline of prayer and Bible study, constantly readying themselves for the unexpected callings of Christ. They are always asking the question, *What should New Hope-in-the-Heart Church start preparing itself to be doing excellently well **ten years from now?***

The pastoral leader, once called "the Teaching Elder," is a *trainer* and *not* an educator. She, he, or they are not preoccupied with communicating correct doctrinal and ideological information, or with ensuring that everyone agrees with each other in interpretations of Scripture and life. They spend their time training people to have excellent skills, so that people can think for themselves with integrity and exercise their spiritual gifts with quality. They are "midwives," helping missionaries be born out of ordinary people. They are "mentors," creating pastors out of formerly needy people. They train others to do ministry. They always relate to people by asking this question: *What are the God-given spiritual gifts that Jesus Christ is calling you to exercise in a concrete way, and how can I equip you to discern and do that ministry with excellence?*

The pastoral leader, once called a "Supervisor," "Overseer," or "Bishop," is a *motivator, not* a coordinator. She, he, or they are not interested in controlling the ministries other people do, and they are never perpetually "looking over the shoulders" of the laity to make sure things are done right, in the right way, and with the right point of view. They are motivators. They inspire people's hearts, energize them, and help them continue to experience the transforming power of God that is changing their lives. These leaders will spend hours crafting and customizing worship to be a powerful, transforming, uplifting, celebratory, and visionary experience that sends people out on fire to continue doing whatever it is Christ has called them to do. They enter every worship service, small group gathering, and chance encounter with Sally or Bob in the grocery store with this question in mind: *How can I help you feel fresh enthusiasm, and renewed willpower, to carry on doing whatever Christ is calling you to do?*

The pastoral leaders of New Hope-in-the-Heart Church are doing very different things from those of the ministers of St. Friendly-on-the-Hill Church. They spend less time one-to-one, and more time one-to-group. They spend less time visiting people inside the church, and more time among the public who never come to church. They spend less time attending denominational meetings, and more time in spiritual disciplines. They spend less time building consensus, and more time encouraging diversity. They spend less time memorializing the achievements of the saints, and more time laughing and learning with laity from the mistakes of people who have been turned loose into ministry.

Administration Team

Only seven or eight persons are needed for the administration team, regardless of the size of the church. These are people who have discovered through their own intense and intentional spiritual disciplines that they have been given a spiritual gift in administration. Moreover, each person on the team believes that Jesus Christ is calling her or him to this ministry of administration. Gifts and calling initially determine whether or not individuals are invited to serve on the team, and whether or not they agree to do so. Their professional experience and training are secondary.

The administration team is organized into "classes," so that membership can be rotated to others in the congregation. The human resources team has a nominations process to discover and recognize people who are gifted and called into such a ministry. Since the congregational meeting is oriented toward vision and celebration, the election of the administration team will probably happen through ballots mailed to all the members of the church.

Once individuals who are gifted and called agree to join the team, they are given extensive training in organization, planning, finance, marketing, public relations, communications, and other skills necessary for their work. They may in fact be trained by professionals within the church who do these things for employment, but who in fact are gifted and called by God in other directions. They may also be trained by consultants from outside the church, or from neighboring churches or denominational offices. The point is that they are gifted, called, and equipped—and therefore, they should be *trusted*.

The administration team manages the day-to-day life of the church. They make and implement decisions regarding property, finance, and church organization—and they do this quickly, with selective consultations as needed, without requiring a consensus from the church. They maintain an extensive communications network with the congregation, so that all the diverse life of the church is accessible and fully known by everyone. Only rarely will they ever need to assist the pastoral leadership team in determining if a particular creative idea goes beyond the basic vision, beliefs, and values of the church. They do not give permission, or withhold permission, for ministry. They do not do or create ministries. Their basic question to every idea or proposal is, *How can we help **you** do it?*

Human Resources Team

Everyone is accountable in New Hope-in-the-Heart Church. Everyone deserves an opportunity to do ministry. Everyone requires assistance to do ministry well. And everyone needs continuing personal and practical support to grow. These are the assumptions of the human resources team. They, too, are nominated and rotated in "classes." They, too, are clearly gifted and called. They, too, will be trained and equipped to do their work with the highest professional standards.

Since everyone is accountable in the church, the human resources team monitors the "mission performance" of all those in ministry, salaried or volunteer. They will review the work of staff, administration team members, small group leaders, and all members of the church. If needed, they can assess leadership according to the basic vision, beliefs, and values of the church, recommend continuing education, personal counseling, or upgraded training, and even remove individuals from leadership.

Since everyone deserves an opportunity to do ministry, the human resources team will design the spiritual gifts discernment process, and help individuals and small groups ponder practical alternatives to design and do ministries. They do not recruit people into an institutional agenda, but they help the mission agenda to "bubble up" from among the people.

Since everyone requires assistance to do ministry well, the human resources team will ensure that careful training is provided for any ministry, and that a standard of excellence is achieved before people start doing ministry. The team may provide training, or may identify professional expertise beyond the church, or may assist the staff in training. As the creativity and diversity of mission increase, the method and content of training developed with the human resources team will become more challenging.

Since everyone requires personal and practical support for growth, the human resources team will create interpersonal networks that can be sensitive and compassionate toward the stresses the leaders in ministry experience. The team will be trained in conflict resolution skills to intercede in particularly difficult situations. It may publicly defend ministry leaders from public gossip or criticism, and it will be prepared to lead the church to participate responsibly in any litigation that might arise.

Clearly, the human resources team is not just involved with salaried staff. They are involved with the whole life and ministry of the church. They will facilitate the nominations process for the administration team, as well as contract negotiations with staff. They will arrange for the outside expertise of consultants and facilitate the internal training and nurture of gifted and called individuals and small groups.

The Core of Church Life

Worship lies at the core of the thriving church organization. The worship services are so motivating and enriching, *that it is **not possible** to be involved in the organization, the ministries, or the small groups of the church **without** regularly attending worship throughout the entire year.*

D. THE CORE OF CHURCH LIFE

BASIC VISION

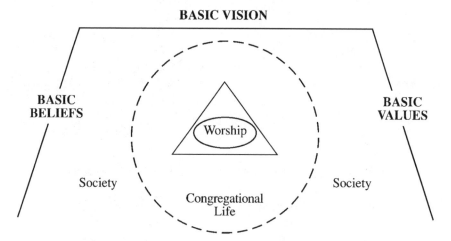

Bob and Sally found this the single most-striking difference between their experience in New Hope-in-the-Heart Church and St. Friendly-on-the-Hill Church. When they attended St. Friendly-on-the-Hill, they discovered that the organization had a life of its own, to which the worship services were increasingly irrelevant. On Installation Sunday, Bob and Sally observed that half the newly elected board members did not even consider it important to be in worship that day to be recognized. The passions and issues that gripped board members, and caused committees to meet late into the night, did not even surface in worship services. Indeed, people were so exhausted by all the organizational meetings, that they felt quite free to take the entire summer off from attending worship. Bob and Sally had the feeling that membership had more to do with "running the church," than with "celebrating the grace of God."

When Bob and Sally came to New Hope-in-the-Heart Church, they discovered that it was not possible for them to grow in faith, or to participate in small groups, or to pursue their callings, without *always, always* attending worship services. They just couldn't do it. It was not that they felt guilty if they missed worship, but that they had personally lost something by missing worship. Worship was essential to their emerging sense of personal mission. It is the shared experience of the transforming power of God that binds the church together.

There are several worship services in New Hope-in-the-Heart Church, each one very different in character from the others. Each has a different style, a different music, a different leadership, and a different day and time of celebration. Whatever the service is like, however, the worship models the very system of thriving church life.

First, worship celebrates and anticipates the transforming power of God that changes people. The atmosphere of expectation and hope is electric. There is great freedom to interact with the music, the drama, or the prayers. Some services celebrate healing of the body, mind, will, or spirit; other services celebrate the mentoring presence of the risen Christ that warms the heart and guides mission; and still other services celebrate cherished truths that open individuals to reverence and awe. Worship reflects the very system of thriving church life, which begins with the inner experience of being changed, feeling different, and experiencing liberation from burdens and addictions.

Second, thanksgiving and assurance lead to a deeper awareness of who God is and what God is doing. The atmosphere reflects the many moods of the people. Singing and praying will be done in many styles, but with great intensity and sincerity. Some services will focus on discerning spiritual gifts or listening for God's unique word for each participant; other services will interpret Scripture in dramatic or interactive ways that make key Bible passages relevant to our lives. Worship reflects the system of church life which leads people to deeper spirituality and intimacy—and indeed, Bob and Sally often worship, not as a couple, but with Fred, Sonja, or their small groups.

Third, insight and discovery lead to discernment of one's own call into mission, and to the integration of all the "personal missions" of the church into one "Body of Christ." The atmosphere reflects the eagerness of people to discover their destiny, and to fulfill themselves through sharing life with others. The music can be anything from new age, to country, to rock, to classical, but it makes people feel close to great things. There is no preaching, but rather a mentoring message that conveys the faith and authentic experience of the speaker, which seems to "hit home" for every individual. Worship reflects the system of church life, which awakens people to their destiny and coaches them in the ways of discipleship.

Fourth, a profound sense of self-worth and purpose overflows into a commitment of generosity. The atmosphere reflects the conviction of the people that what is happening to them in this brief time is too precious to end, that the experience of change should continue through the week, and that others should be invited to share it. People begin to recognize the risen Christ in new ways, and form covenants or commitments to "walk with Christ" in the coming days. Worship reflects the system of church life in which only excellence is good enough, and so seeks to equip and train people to maximize their destiny in mission.

Finally, a profound sense of "joyful discontent" or "joyous restlessness" motivates the people to leave the service intent on sharing faith and new life among the public. The atmosphere is charged with purpose, movement, and the contained excitement of people who are just packing for a long journey. Whatever the style of music, it is like a marching cadence. People want to linger and get going, all at the same time. Worship reflects the thriving church system, in which people "break out" into all manner and style of ministries.

The worship that lies at the core of the thriving church organization articulates and celebrates the basic vision, beliefs, and values of the church all the time. It motivates and nurtures the quest for spiritual discernment, personal value and worth, and divine callings. It builds upon, and spiritually feeds, the small groups and personal missions of the people. What is important in the worship of New Hope-in-the-Heart Church is not what people know, but how people feel. It seeks not to build their intellect, but to energize their willpower.

Worship at St. Friendly-on-the-Hill Church sent people home contented, raised money for experts to do mission, and encouraged church officers not to miss their management meeting during the week. Bob and Sally knew that they could be content, give money to charities, and still attend their management meeting through the week, without ever attending the worship service. Worship at New Hope-in-the-Heart Church sent people straight into the coffee shops and public places following the service to share their enthusiasms, created covenants of commitment for people to do mission themselves, and encouraged participants not to miss their small, spirituality cell group during the week. Bob and Sally realized that they could never fulfill their visions, live up to their covenants of complete generosity, or deepen spirituality among intimate friends, *unless* they regularly attended the worship services.

Two Different Systems, Two Different Organizations

Just as a system will produce only what it is designed to produce and nothing else—so also, *an organization will accomplish only what the system allows it to accomplish and nothing else!*

The bureaucratic, consensus-building, and centrally controlled organization of St. Friendly-on-the Hill Church is the natural outcome and fulfillment of a particular system of church life. If the system of the church is all about belonging, that organizational model will make it happen. It will protect a heritage, preserve an identity, initiate and mold newcomers into a common way of life and point of view, and multiply institutional offices in which people can have their place. It will confront society on the outside, keep the membership content on the inside, and contribute money to important charities.

The trouble is that on the brink of the twenty-first century, more and more people like Bob and Sally don't find that system to be meaningful, and they don't have time to waste in that organization.

The streamlined, entrepreneurial, self-directed organization of New Hope-in-the-Heart Church looks threatening and bizarre to some, but that is only because they evaluate it from the standpoint of the old system. If they change systems, they discover that this new organizational model is the natural outcome and fulfillment of a new system for church life. It will celebrate a vision, encourage diversity, attract newcomers to a process of self-discovery and personal fulfillment, and *get out of the way* of the really important developments of spirituality and mission. It will engage society in respectful dialogue, even as it celebrates the joyful conviction of the membership. And it will not only raise money for important charities, but it will release multitudes of trained, motivated people to do charitable work.

Bob and Sally probably never really thought about it. They never really said that they were fed up with institutions "controlling" their lives, and angry at other people trying to force them to adapt and mold themselves to an institutional mission agenda. They may not have been consciously aware of the many addictions that robbed life of meaning, or of their yearnings to have a deeper association with infinite meaning, or of their desires to have a purpose and destiny that could benefit others in a way that was purely positive. They probably just talked about freedom, and sang about a "second chance," and read self-improvement books, and dabbled in curiosities, and dreamed about being "a somebody."

Then they went to New Hope-in-the-Heart Church—and felt like they had been heard at last. St. Friendly-on-the-Hill Church had offered them *a home.* New Hope-in-the-Heart Church offered them *a way.* Frankly, they never had time for St. Friendly-on-the-Hill—but they were ready to take all the time in the world for New Hope-in-the-Heart!

Part 3

FROM HERE TO THERE: TRANSFORMING THE CHURCH ORGANIZATION

Transforming the Systems of Church Life

Bob and Sally Public are now joyously involved in New Hope-in-the-Heart Church. They have been changed, gifted, called, equipped, and sent. Even now they continue to feel the transforming touch of God in their lives, and they continue to discover new dimensions to the gifts they have been given. Their own sense of calling has led them to appreciate the many diverse callings of people around them, and they value more than ever the great basic vision of the church which allows all these missions to happen in the Body of Christ. The fact that they have a sense of their own destiny, that the church has invested itself to train them, and that the church has trusted them to do ministry, fills them with a deep sense of worth and responsibility.

Yet Bob and Sally have not forgotten St. Friendly-on-the-Hill Church. After all, they really were friendly, good people. True, some people feel rejected and mad that Bob and Sally left the church. A few others can't get over their sense of guilt that somehow they failed Bob and Sally. And a few more still think Bob and Sally left because the nursery wasn't carpeted, or because the hymnbook wasn't good enough, and they are still tinkering with the program in the belief that Bob and Sally can be lured back again. Most of the people, however, remain very friendly with Bob and Sally, and marvel at the change in their lives. Some of their teens are involved in Bob's drug addiction ministry; and some of their members have talked to Sally about her dream of an elder day-care center. The model railroad youth ministry, of course, has been described in the local newspaper.

Some of the St. Friendly-on-the-Hill people begin to talk with Bob and Sally more seriously. They actually came to visit as representatives of the church, seeking only to listen and learn from Bob and Sally. Others are actually surveying complete strangers in the community to discover what they can do to address public interest more effectively. Bob and Sally are deeply moved. Perhaps New Hope-in-the-Heart Church can help St. Friendly-on-the-Hill, not simply to imitate their church life but to discover some new way of thriving that is right for the unique context of St. Friendly-on-the-Hill.

Bob and Sally talk about it with the woman who has been their mentor, small group leader, and spiritual guide throughout their church experience. This is the woman who first visited them as newcomers to the church, who sat with them in worship, and who guided them into the small group spirituality of the church. Edith tells them a remarkable story:

"You know," Edith says, "New Hope-in-the-Heart Church was not always this way. In fact, some years ago, it was a traditional, declining church just like St. Friendly. The congregation at the time was called 'Old Faithful Church.' Back in the forties and fifties it was a really big church, but by the eighties only about thirty people worshiped inside the big, old, beautiful building. Basically, they were great folks, who were in deep trouble. Then one day things began to change—really change. Funny to say, when things began to change, almost everyone between fifty and sixty years of age left the church. It seemed like the only remaining ones were either under forty or over ninety! But I guess they figured they didn't have anything to lose, so they kept on changing. Eventually they tore down the old building, relocated, and things started happening in a brand new way. Looking back on it, I think even they thought it was a bit crazy. Now, I guess, it looks like the power of God."

The systems in which congregations live are so subtle and powerful that the people of St. Friendly-on-the-Hill Church cannot imagine an organizational alternative. However, their own appreciation of the heritage of the Christian church disconcerts them.

They find themselves unsettled and confused when they read Scripture. They cannot understand how the early church described in Acts and New Testament letters could work. The stories of Paul in Athens, or Lydia in Philippi, or Peter with Cornelius are strangely compelling. They try unsuccessfully to force the terms "bishop" and "elder" to mean the same as they do today. Talk of "spiritual gifts" suggests an uncomfortable supernaturalism to the modern, scientific mind. The conversion and enthusiasm of the masses seems disrespectful in a multicultural society. And yet—and yet—there is something profound here, if only they could grasp it.

They find themselves troubled by instances in church history when religious life was lived differently—and worked—and was criticized because it dared to be so popular. They read of the Spirit-filled Montanists attacked by Augustine; or of the early monks and hermits who seemed equally at home in caves, on pillars, in soup kitchens, or leading armies into battle. The Reformation included an astonishing variety of organizational models. Closer to modernity, they learn of Wesleyan cell groups. Older members of St. Friendly-on-the-Hill recall a revival church quite different from the one they support today. Perhaps these are all anachronisms limited to bygone days—and yet, and yet—there is something profound here, if only they could grasp it.

They find themselves disturbed by churches and religious movements within their own community that are thriving. Such groups seem to attract all ages, all races, all cultures. They grow in participation and membership; their financial resources seem inexhaustible and they take incredible risks; their presence seems to be felt in the coffee shop next door, and their missions seem to extend to other countries. It is easy, too easy, to accuse them of pandering to the public with a "soft gospel." It is too easy to retreat into self-righteous identity primarily defined as opposition to others. There is something profound happening in the religious world today if only they could grasp it.

The people of the church today are growing restless. Some, of course, are merely in a panic about decline, and are looking for miracles that will fix the old organization and breathe new life into the old system. Many others, however, are not merely motivated by a longing to recover the good old days. Even if they cannot envision an alternative church system to the one which dominates their lives, they are rejecting the system in which they currently live. Even if they cannot imagine an organizational alternative, they are rejecting the one they have. They are coming to a place of courage and risk, in which they prefer mystery and potential chaos to the meaningless frustrations of their church life.

The truth is that New Hope-in-the-Heart Church was once like St. Friendly-on-the-Hill Church. Courageously, painfully, enthusiastically, they broke free of the bondage of the old system. They experimented and explored, failed at times and learned from their mistakes, and began to envision a whole new system. They then allowed the system to generate a new organizational model.

Here is how it happened.

The Coming of the Vision

The first, biggest, and most difficult step for the people of Old Faithful Church was to admit, to themselves and the world, that many of the things to which they were "faithful" were not authentic callings but deadly addictions. It is very hard for a group of addicts to admit an addiction. It means recognizing absolute helplessness to liberate themselves by their own power. It also means recognizing that no emergency capital assistance from denominational offices, no expert consultants, no new program gimmicks, and no "messianic" pastoral call to a new minister will liberate them from their addictions. Nothing human will liberate them from their addictions. Only a Higher Power can do that. Only God. Only Jesus Christ.

The church initiated a time of deep spiritual searching. They needed a new vision that would liberate them from past addictions. They began to listen closely to the public, and they began pondering the key question, *What is it about our experience of Jesus Christ that this community cannot live without?*

The church realized that it could not simply send the board away on retreat, expecting them to return with an authentic, dynamite vision that would transform the church. Instinctively they knew that visions of biblical proportions would only be revealed, not created, and that they would come in their own time. They did go away for a retreat, but that was only one part of a whole spiritual strategy that would continue six months to a year.

1. *Worship.* The church started experimenting. They cleared away the "hardwood," moving aside pulpits and chancel rails to create space for movement. They used the organ sparingly, and tried electronic keyboard and alternative instruments. They used drama and dance, and gave permission for spontaneity and movement. They suspended use of the "Common Lectionary" for six months and devised their own Bible discipline by reading all the "vision revelation" passages of the Scriptures. Preachers stopped preaching, and courageous people started sharing their faith stories. Most of all, they started laughing at themselves (at their mistakes, seemingly amateurish experiments, and silly self-consciousness).

2. *Prayer.* Together and individually, people started praying for new vision. They kept and shared spiritual journals of "night dreams" and "day dreams." They experimented with different kinds of prayer, but mostly they stayed away from "prayer books" and other "off-the-shelf" resources. They made prayer personal, sincere, and authentic. They formed prayer "triads" with covenants to pray at specific times of the day, no matter where they were or what they were doing.

3. *Dialogue with strangers.* The church cut meetings and management time by two-thirds by entrusting it to three persons, and spent most of their time in public places listening and talking with complete strangers. They consumed a lot of coffee and doughnuts! After the listening and dialogue, they would gather in someone's home and talk about what they had heard. They began to understand their addictions, and perceive the spiritual yearnings of the public.

4. *Listening to the "fringe."* Since most biblical visions were revealed to people who were *not* insiders in institutional life, they sought and listened to people who were not active, or who were turned off, or who had simply drifted away. In fact, these were the people the church brought to the retreat!

In the end, the vision came to a forty-year-old divorcee named Marlene, and found expression in the song "Spirit, Spirit of Gentleness."

> You call from tomorrow, you break ancient schemes,
> From the bondage of sorrow, the captives dream dreams;
> Our women see visions, our men clear their eyes,
> with bold new decisions, your people arise.

It caused simultaneous excitement and consternation. It caused some people to jump up and down with enthusiasm, and other people to leave the church. It wasn't just that the old cathedral building was eventually torn down, and that the congregation relocated into a very different facility. The joy and the pain resulted from the fact that the "Old Faithful Church" system was laid to rest with mingled thanksgiving and relief, and the "New Hope-in-the-Heart Church" system was born.

These are the ten keys to authentic, motivating visions that churches on the brink of transformation have discovered:

1. It's a "Song in Your Heart": Authentic visions are not statements, essays, or understandings of the mind; they are a rhythm, beat, tune, hymn, song, verse, or lyric of the heart.

2. It makes your blood beat faster: Authentic visions do not initially make your brain work harder, but they create energy to stand, tap, act, or move. Visions create willpower. Thinking is important, but it comes later.

3. It can only be communicated without words: Words will always be inadequate, and no two persons will describe the vision the same way. Visions are communicated by a hug, smile, kiss, dramatic action, eye contact, and surprising intuition.

4. It is only real when shared with strangers: It is usually embarrassing to repeat it to friends, but among strangers it creates friends. Confirmation comes when the eyes of complete strangers light up in recognition.

5. It makes you feel like nobility: Authentic visions never motivate you to join an organization or be a member of a club, but they make you feel like a key part of a great destiny of personal fulfillment and universal significance.

6. It makes you want to do something—and do it now! Authentic visions provide no patience with committees or processes of approval. They fill a person with instant eagerness and profound immediacy.

7. It only comes after waiting in prayer and Bible study: Authentic visions are never planned, scheduled, or created. They are only revealed in the context of deep spirituality and dramatic change.

8. It only comes to individuals: Authentic visions are never revealed to committees, boards, or groups, but only to receptive individuals—who may not even realize how receptive they are!

9. It only survives as team vision: Protected by the individual it dies, but when shared and refined the authentic vision collects and unites the people.

10. It is always "Jesus Christ": Authentic visions convey an immediate experience of God as powerful and transforming. They connect with the second "person" of the Trinity, Jesus Christ, as the transfiguring, healing, transforming agent of divine will.

Old Faithful Church learned one more thing about authentic visions. They are explosive. And if you are handling dynamite, you need to handle it with care. Systemic change in the church is always extremely stressful. Therefore, they needed some kind of plan, the details of which would need to be invented as they went along, but the broad outlines of which could help them anticipate in advance the stresses at each stage of transition. The plan should integrate simultaneous "de-construction" of the old system, and "re-construction" of the new system. They would not move forward to the next stage of the plan, until the stresses erupting from the previous stage had been fairly resolved.

Chapter 7

Stage 1:
Shared Vision

The vision of Marlene spread to others, but the church wanted to build as large a team as possible to share the vision. Therefore, they did not immediately restructure the board, rewrite the mission statement, or revise the constitution. Instead, they sought to extend the intense spiritual discipline that had allowed the vision to emerge, building a spirituality that was freeing and open to creativity into the daily and weekly routine of church life. They were not seeking consensus, either as unanimous approval or as common agreement. Already, they knew that some people would leave the church, and they were willing to pay that price. They were seeking team vision, in which the largest possible number of people would intuitively celebrate the still mysterious direction in which the power of God was taking the church.

The goals of the first stage follow.

STAGE 1: SHARED VISION

GOALS

1. Build Congregational Commitment to Transformation
2. Create Visionary, Motivating Congregational Meetings
3. Focus on Discovery of Spiritual Gifts
4. Flex the Leadership Priorities

De-construction	Re-construction
1. Stop preaching "renewal."	1. Start preaching "transformation."
2. Leave the church building to meet.	2. Meet in "public" locations.
3. Suspend Parliamentary Procedure.	3. Initiate "Common Sense Procedure" ("Be Brief, Be Clear, Be Generous").

4. Reduce management meetings by 50 percent.

4. Build into committee meetings the P.A.L.S. strategy.

5. Reduce review of reports to 20 minutes.

5. Maximize opportunities for singing, praying, and sharing.

6. Reduce budget agenda to 10 minutes.

6. Expand mission discernment.

7. Detach nominations from the board.

7. Attach nominations to congregation.

8. Do not assign people to tasks.

8. Do commission individuals to exercise spiritual gifts or calling.

9. Declare the constitution to be "clay."

9. Allow the board to "mold" the rules.

10. Declare the committee mandates to be "clay."

10. Allow committees to experiment.

11. Declare staff job descriptions to be "clay."

11. Allow staff to re-prioritize time.

12. Surrender commitment to multiple-committee, overlapping-accountability system.

12. Build enthusiasm for the small-group, individual initiative, high-trust system.

13. Surrender commitment to "enabling" "one-to-one."

13. Build enthusiasm for "training" "one-to-group."

14. De-emphasize long-term, all-inclusive large groups.

14. Initiate short-term, diverse learning opportunities.

15. Don't send the board on retreat.

15. Do send church leaders plus marginal members on retreat.

16. Reduce administrative task groups.

16. Multiply ministry teams.

17. Stop writing mission statements.

17. Start looking for the Song in the Heart.

18. Minimize recruitment to offices.

18. Maximize spiritual gifts inventories.

19. Reduce the "busi-ness" of management.

19. Answer the question, What is it about our experience of Christ that this community cannot live without?

Stress Points

1. changing the location of the meeting
2. loss of control by the long-standing membership
3. finance no longer the cornerstone of the agenda
4. inability to shift thinking from "offices" to "gifts"
5. insecurity about nominations from the floor
6. too much freedom given to the staff
7. energy required to change too demanding
8. inability to surrender commitment to unanimous consent

9. inability to endure some immediate membership loss
10. inability to "catch" the vision or "endorse" the vision.

Build Congregational Commitment to Transformation

The congregation needed to abandon the dream of church renewal, which had been tried for years and never worked. "Church renewal" was all about programmatic change, and the congregation knew that just tinkering with the old system to make it work better simply perpetuated their bondage to old addictions. No new or revised program, curriculum, staff position, or piece of property would bring real life to the church. In order for the team vision to grow, people needed to understand that church transformation involved systemic change. A whole new system of church life needed to be born. The contrasting images of the "croquet game" and the "jai alai game" provided a helpful metaphor for people as they tried to grasp the paradigm shift at stake.

Create Visionary, Motivating Congregational Meetings

Every meeting of the church (annual congregational meetings, board and committee meetings, membership training and group meetings) needed dramatically to cut the governance agenda. Flexibility, spontaneity, spirituality, and high trust needed to be increased. In order to create visionary and motivating meetings, the priority given "control" needed to be checked. Permission to disagree, experiment, and take initiative needed to be encouraged. The congregation needed to expand the limits of tolerance, and lay a foundation for the future identification of basic vision, beliefs, and values. At the same time, they needed to give priority to listening to the estranged public and the fringes of congregational life.

Focus on Discovery of Spiritual Gifts

The congregation needed to relearn their biblical heritage regarding spiritual gifts, and resist the temptation to recruit people for offices that fulfilled the institutional agenda. This would lay the foundation for future organizational "flattening" and self-directed mission. Therefore, the congregation needed to open up the nomination process, reduce offices, and fill offices only when the spiritual gifts clearly emerged. Workshops and meetings initiated spiritual gifts discernment inventories, personal discovery processes, and other counseling sessions to help people discover what activities really excited them which they intuitively did well. If certain tasks didn't get done, that was O.K.

Flex the Leadership Priorities

Both salaried and volunteer leadership in the church needed more freedom to prioritize time. For the clergy, this meant shifting ministry from one-to-one pastoral care, to one-to-group training for others to do pastoral care. For the laity, this meant entrepreneurial freedom to respond to individual callings. Together these shifts laid the foundation for future "proscriptive," rather than "prescriptive," management. The congregation needed to do everything possible to build trust, rather than enforce accountability, so that people were released from organizational duties to become more involved in spirituality and mission. They created a corporate "sense of humor" which forgave failure, and regarded mistakes as learning opportunities.

The chart for Stage 1 indicates the parallel tactics the congregation used for simultaneous de-construction and re-construction. This helped the congregational leaders to monitor the progress of congregational transition, and identify unexpected obstacles or unsuspected opportunities.

Perhaps the single, most powerful tactic for Old Faithful Church was the deliberate transition from committee life to small group life. Some committees were simply converted into spirituality cell groups, and were often easily multiplied to reflect different styles and perspectives. Other committees ceased to exist, either because they had no clear focus anyway, or because God had yet to call forth spiritually gifted people to address the issues of that committee. Still other committees were radically downsized and amalgamated, their work entrusted to a few gifted people.

In Stage 1, the congregation had already begun to experience stress. The ten stress points in the chart name some of the most severe challenges. In retrospect, however, the people of Old Faithful Church, who were rapidly being transformed into New Hope-in-the-Heart Church, realized that all the controversies in this stage boiled down to three great "stress themes."

"I Demand an Explanation!"

The first stress theme was that most of the middle-class folks who composed Old Faithful Church were reasonably well educated, North

American people who valued reason and distrusted emotion. Religion for them needed to be understandable and enlightened. Faith was something that could be communicated, taught, and explained. Mission was something that could be planned, scheduled, and organized. To be faithful meant to be responsible, to be held accountable, and, therefore, to be in control of what was going on. Even their worship was essentially an educational, understandable, and rational experience. They believed that if only one correctly understood the right things, one would automatically do the right things.

In short, the people of Old Faithful Church wanted a controllable experience of the Holy. They translated "sin" as "ignorance" and "grace" as "insight." The religious experiences that shook them most profoundly were gratuitous evil on the one hand, and miraculous grace on the other. Both needed to be rationalized, interpreted, and explained. It took immense courage for some of them to admit to their corporate church "addictions," because this was tantamount to admitting that their sense of control was all a sham. More than this, they admitted that the power to escape addiction lay beyond their capabilities.

Thus, the stress theme that emerged was the troubling discovery that the Holy is always, always uncontrollable. The Holy was simultaneously their salvation (liberating them from addictions) and their doom (carrying them into the depths of the irrational). Ultimately, faith could not be taught but only given. Mission could not be planned but only allowed to erupt. Worship was always unpredictable, emotional, and a little scary. To be faithful meant to be thankful, joyous, and perhaps a little crazy.

The recovery of the merit of the irrational was quite stressful for many of the middle-class, well-educated North American people of the church. All the "vision stories" of the Bible seemed to contradict their religious assumptions. Their rationalizations of the transformation of Saul on the Damascus road seemed to collapse before what, to them, was an incomprehensible passage of Scripture in which even the converted Paul wrote:

> I do not understand my own actions. . . . For I do not do the good I want, but the evil I do not want is what I do. . . . I delight in the law of God in my inmost self, but I see in my members another law at war with the law of my mind. . . . .Wretched man that I am! Who will rescue me from this body of death? Thanks be to God through Jesus Christ our Lord!
>
> (Rom. 7:15, 19, 22-24)

The other side of the coin for the admission of one's helplessness with habitually destructive behavior patterns that rob life of meaning, is the recognition that only the uncontrollable Holy can rescue you from them.

"Someone Needs to Tell Me What to Do!"

The second stress theme involved the deep-seated desire of many current leaders in the church to control the thoughts, behavior, and mission of other people.

For some leaders, this need to control the activities of the church was born out of the declining church system in which they unconsciously lived. Their task in the system was to protect the ethos, heritage, or identity of the church from radical change, so that the membership could always maintain the continuity of spirit the "belonging" to which was so meaningful. Everything in the church needed to be controlled by a slow, manageable process of consensus which could not be circumvented or sidestepped in any way.

For still other leaders, this need to control people in the church was born out of the inner conviction that the people who "know best" should guide others. This might mean that experts should be given power to tell others what they should do or think. Or it might mean that those highest in seniority should be given power to shape policy and practice. Or it might mean that "prophets" and "professors" should have power to design church life in accord with whatever was politically just (correct) or doctrinally pure.

Sadly, for a few leaders of Old Faithful Church, this need to control people was born out of a personal need simply to have power. These leaders had filled vacuums created by the increasing nomination vacancies in the life of the church. The truth was that they simply enjoyed making decisions for other people, and forcing people to follow their own agenda. Such people needed to be on every ad hoc committee, and they needed to be recognized as the "right hand" of the minister.

Whatever the reason for the need to control, all these leaders assumed that it was of paramount importance that everyone in the church agree with one another about issues, policies, dogmas, and perspectives. The assumption that the church needed to speak with one voice had led Old Faithful Church into never-ending factional feuds, as people competed for control of the agenda. In a sense, the irrational Holy Spirit had been given an opportunity to transform the church, partly because many of the "controllers" had left the church already, died, or reached exhaustion—allowing the meek to stand up for themselves and inherit the earth.

"I Don't Get It . . . and I Don't Want It!"

The third stress theme was that some people simply didn't get it. They just couldn't catch the vision. They listened attentively and participated in discussion with generosity, but they emerged shaking their heads. The excitement was not there.

—Some were in denial. Deep in their hearts they just could not recognize self-destructive behavior patterns to which their church was addicted.

—Some were "paradigm blind." They could not conceive of a system different from the one they were experiencing, and continued to search for that new program which would make the past vital again.

—Some were cynical. They saw the addictions, they realized no new program would rescue them, but they did not really believe in the transforming power of God that could liberate them.

—Some were "spiritually inert." They were satisfied with themselves and with declining church life. They did not understand the content or the usefulness of "spiritual gifts." They considered the experience of the biblical church in Acts to be an idealized, inspiring legend.

—Some were "righteously indignant." They welcomed decline as the verification of their righteous identity. They were the "righteous remnant" who would remain loyal to the agreed "truth" that had the consent of the chosen people. Newcomers could never change the church, but must be initiated into its elite identity. The very idea that the doctrinally impure or politically incorrect public should be consulted by the church made them hurt and angry.

For whatever reason, some of the people of Old Faithful Church simply could not comprehend the emerging vision that was exciting the rest of the people. They complained . . .

that there was no need to change;
that it was just "change for the sake of change";
that after all was said and done, nothing would change anyway;
that change was a lot of work, and not really worth the effort;
that it was the public who needed to change, and not the church.

Sometimes these people quarreled with the church, but more often than not they seemed to "talk past" each other. Like ships passing in the night, they never seemed to perceive the nature and direction of the other's voyage.

Those who were in denial, the "paradigm blind," and the cynics, all tended to stay with Old Faithful Church through the transition. The emerging system of thriving church life permitted failures and mistakes as a vehicle of growth, and all these people readily said, "I told you so!" whenever mistakes were made. The church did not let such negativity undermine the enthusiasm. They loved the "naysayers" anyway, and carried on. Over time, many of those who were in denial began to recognize addictions they had never perceived. Many of the "paradigm blind" never did understand the emerging new system, but they did come to appreciate it. And even years later, some of the cynics came to an eye-opening moment of personal transformation when they finally "got it!"

Many of those who were "spiritually inert" left the church. They felt it was too demanding, or too unpredictable, or too frenzied, or too bizarre. The church let them go, knowing that God was always working in their lives. In time, some of them returned. They discovered they didn't feel comfortable anywhere else. They realized they were under less pressure there, than in declining church neighbors vigorously recruiting people to serve committees. However crazy life in Old Faithful Church seemed to be getting, everybody did seem to be having a good time. As the trials and tribulations of life continued to open the door for God, the "spiritually inert" began (almost despite themselves!) to go deeper into faith. Of course, when they returned, the people of the church welcomed them with open arms— because sitting on the sidelines to watch was a legitimate option, too.

Finally, most of the "righteously indignant" left the church permanently. Those whose righteousness was doctrinal, tended to go to conservative, "fundamentalist" churches. A few hopped from church fortress to church fortress, always looking for pure harmony. Those whose righteousness was ideological, tended to join charities, political parties, and social "movements," and united themselves with churches that were purposely small. Both groups tended to criticize the transition of Old Faithful Church in the media and in public conversations, saying that Old Faithful Church was "watering down the gospel."

Chapter 8

Stage 2: Congregational Spirituality

Once the church had addressed the stresses of the first stage, they were ready to move on. Broad ownership for the team vision had been gained. Governance had been cut back, and a new emphasis on vision and motivation had begun releasing congregational energies in creative ways. People were coming to understand church involvement to be a matter of discerning and using spiritual gifts, rather than serving offices. More and more small, spirituality cell groups or ministry teams were emerging among the congregation. A greater atmosphere of trust allowed the clergy and lay leadership more room to reorient their time toward training others in ministry.

During the visioning time of the church, the congregation had already begun experimenting in worship. Now they began to concentrate on worship and congregational spirituality, because they recognized that this would be the bedrock upon which any further church transformation would be built. Worship and spirituality were at the very core of their vision.

Charted here is Stage 2, followed by a discussion of its goals.

STAGE 2: CONGREGATIONAL SPIRITUALITY

GOALS

1. Create a Climate of Expectation
2. Involve Everybody in Listening for God
3. Make Worship Dramatic and Diverse
4. Increase Congregational Communications

De-construction	Re-construction
1. Surrender informational worship.	1. Build motivational worship.
2. Stop aiming at the "head."	2. Start aiming at the "heart."

3. Stop preaching.

3. Start faith sharing with spontaneous dialogue.

4. Surrender Sunday morning.

4. Experiment with worship through the week.

5. Eliminate "code" words and repetitious services.

5. Use everyday language and create variety.

6. Surrender "off-the-shelf" liturgy.

6. Create authenticity.

7. Do not call for financial offerings.

7. Call for gifts of the whole life.

8. Replace ushers.

8. Train counselors.

9. Set aside the Common Lectionary for worship service use.

9. Create your own lectionary for worship service and home use.

10. Reduce "reading" Scripture.

10. Increase "acting out" Scripture.

11. Reduce organ music by 50 percent.

11. Increase current vocal and instrumental music.

12. Clear away the "hardwood."

12. Create open chancel area space.

13. No longer settle for "friendliness."

13. Aim at intimacy.

14. No longer settle for "knowledge."

14. Aim at ecstasy.

15. Reduce worship committee time.

15. Meet once a year for worship policy.

16. Cancel worship committee management.

16. Create a design team: faith sharer, drama coach, music coordinator.

17. Stop emphasizing grace before meals.

17. Start building "prayer triads."

18. Decrease emphasis on Holy Spirit's leading individual journeys.

18. Look for the Spirit to provide spiritual gifts for individuals.

19. Cease relying on word-of-mouth communication.

19. Create biweekly newsletters and quarterly videos.

20. Eliminate bulletin inserts.

20. Create information booths.

Stress Points

1. Complaints from traditional choirs and music programs
2. Potential loss of organist and music leaders
3. Refusal to do adult education because "we don't need it"
4. Liturgical conservatism
5. Worship not solemn or respectful enough
6. Fear of intimacy
7. Fear of ecstasy
8. Refusal to pay financial cost of communication
9. Inability to pray
10. Retraining required by ordered ministers
11. Heritage protection
12. Fear of losing doctrinal or ideological purity.

Create a Climate of Expectation

The key to transformation is not the mind but the will. Therefore, worship needed to focus on motivating and liberating the will from destructive addictions, rather than educating and communicating to the mind important information. Worship should be aimed at the "heart," rather than the "head."

The congregation believed that corporate transformation could not be achieved without personal transformation—and personal transformation could not be achieved without the intervention of God. The subtlety and influence of addiction demanded the intervention of divine power greater than oneself. Each worship service should be a spiritual journey of change: along the Damascus road to transform destructive critics into apostles of love (Acts 9), or along the Emmaus road to nurture disciples to have greater clarity of faith and purpose in mission (Luke 24), or along the Gaza road to celebrate the answers and insights that satisfy one's innermost longings (Acts 8).

Every worship service in the church would create a climate of expectation for personal change. It would be an experience of "healing" in the most holistic sense of that word. Services would become less "wordy" and more "experiential." Whenever possible, worship would engage all five senses and encourage spontaneity. In every service, participants should be able literally to see the personal impact of God in the behavior of others in the service, as people smiled, swayed, laughed, cried, remained quiet, or exclaimed aloud. In every service, people should emerge with positive feelings, not simply newly acquired knowledge. They would "feel better," be more "joyous," and be highly motivated to learn and serve throughout the week in their small, spirituality cell groups and other disciplines.

A quality of mystery and surprise should surround each service. The impact of the service would have an unpredictable character, so that those who came would never be sure exactly how they might be changed by the time they left. No one looked for dramatic and complete transformations in an hour. However, they did expect a continuing experience with the healing power of God, which would link with their spirituality disciplines through the week, and, in the long run, enable them to be free from the self-destructive behavior patterns (addictions) that dominated their lives and robbed life of meaning.

Involve Everybody in Listening for God

Although intense thanksgiving would be the outcome of worship, that thanksgiving would be expressed primarily through an overflow of generosity through the week. Worship for Old Faithful Church was no longer a time when dutiful "followers of the Cross" obediently "gave thanks," "gave offerings," and "gave praise" to a God who passively waited expecting "his due." Worship had nothing to do with "giving God" anything. Instead, the focus shifted to waiting and listening for what God would give to people.

Every worship service would emphasize a profound readiness for revelation. People would "listen" with heart and mind for that "Word" which would speak directly and powerfully to the individual person. They would not only feel differently, but they would be equipped and motivated to live the rest of the week and communicate new hope to others. Listening to God would not create people who followed the cross in obedient self-denial, but who walked with the risen Lord in joyous self-affirmation.

The process of listening for God was linked directly to the discernment of personal mission. Even as people needed to discover their spiritual gifts, so also they needed to hear their calling. Congregational worship and personal devotions helped mentor maturing Christians to discover that concrete use of their spiritual gifts to which Christ called the individual person. This created a "corporate atmosphere" with a "Do it!" attitude, which welcomed creativity and thrived on imagination.

Make Worship Dramatic and Diverse

As the church surrendered its addiction to consensus and uniformity, it increasingly valued variety and diversity. This needed to be reflected at the very heart of church life, namely, worship.

Initially, Old Faithful Church brought variety into its single, Sunday morning service. They renovated the sanctuary to make room for more leadership options, especially options that incorporated dramatic movement. They also rewired the sanctuary and upgraded the sound system. Finally, they removed the pews, and installed far more comfortable and flexible seating, with space in the center of the room for speakers and musicians. Music pervaded the service, but in various styles, rhythms, volumes, and groupings. From Sunday morning to Sunday morning, each service was created differently.

In addition to Sunday morning, they experimented with other services on weekdays, weeknights, and weekends. Each had a different style of music, with different perimeters of activity. Some seemed quite "traditional," while others seemed quite "contemporary." Very different kinds of people began attending the different services. Sometimes people "crossed over" between services, but usually they did not. Attendance for some was large, and for others was small, and for still others was seasonal. The church took seriously the words of Paul: "I have become all things to all people, that I might by all means [rescue] some" (1 Cor. 9:22). All worship services became dramatic, interactive, and experiential. The use of printed material (bulletins, hymnbooks, prayer books) was trimmed. They were not planned as "informational events," but as "motivational events" that would excite people to do further study, prayer, and service during the week.

Increase Congregational Communications

Since the worship service was no longer the key time for sharing information in the congregation, new communications vehicles needed to be created. Moreover, as the congregation became increasingly diverse, and as missions multiplied, there was an urgent need to share opportunities for small group, mission, and spiritual gifts discernment. Finally, as stress during this stage of transition grew, the congregation needed to do everything possible to prevent misunderstandings.

Communication became as diverse and intentional as congregational life. Therefore, the church initiated shorter newsletters, delivered more often. Telephone ministries were devised in which trained laity (who enjoyed talking on the phone!) regularly helped defined circuits in the church know what was going on. They even established a separate telephone line with recorded messages that were updated daily. One small group of video enthusiasts began quarterly "information videos," which were duplicated and distributed among the groups of the church. Finally, an elaborate, visual, interactive "information area" was created in the vestibule and refreshment room of the church following services. These were maintained by small groups and individuals. Most of them were "staffed" by volunteers who could speak knowledgeably about the mission topic, and were equipped to accept financial contributions (cash, credit, or debit) on the spot.

Since governance was being cut, and committee life was being reoriented to spirituality, the church secretary spent less time typing and duplicating agendas, reports, and statistical information. The secretary now spent more time as a communications expert. The office was equipped with quality fax and copying equipment, and filing cabinets were moved downstairs. Computers linked the church office with other offices, music rooms, and Sunday school rooms. Whenever possible, information was placed on disk, and laity were encouraged to borrow, use, and print information for themselves.

The chart for Stage 2 indicates some of the parallel tactics for de-construction and re-construction that the congregation used. These charts were shared widely in the church, adjustments and additions to which became the primary focus of board meeting agendas.

Perhaps the single most powerful tactic of Old Faithful Church was creating a leadership team entrusted with the design, volunteer recruitment, and implementation of worship services. This team replaced the old worship committee, and comprised three persons:

The "faith sharer" gave topical focus to the services, and oriented the services to Scripture. She or he would lead, or guide others to lead, in the prayer experience of the service. Similarly, if this person did not give the "mentoring message," he or she would train and guide other volunteers to do so.

The "music coordinator" crafted the musical background for the service, involving a variety of ensembles and soloists, in a variety of musical styles and moods. He or she would choose songs, hymns, or choruses relevant to the topic and prepare them for overhead projection or other use. If this person did not personally play electronic keyboard or other instruments in the service, he or she would train and guide volunteer musicians.

The "drama coach" translated Scriptures or topics into brief, realistic "chancel" dramas involving from one to a dozen persons. She or he would script, direct, and produce at least one such drama for each service. In addition, he or she would help choreograph dance with the music coordinator.

At first, only the "faith sharer" was a salaried member of the team. This was "the minister" left over from the old system of church life. The church rapidly developed the other two functions into salaried positions as well, recognizing that time and expertise were crucial to the goal of high-quality worship services. This team was entrusted to craft each service, and free to experiment in any way it wished within the perimeters of the basic vision, beliefs, and values of the church.

Once again, the congregation experienced significant stress throughout this transition stage. The chart indicates a number of stress points, but the congregation soon realized that all the conflicts and complaints were related to five basic "stress themes."

"The Only Good Music Is Organ Music!"

The first stress theme related to music. Even in the most "traditional" of the multi-track worship services, the organ was used much less than previously. Electronic keyboard, guitars, percussion, and other instruments never eliminated the organ, but they did move the organ to the sidelines of worship. Naturally, this upset the organist left over from the old system. Although many organists are in fact very versatile musicians who are skilled in a variety of musical styles, it happened that the organist of Old Faithful Church was limited to pipe organs and classical music. In addition, there were many people within the church who loved (and raised money to repair!) the pipe organ, and who regularly listened to classical music at home. They believed that the organ was the only "proper" instrument for worship.

The church, however, remained committed to the advice of Paul. The gospel was more important than the vehicle through which the gospel was delivered, and they wanted to become all things to all people, so that by all means some might be rescued. Since the vast majority of the public did not regularly listen to organ or classical music, they chose to communicate the gospel through the kind of music to which the public did listen. Rock, country, rhythm and blues, rap, and other styles, with appropriate instrumentation, dominated the music of worship.

Ironically, even as the organist of Old Faithful Church left, the congregation hired a musician from another church who was an accomplished organist, but whose zeal for ministry was constrained by the declining church system. He became the music coordinator. The legitimate appreciation of members of the church for organ and classical music could still be addressed in the more "traditional" track of worship, and in regular recitals sponsored by the church on the first Monday evening of the month.

"Choirs Should Give Great Performances!"

The new system of church life no longer required large, robed, massed choirs sitting at the front of the sanctuary. Instead, a small band with drums, keyboard, and guitar usually sat at the front of the sanctuary, and small musical ensembles or individual soloists would come forward from the congregation as needed. Many would dress informally, and no one ever wore choir robes. Since music constantly provided the background to 90 percent of the service, and since the service tended to flow without break from one musical form to another, the old "choir anthem" was not highlighted as before. And finally, singing was no longer led by a choir familiar with the pronunciation of difficult words, but by individual song leaders well acquainted with the style and rhythm of the music.

In Old Faithful Church, the choir had been the bedrock of worship music. Their decision to give or withhold enthusiasm for a given hymn often determined whether that hymn would ever be sung again. Special services at Christmas and Easter tended to showcase the choir and gave them a certain prestige for concert performance. Indeed, several choir members with voice training resented anyone else's having a solo.

All this came to an end in the new system. The power to design music in worship went to the leadership team. Music involved far more people, with a wide variety of musical taste and skill. Current music tended to de-emphasize words and introduce rhythm, volume, and lyrics that trained classical voices found uncomfortable. And Christmas and Easter were definitely not key concert occasions.

Fortunately, the new music coordinator understood their stress. Although he let go the paid soloists, he guided the choir members in two ways. First, he helped them form several small, spirituality cell groups, the interest among whom was a particular style of music. One small group loved classical, another loved country, and another loved Dixieland jazz. Each group was given opportunities to contribute to worship services. Second, he helped many of them discern a new calling as trainers. They began giving music lessons to the increasing number of "amateurs" who felt that they had gifts and callings that could make music into a mission.

"I Don't Know How to Pray"

Not a few people in Old Faithful Church discovered that when it came to spirituality, they really didn't know how to "do" it! They were very good at parliamentary procedure, attending meetings, supervising task groups, and organizing meetings, but many complained (some with tears in their eyes!) that they did not know how to pray.

The church discovered that this inability to pray was tied to the hesitancy of many church "insiders" to move beyond mere friendship to real intimacy. Both prayer and intimacy involve the risk of vulnerability to forces beyond the self. Both deliberately open the self to be filled, molded, influenced, and changed by another. Both require a rather frightening trust.

It had been a shock to discover that the very "friendliness" they had valued so much as a declining church, was in fact an addiction that was robbing life of intimacy with God and others. The chatty, jovial, kindly, and welcoming conversations around the coffee urn following declining church services, had become shields behind which many church members concealed their real feelings and thoughts. Small group spirituality pushed them to step around the coffee urn, to reveal the best and worst about themselves, to accept one another, and to support one another in change.

Prayer, as an intimate conversation with God, carried the same anxieties. The real issue was not that some doubted the existence of God, nor even that some doubted God's taking an interest in their small lives, but that God was the last person in the universe with whom people wanted to be close. Who wants to be vulnerable with a pillar of smoke by day and a pillar of fire by night?

The church managed to help many people using two broad strategies. First, they did not judge, but rather accepted people who doubted either the existence or the interest of God. They simply taught them to pray as if God existed and were interested in their lives. Some found "San Manuel Bueno," the little-known story by the turn-of-the-century Spanish Christian existentialist, Miguel de Unamuno, valuable. Others simply remembered advice given to a desperate John Wesley: "Pray for grace until you receive it, and when you receive it pray for grace."

Second, they encouraged prayer in the intimacy of small groups or "prayer triads." As the trust invested in two or three persons proved to be worth the risk, individuals were willing to trust more. They could risk sharing deep questions, or profound struggles regarding their relationship with God, supporting one another to overcome such obstacles. This confidence helped people risk "looking foolish," as they struggled to set aside self-interest to open themselves to God's power to bring change.

"Tell Me What to Say to God!"

Initially, Old Faithful Church had abandoned literate liturgical worship altogether. Responsive and unison readings, historical affirmations using obscure terminology, printed hymnbooks and prayers borrowed from other people, all seemed—for this congregation—to be barriers to authentic worship. Just as "coffee urn friendship" seemed to block real intimacy, so also the "familiar liturgies" seemed to block an authentic connection with

God. A literate liturgy had become an addiction for this congregation. It had become a repetitious incantation that produced the illusion of faith, without the reality of faith.

However, it was not long before the church needed to reconsider the matter. After the first outpourings of spontaneously expressed faith and joy, many people frankly seemed to be at a loss for words. Their own spiritual awakening seemed to plateau. Worse still, words that once were authentic became merely pious with constant repetition. They began to value afresh the assistance of spiritually mature friends who seemed to "say the words I am feeling inside," or whose words "move me into deeper waters."

The difficulty is this: How does the church know when liturgy is feeding an addiction or fueling the faith? The church never did have any final answers to this question, but they did put together some basic guidelines.

1. Liturgy ought to supplement the flow of personal interaction with God, but not replace it. It would be prized only insofar as it could enhance, deepen, or stimulate the movement of spiritual growth toward healing, listening, missioning.

2. Liturgy must be handcrafted or customized to reflect the context of this specific church. They never simply reproduced "off-the-shelf " resources. Historical liturgies and prayers were used effectively, but only if some wordings were modernized, and only if explanations regarding the origins and contexts of such liturgies helped participants link them to their own experience.

3. Liturgy must use the simplest, most common language of the people, and avoid insider jargon at all costs. It should not serve as an educational vehicle for the institution, but only assist the outpouring of the people's yearning and praise.

In short, the church decided that a literate liturgy could be useful but never sacred. It could help people articulate their innermost thoughts and feelings, but it could never communicate the voice of God.

"I Was Never Trained to Do This!"

The last stress theme involved training. The clergy of Old Faithful Church discovered that they had never been equipped for this kind of worship leadership. They had been trained to use a common lectionary, not to develop their own lectionary responsive to the unique spiritual needs of the church. They had been trained to weave together historical and current liturgical resources that celebrated the Christian year, not elicit personal expressions of joy and yearning from people who cared little about "feast days." And perhaps the most stressful discovery of all was that they had been trained in expository preaching, complete with notes or full text, pulpit, and cassock albs—and now they needed to deliver "mentoring messages" with nothing but a microphone and honesty. The clergy were delighted by the dynamism and participation of the new worship, but recognized they needed to be retrained.

The clergy felt their new vulnerability very deeply. They had been trained to avoid personal anecdotes in favor of textbook and imaginative illustrations, but now they needed to reverse themselves. They needed to share their own spiritual struggles and victories in ways that coached others with experiences in life not dissimilar from their own. On the one hand, they were uncomfortably "the same" as every person in the room. On the other hand, they were uncomfortably called to be spiritual guides to everyone in the room. There was no place to hide. Authenticity, sincerity, honesty, and profound personal faith were the characteristics of a vulnerable mentor.

The lay leaders of Old Faithful Church were having an equally stressful time. They had been trained to greet people and usher them to the right pew, not to counsel "on the spot" with emotionally excited or troubled worshipers. They had been trained to read a scripture, not act out a scripture. They had been trained to read a responsive liturgy, not invent a prayer on the spur of the moment. And perhaps the most stressful discovery of all was that they had been trained to listen passively to expert preaching—and now they needed to publicly share their faith story so that "newcomers" to the faith could be encouraged. The lay leaders were delighted with the healing, transformation, new faith, and growing worship attendance, but they recognized they needed to be retrained.

These stresses led the church to budget far more money for adult continuing education. They sent individuals to theological colleges and seminaries to take courses previously never considered. They sent their leaders in teams to spend time with other thriving congregations, to observe and learn together. They brought into the church outside consultants to train individuals in their new leadership roles. The clergy found themselves training the lay leaders in communication and counseling skills—while lay leaders found themselves teaching the clergy new skills in motivational speaking and the proper use of audio-video technology.

In the end, the new worship blurred the distinctions between clergy and lay leadership. Often, newcomers could not tell which was which. Even the sacraments included both clergy and laity. In the old system, the clergy took the lead and the laity helped. In the new system, the laity were taking the lead while the clergy helped!

Chapter 9

Stage 3:
Redefining Leadership Roles

Once Old Faithful Church had addressed the stresses generated by the transformation of worship and spirituality, it was ready to move on to the next stage. Their experience with worship underlined the fact that leadership roles in the new system of church life would be very different. Now they concentrated on the full scope of changing leadership expectations. These were the goals for this stage of the transition.

STAGE 3: REDEFINING LEADERSHIP ROLES

GOALS

1. Shift Clergy from "Enabling" to "Training"
2. Shift Lay Leadership from "Managing" to "Futuring"
3. Shift Lay Participation from "Fund-Raising" to "Ministry"
4. Insist on Quality

De-construction	Re-construction
1. Reduce "descriptive" committee mandates.	1. Develop "proscriptive" mandates.
2. Eliminate executive "approval."	2. Initiate executive "management."
3. Remove financial statement from board's agenda.	3. Focus board on policy and long-range planning only.
4. Reduce by 50 percent eldership energy attending meetings.	4. Eldership spend time among the public listening for spiritual needs.
5. No longer accept leadership without training.	5. Train leaders intensively.
6. Stop training elders to be bureaucrats.	6. Start training elders in relational skills.

173

7. Surrender the assumption that clergy do ministry and laity manage or support it.

7. Create the attitude that laity do ministry and clergy manage or support it.

8. Abandon the "chaplaincy" role of clergy.

8. Equip laity for visitation.

9. Cut back clergy time with the "churched."

9. Increase clergy time with the "unchurched."

10. Eliminate long-term counseling by clergy.

10. Refer long-term counseling to others.

11. Stop searching for "chairpersons."

11. Start searching for cell group "pastors."

12. Stop crisis personnel committee meetings to deal with complaints about salaried staff.

12. Start regular personnel committee meetings to evaluate and support.

13. Broaden personnel committee focus beyond staff.

13. Include performance reviews for lay volunteer leadership.

14. Clergy release responsibility for pastoral care.

14. Laity accept responsibility for pastoral care.

15. Clergy reduce visitation agenda 50 percent.

15. Create trained pastoral care teams.

16. Clergy stop giving time to everyone.

16. Start mentoring a gifted, trusted few.

17. Cease underfunded continuing education.

17. Triple the budget for training.

18. Stop just sending individuals for education in colleges.

18. Start sending teams for on-site observation in parishes.

19. Reduce denominational meetings by 50 percent.

19. Increase ecumenical associations both mainline and evangelical.

20. Continue to decrease energy for recruitment.

20. Accelerate discernment of spiritual gifts.

Stress Points

1. Hesitance to give committees power to implement
2. Finance committee's loss of control of program
3. Reluctance of elders to exercise their role among the public
4. Not enough visitation by clergy
5. Clergy's feelings of guilt or discomfort while among the unchurched
6. Pastoral care and counseling made secondary priorities for clergy
7. Difficulty recruiting, training, and trusting the Personnel Committee
8. Personnel evaluation now extended to include lay leadership
9. Influence achieved through participation rather than patronage

10. Clergy accused of taking too much authority
11. Laity uncomfortable receiving pastoral care from other laity.

Shift Clergy from "Enabling" to "Training"

In the old system of church life, the clergy were burning themselves out trying to visit every person in the parish, or personally counseling outsiders experiencing grief, seeking to be married, or just plain troubled about something. They took care of folks. It is true that the "enabling" style of ministry that they had been taught in seminary, at its best, was intended to "empower" individuals to solve their own problems. However, the facts of life in the old system always seemed to lead the clergy and the congregation toward unhealthful codependency. More and more people seemed to need visits from the minister, and the minister needed to be needed. Parish ministry was becoming an unhealthy form of "chaplaincy," in which the minister moved "room-to-room" in order to "take care" of people. The minister tended to function always with the unspoken assumption, "Tell me where you want to go, and, wherever that is, I'll help you get there."

In the new system, the clergy operated with a different assumption: "Tell me where you believe Christ is calling you to go, and I will help send you there." Visionary clergy knew where they were going, and they were not going to allow others to sidetrack them from their quest; similarly, they believed God was calling every individual to a specific mission-destiny, and they refused to allow their own personal needs to sidetrack others from their quest. The new role of clergy was to train others in ministry, or, to say it another way, to equip others to pursue their spiritual callings (whatever those callings might be). They tended to work not one-to-one, but rather one-to-group. When they worked one-to-one, it was only with the view of equipping the other person to go and do ministry, and then to train yet another person to go and do ministry.

Shift Lay Leadership from "Managing" to "Futuring"

In the old system, the elders, deacons, board members, and lay leaders concentrated on control. They spent endless hours in meetings: setting policy, approving proposals, adjusting the budget, devising clever fund-raising strategies, supervising staff, and generally monitoring the institutional mission agenda to which everyone must be obedient. They maintained the ethos of the church. It is true that the "management" leadership style of the program church, at its best, was intended to free the experts to do ministry. However, the facts of life in the old system always seemed to hinder and slow ministry, rather than help and accelerate ministry. Lay leaders became "burned out" serving multiple offices, or "bored to tears" sitting in too many meetings. Lay leaders always tended to function with the unspoken assumption, "Tell me what you want to do, and I will tell you if you have permission to do it, and, if so, how it must be done."

In the new system, lay leaders operated with a different assumption: "Tell me what you feel called to do, and, no matter how crazy it may seem, I will help you do it with excellence." They spent hours, not inside the church buildings in meetings, but inside public places, listening for the emerging needs (spiritual and physical) of the community. They entrusted the annual budget to a gifted few, and concentrated all their attention on what must happen in ministry five or ten years down the road. Most lay leaders in the new system never looked at a financial statement. They spent all their time in two basic activities:

1. *Faith-sharing.* They are constantly engaged in dialogue about faith. They are constantly talking about what really makes life worth living, and what truly motivates action. They are forever discovering new growth in themselves, and always articulating their own experience of the transforming power of God.

2. *Mentoring.* They are constantly "mentoring" or "midwifing" new ideas into being, no matter how different they might be from current practice, and regardless of whether or not they personally agree with them. They are perpetually helping others to see the "burning bushes" in their lives, and to hear the voice of God saying "Here am I!"

Lay leaders in the new system never purposely maintain a heritage. They are too busy encouraging new eruptions of the divine into human life.

Shift Lay Participation from "Fund-Raising" to "Ministry"

In the old system, lay participation essentially meant raising money to pay others (presumably "experts") to do ministry. Laity could rest content if they fulfilled their annual financial pledge, and serve standing committees that supposedly freed professionals to do all the pastoral care, advocacy, evangelism, teaching, and liturgical leadership that together constituted "ministry." They maintained the machinery of ministry. It is true that the emphasis on the financial offering in church, at best, symbolized one's complete obedience to the cross of Christ. However, the facts of life in the old system always seemed to highlight the "pocketbook" and never the "heart." Lay participation could only get motivated in times of crisis ("A tornado tore the roof off the building!"), and could only get excited over accountability ("What are we paying these people for, anyway!"). Lay participation always seemed to ask the same question: "What will it cost?"

In the new system, lay participants asked a new question: "What can I (personally) do?" They no longer raised money to pay experts to do ministry. They did the ministry themselves. They raised money for only two reasons. Either they raised money to extend their personal missions to more people, or they raised money to hire professionals to train them to do personal mission better. Lay participation involved two basic activities, neither one of which could be fulfilled on Sunday morning:

1. *Using Spiritual Gifts.* They discovered which biblical gifts filled them with enthusiasm, and then constantly looked for creative ways to exercise those gifts. They loved to refine, perfect, and deepen those gifts; cooperate with similarly motivated people to share those gifts; and listen for God's direction to use those gifts.

2. *Healing.* Everything they did aimed at healing, meaning the transformation of individuals and society toward health, wholeness, and harmony. They made contact with the "heart" and then worked outward toward the "mind." They first addressed the shackled will, and then nurtured the knowledge of insight.

Lay participants in the new system no longer consumed information, in order to contribute more money. They perfected spiritual gifts, in order to perform ministry.

Insist on Quality

In the old system, Old Faithful Church had made a virtue out of accepting mediocrity. They recruited people whose sense of duty made them willing to serve committees and fill offices. The very fact that volunteers were willing to set aside personal enthusiasms and sacrifice personal enjoyment, in order to fulfill the institutional agenda, underlined their importance to the system. All the church asked was that reluctant nominees simply promise to "do what they could." Duty was all important—occasional competence was a bonus. It is true that, at its best, the church would offer extra training. However, the facts of life in the old system dictated that they never budgeted for it, and few people wanted to be trained in something that deep inside they did not want to do. What they brought to the church out of duty would be "good enough."

In the new system, the only virtue was excellence. Enthusiasms abounded. Like racehorses champing at the bit, the problem was not to get them moving but to rein them in long enough for training, so that when they started running they wouldn't break a leg or knock something down. However excited the church was about spiritual gifts, it knew that God expected those gifts to be exercised with integrity and skill. An old fellow Christ called to play music on the street corner and talk to people about religion, could not be released into ministry until he had been given accordion lessons and educated to be a walking encyclopedia of local social services. A young woman Christ called to lobby municipal government about antipornography legislation could not be let loose on city hall until she understood perfectly the machinery of government, and could articulate the faith that lay behind the cause.

High quality was essential to the emerging system of the church, for two reasons:

1. *Only **high** quality could build credibility.* The church was committed to ministry with long-term impact. Such ministry required the wide public respect that recognizes professional standards and lasting, positive results. The ministry needed to be accessible, safe, relevant, productive—and good.

2. *Only **high** quality could build confidence.* The people sent into ministry should not be timid or easily defeated. If they were to walk with the risen Lord in the real world, they needed the self-assurance and courage that only high quality training could give.

High quality was a never-ending quest in the new system. People could continue in ministry only if they were constantly growing in faith and upgrading their skills. Continuing adult education, oriented to specific mission and practical ministry, became a way of life.

The chart for Stage 3 identifies some of the key strategies Old Faithful Church used to help people change their leadership expectations. Once again, these strategies were widely shared with the congregation. Specific, concrete examples were provided to demonstrate how these strategies changed the weekly routine of the clergy and laity. The newsletter printed personal "testimonies" sharing the continuing struggle of both clergy and lay leaders as they sought to adapt to a new system. In this way, no one felt alone in experiencing stress.

Perhaps the single, most powerful strategy for this stage of transformation was the reorientation of the traditional "eldership" of the church. Elders trimmed by 50 percent (and more) the time they spent in management (e.g., policy formation, supervision, and permission giving). In groups of three or four, they purposely devoted hours to sitting in public places watching people and eavesdropping on their conversations. Later they returned to an elder's home to discuss the spiritual yearnings they had perceived, and their own sense of shock about the image of the church in the community. They prayed for the people they had seen and heard. They imagined what they might say to such people (if they had the chance), and before long God gave them the chance.

Simultaneously, the church stopped treating the eldership as an office. It became a calling, revealed only as individuals pursued an intense process of discerning their spiritual gifts. The role of "elder" was returned to the biblical model of "pastor." These lay leaders were emerging as the cell group leaders, shepherds, caregivers, or *pastors* of the congregation. The pastoral leader (formerly known as the senior minister) stopped trying to care for everyone, and began to concentrate on mentoring these key lay shepherds. The pastoral leader spent many hours teaching, coaching, encouraging, and troubleshooting with this group. In the end, they emerged equipped with the same knowledge and skills in pastoral care, Scripture, and prayer as the pastoral leader obtained from seminary—and more. They began to uncover and train others whom God had gifted and called into this ministry. By the way, the church no longer called them *elders*, since nobody among the public knew what that meant. They simply called them "friends."

It is not difficult to imagine that stress in the congregation reached new heights during this stage of transition. Some felt that these changes compromised an identity which, for them, was too precious to lose. The minister should be a visitor and caregiver, available around the clock; lay leaders should be managers and administrators; lay participants should be beneficiaries and fund-raisers. They said, "I won't change!" Many were frankly excited by this new vision of leadership, but felt threatened by their inadequacies. They weren't trained or equipped, they had no confidence in themselves or in their faith, and the public, frankly, scared them to death. They said, "I can't change!" Three stress themes emerged in this stage of transition.

"Nobody Can Care for Us the Way the Minister Can!"

The first stress theme was that many people felt that a visit from a lay leader, no matter how pleasant or helpful, simply could not be a substitute for a visit from the minister. Oddly enough, the people who held this view were not necessarily the very elderly, the hospitalized, or those chronically ill or limited. The most vocal people who held this view were board members, who wanted to believe this was what others thought. The idea that anyone else might offer pastoral care (or that they themselves *should* offer it) was deeply troubling. Indeed, for some, part of their hidden motivation to be board members was their codependency relationship with the minister. The more hours they sacrificed participating in management, the more attention they would "deserve" from the minister in times of personal crisis.

Many held this view, however, for more legitimate reasons. Once the church began to understand their reasons, however, it could help these people accept the change. Three basic reasons were discovered:

1. *The pastoral visit is **sacred**.* Whether or not the sacrament was shared, the visit was often experienced as a sacred time in which God became "real" to the person in a way unlike that of more mundane visits of friends. The church responded by dropping the use of "titles," such as "Reverend" or "Doctor," in reference to its pastoral leader. They also "laid hands" on their emerging lay "friends" in worship, and made sure that they brought to their calling a profound spirituality. Laity who visited were well equipped to empower prayer, oriented toward healing (not idle chatter), and freed to creatively share the sacrament of holy communion when asked.

2. *The pastoral visit is **skillful**.* People expected a visit to be well considered, planned, and consciously supportive or therapeutic. Traditionally, the only person in the church who could do this was the minister. The church responded, not only by training its emerging lay "friends" to the highest professional standards possible, but by communicating the content of that training widely and repeatedly among the congregation. "Stories of Effectiveness" were circulated in the newsletters. The church deliberately recognized and celebrated a different focus of activity around its pastoral leader.

3. *The pastoral visit is* **confidential.** In the end, this was the most powerful reason people wanted only the minister to visit. In the power politics and gossip mill of life in the former church, the lay leaders had lost credibility. This reality took the longest time to overcome. The church began regular "mutual mentoring" sessions through the year for the emerging "friends." These were led by the pastoral leader. Confidentiality was repeatedly stressed, but these sessions provided a safe environment for the "friends" to help one another troubleshoot difficulties as they arose, and unburden themselves of some of the emotional stresses of caregiving. Slowly people trusted that their personal affairs could be responsibly and discreetly addressed.

After the initial, drastic adjustment to the time spent by the pastoral leader in visitation, involvement in visitation was cut much more gradually. It took time for some people to shift their expectations, and some never did to the day they died. Neither the church nor the pastoral leader would ever abandon them.

"Craziness Will Wreck the Church!"

The transformation of leadership in the church included shifting power in order to design and implement program "downward" and "outward" to the people. This both freed the elders to become the "pastors" God called them to be, and empowered individuals to exercise the spiritual gifts God called them to use. The strategy to eliminate "prescriptive" committee mandates, however, was controversial. The "proscriptive" mandates the church initiated simply defined the boundaries beyond which a committee could not go. In a sense, the church no longer told them what to do, but what they could *not* do. Their new freedom to do anything they wished, right away, within the boundaries that had been established, opened the door to all kinds of innovation and experimentation.

Once again the issues of "control" surfaced in church life. Some church insiders were afraid that work they considered vital would not be done, and work they considered unimportant, or (worse still!) bizarre, or (worst of all!) illegal and immoral, would multiply. This profound lack of trust was deeply resented by many members of standing committees, who felt passionate about their ministry and who had long complained about the slow, insensitive church bureaucracy. As tempers flared, the church responded by first calming people down. Much of this was irrational overreaction. The truth was that nothing illegal or immoral would happen, and the basic values and belief emerging from within the deepening spirituality of the congregation would guard against abuse. The proscriptive mandates imposed spending limits and other basic boundaries, which would prevent program committees from destroying the church. The committee members were responsible people who deserved to be trusted. Accountability was, in fact, even more intentional. A human resources team with oversight of both salaried *and* volunteer leadership was initiated and carefully trained. They would meet regularly to plan training for all leaders, monitor work performance, build understanding, and, if necessary, reconcile complaints.

In the end, this stage of transition resulted in a different *attitude* about leadership. Behavior patterns that initially required forethought became unconscious and intuitive. Salaried and volunteer leaders spontaneously acted in different ways, because they *thought of themselves* in different ways.

"I'm Good Enough Now, and Don't Need to Improve Anything!"

The quest for excellence now demanded of all church leaders was very disturbing for some staff and volunteers. While many celebrated the opportunities for personal growth, and the incentives for improved missions, which the quest implied, others were offended or frightened. These people were quite comfortable on one or more of the following life plateaus.

1. *The faith plateau.* These people believed they no longer needed to grow in faith, spirituality, or relationship to God. Confirmation at the age of fourteen had been their certification of faith-sufficiency. They knew what they needed to know, believed what they needed to believe, and had memorized what needed to be memorized.

The church now challenged them for spiritual growth. Membership no longer meant simply the right to vote and hold office. It implied a covenant to go deeper in a relationship with God. They were being challenged to ask truly tough questions, and discover for themselves truly profound answers.

2. *The relationship plateau.* These people believed they had no need to deepen relationships with friends they had, or broaden their friendships with strangers. They were content with their friendships around the coffee urn following worship, their circle of influence in church politics, and their supper club with whom they had eaten "potluck" for more than a decade.

The church now challenged them to build deeper, multiple relationships. Membership no longer meant mere "friendliness." It implied intimacy, trust, confidentiality, compassion, and mutual support. They were being challenged to befriend strangers, and understand those beyond their cultural, racial, economic, or aesthetic experience.

3. *The skills plateau.* These people believed that their skills were "good enough" for the church. They had no desire to work toward self-improvement. If something went wrong, they tended to blame the church for failing to provide adequate supervision of their work. If their performance was criticized, they tended to perceive this as personal rejection.

The church now challenged them to constantly upgrade their abilities. Membership no longer meant obligations to perform institutional tasks. It implied callings to participate in Christian missions. They were being challenged beyond mere adequacy, to genuine quality.

The church recognized that the real issue here was not acceptance of individuals, but excellence of ministries. Hidden within each of the "life plateaus" were personal and corporate addictions that held people back from self-fulfillment and Christian mission.

The church reassured those who were offended by the quest for excellence that their "salvation" or "acceptance" by God was not being questioned. The church simply loved them enough to wish for them abundance of life and effectiveness in mission. The church reassured those who were frightened by the quest for excellence that they did not expect instant achievement of an abstract standard of excellence. They simply expected everyone in leadership in the church to develop a strategy for personal growth, a process to gain sensitivity to strangers, and a plan for skills development.

Chapter 10

Stage 4:
Streamlining Organization

Now that Old Faithful Church had built a new and deeper spirituality in church life, and a new and different attitude about church leadership, it was ready to overhaul the organization. The structures of church life had been declared "clay" in the first stage of transition, but they had not yet been changed. The experiences in stages 2 and 3 had initiated systemic changes, but now there was a need to follow through on those experiments and make sweeping organizational adjustments appropriate to the emerging church life. In short, the *system* of church life was now different, and it called forth a whole new organizational model.

STAGE 4: STREAMLINING ORGANIZATION

GOALS

1. Establish the "Energy Field" of Basic Vision, Beliefs, and Values
2. Create the Stability Triangle
3. Shift Program Development to Spirituality Cell Groups
4. Multiply Entry Points into Church Life

De-construction	Re-construction
1. Reduce the constitution to a brief summary.	1. Identify and celebrate the "Energy Field."
2. Reduce repetition of creeds.	2. Increase singing the visionary song.
3. Reduce and consolidate standing committees.	3. Match committee activity to public use.
4. Trim overall board to no more than: 4 per 100 members in churches of 250 and fewer;	4. Use spiritual gifts inventories to identify administration gifts.

2 per 100 members in churches of 500 and fewer; 1 per 100 members in churches of 750 and fewer; etc.

5. Transform the "personnel" committee from mere supervision.

5. Create a human resources team to empower excellence.

6. Remove initiation barriers for involvement.

6. Create "hooks" to engage the public.

7. Stop counting membership.

7. Emphasize participation.

8. Accept unfilled vacancies on the board.

8. Appoint only gifted, called volunteers.

9. Eliminate finance and management from the board agenda.

9. Focus on "futuring" and evangelism.

10. Eliminate policy and approval from executive.

10. Do coordination, communication, and finance.

11. Eliminate the finance and property committees as standing committees of the board.

11. Make finance and property committees advisory to the executive.

12. Stop using ad hoc committees for policy or research.

12. Editorial task groups refine resources.

13. Do not expect congregational meetings to manage program.

13. Define, refine, celebrate the "Energy Field."

14. Congregational meetings don't evaluate reports.

14. Reports mailed to "shareholders."

15. Congregational meetings don't do management.

15. Build team vision and enthusiasm.

16. Eliminate "descriptive" committee mandates.

16. Empower "proscriptive" mandates.

17. Cut committee role in program design.

17. P.A.L.S. groups design program.

18. Cut committee role in implementing disciple individuals for ministry.

18. P.A.L.S. groups implement program.

19. Surrender historical or geographic church names.

19. Rename the church after the vision.

20. Eliminate elders' visitation districts.

20. Train and regularly upgrade P.A.L.S. Group leaders.

Stress Points

1. Board members committed to control, pressured to leave office
2. Traditional emphasis on consensus decision-making abandoned
3. Control by way of central nominations process abandoned

4. Wrong expectations of board maintained by inactive members
5. Occasional mistakes by committees
6. Money risked investing in people, rather than saved for "rainy days"
7. Affordable mission no longer the priority
8. The finance and property committees no longer the focus of power
9. Laity expected to do ministry
10. Laity expected to do high-quality ministry
11. Clergy now doing things they may not have been trained to do
12. Rapid escalation of the need for adult faith development and training
13. Welcome systems for newcomers quickly overburdened
14. Veteran members panicked by some creative ideas.

Establish the "Energy Field" of Basic Vision, Beliefs, and Values

This was the first goal of Stage 4. The process of the first three stages led the congregation to discern, refine, and articulate the essential perimeters of church life. Stage 1 ("Shared Vision") helped them identify the "Song in the Heart" that motivated all church activity. Stage 2 ("Congregational Spirituality") helped them articulate the bottom-line "essentials" of faith that directed all church activity. Stage 3 ("Redefining Leadership Roles") helped them exemplify the behavioral norms and interpersonal values that shaped all church activity.

Now the congregation named and celebrated these essentials of church life. These now formed the boundaries beyond which groups and individuals could not go, and still be a part of the church, but within which they could do anything at all—immediately. Just as church worship found a new character and style in the second stage, and just as church leadership found a new attitude in the third stage, so now the church as a whole found a new identity. It was not an identity shaped by heritage but by purpose. At this point, the congregation decided to rename itself. Like a butterfly emerging from the cocoon, they laid aside their old identity as "Old Faithful Church" and publicly identified themselves as "New Hope-in-the-Heart Church."

Create the Stability Triangle

The Stability Triangle (including the pastoral leadership team, human resources team, and streamlined administrative team) began to replace the old multicommittee, redundant-management official board. A much smaller number of gifted and called people would eventually be entrusted to administrate the direction and progress of the whole church. The number of church "offices" and church "meetings" would be dramatically cut.

This process would actually not be completed until Stage 5. New Hope-in-the-Heart Church made the transition easier by making the board executive a transitional "steering committee." Temporarily, the old executive would

—steer the transformation of former program committees;
—develop effective communications systems;
—manage the day-to-day life of the church.

Eventually, the executive will be replaced by the new administrative team. This new team will combine the work of communication, coordination, finance, property management, and executive policy clarification.

People work very differently in the new organizational model. Members of the pastoral leadership team serve as visionaries, motivators, and trainers. They invest time listening to public yearning, doing long-range planning, motivating and transforming worship, equipping lay leaders, and nurturing small spirituality cell groups. The human resources team combines personnel oversight with nurturing the process of discerning spiritual gifts. They invest time arranging appropriate training for emerging mission, maintaining standards of excellence among both salaried and volunteer leaders, interpreting leadership activities for the congregation, and evaluating performance. The administrative team manages the church in the way just outlined. In other words, the human resources team "grows ministers," the pastoral leadership team "trains ministers," and the administrative team "deploys ministers."

The role of the Stability Triangle is *not* to design an institutional mission agenda and recruit people to implement it; *but rather* it is to facilitate whatever mission God calls forth from the people. They maintain the energy field of basic vision, beliefs, and values, and help people apply it to their particular calling.

Shift Program Development to Spirituality Cell Groups

New Hope-in-the-Heart Church gradually began to phase out program committees—a process that would be completed in the fifth stage. Such committees were now "in the way" of the new system. They were originally designed to implement an institutional mission agenda rather than facilitate individual callings. As a result, they were not readily adaptable to the many diverse, emerging missions that God was calling forth from the people. They tended to force unique callings into preformed mission categories, and, because they had no real power, generally slowed down the speed of mission. All "program," now understood simply as "mission," would emerge from small spirituality cell groups. Callings would emerge from the depths of intimacy, prayer, and Bible study in the small groups. The people most motivated for the mission would have immediate and direct power to undertake it.

In the same way, the church began to phase out traditional choirs, clubs, and generic groups for men and women. The diverse interests of these groups were transformed to become the shared enthusiasm that gathered a small group. That enthusiasm or interest would be purposely set in the spirituality and personal growth process of the small groups. For example, choirs did not gather specifically to rehearse music for Sunday worship. They gathered to enjoy a certain style of music, while sharing spiritual growth with intimate friends. Occasionally the pastoral leadership team would ask them to participate in worship, but their shared musical interest would also find expression in some broader, more public calling.

Of course, all this meant that the mission agenda of the church was no longer predictable, just as it was no longer controllable. There could be surprising gaps in the mission of the church, just as there could be extraordinary imagination. Nevertheless, the role of the Stability Triangle was not to fill the gaps but simply to coordinate and facilitate a growing diversity of missions.

Multiply Entry Points into Church Life

Progress into the heart of church life used to be marked by one's advancement through the bureaucracy of church management. The public had been recruited through a limited number of controlled "access" points, one of the primary ones being the physical entrance to the church building itself. They would then be initiated through an educational process, and then be permitted to celebrate baptism, join the church, and so on. However, all that had been removed by New Hope-in-the-Heart Church. Their commitment to engaging the full diversity of public yearning meant that they needed to devise a wide range of potential "entry" points and "pathways," through which the public could navigate their experience of church life with ease.

Varied worship, multiple small shared-interest groups, and opportunities to discern spiritual gifts all formed easy "entry points" for newcomers. The emphasis on healing, feeling, and personal change took away the forbidding challenge of "learning" volumes of new religious information. Personal faith-sharing and mentoring strategies eliminated the need for special "meetings" for newcomers. Membership was redefined and postponed for later in the spiritual journey. In short, the church removed the "initiation" processes that had once guarded church life.

In the same way, the pathways of involvement were marked, not by institutional commitment, but by personal growth. The pressure to pledge to a unified budget was replaced with opportunities to give to any specific mission that spoke to one's heart. People could come and go, speak or be silent, as they chose and without pressure. There were no institutional penalties for disagreement.

The chart of Stage 4 identifies some of the strategies New Hope-in-the-Heart Church used to transform its organization. However, perhaps no single strategy had more impact on the church than the process of cutting back, amalgamating, and eventually eliminating program committees from the life of the church.

They began by cutting back committees. They chose to allow offices to remain vacant, and simply canceled committees that only existed on paper—no matter how "necessary" the denomination considered them to be. They refused to feel guilty about this, believing simply that God had yet to draw those gifts and callings from among the people.

Then they began amalgamating committees. They broadened the topical area of committees, permitting unique, creative ideas that blurred traditional distinctions between work areas. People were allowed to give their energy to that piece of the topical area which excited them most. They acknowledged that no committee could do everything. Committee mandates could now be shifted easily from "prescriptive" to "proscriptive." This encouraged people to give energy to that which excited them, rather than to that which the institution deemed important. Freedom to experiment encouraged higher "learning curves" and deepened spiritual growth.

Next, they started transforming the committees into small spirituality cell groups. Mission was "hived out" to groups ranging from three to ten persons. These people implemented the P.A.L.S. strategy, forming spirituality groups of prayer, action, learning, sharing, organized around a common enthusiasm or interest.

Finally, they began to eliminate the need for any committee altogether. They allowed the multiple small groups simply to pursue their callings. Initiative to gather more people, meet with other groups, or coordinate with inside or outside bodies, was left entirely to the discretion of each small group. The church provided leadership training, and sought to facilitate their mission in every way possible.

Such a strategy helped New Hope-in-the-Heart Church to convince people that they did not have an agenda to fulfill but rather a mission to perform. People no longer "burned out" as they obediently did what they were told was right, but they found immense satisfaction pursuing what they felt called to do.

Once again, a new set of stress themes emerged in church life.

"I Hate Small Groups!"

Some people just did not like small groups. They understood and appreciated them, and recognized that they addressed the spiritual yearning for intimacy among the public. They even welcomed the multiplication of small groups, and accepted with joy the shift of mission initiative from committees to the small groups. However, at a personal level, some folks simply did not enjoy small spirituality cell groups. New Hope-in-the-Heart Church noticed that this view was particularly common among people between forty-five and sixty; among former, veteran official board members; and among the very well educated. The reasons varied from person to person (the culture of the "Post War Generation," preference for a more traditional learning method, introverted personality types, etc.).

The church loved these people, too, and did not judge their reasons. They simply recognized that the spiritual yearning of some folks is not for intimacy. Therefore, the church took action.

1. *They made room for large spirituality groups.* The large groups had presidents and secretaries, agendas and projects, and large meetings. They resembled the large groups (e.g., women's and men's clubs) of the past, except that:

—they devised a matrix of authentic spirituality;
—they included processes for discerning spiritual gifts;
—they involved participants in hands-on mission activities;
—they had the same powers of initiative the small groups had.

2. *They encouraged large groups to "hand off" pieces of mission for smaller task groups.* This created a less competitive environment, fostering deeper personal relationships.

In the end, the church discovered that some people moved from large to small groups, some participated in both, and some always remained with the large groups. The church also discovered that these large groups formed yet another important "entry point" for some newcomers. They provided a place of relative anonymity from which some could "observe" the life of the church. Many small group leaders often circulated among the crowd in large group events, seeking potential new participants for small groups.

"How Dare You Not Agree with Me!"

The organizational changes in this stage meant that power cliques could no longer veto activities in the church. All kinds of "minority" groups were encouraged. Small groups with special interests and unique perspectives abounded. *What had been eliminated, however, was the power of one minority group to insist that everybody else had to agree with them!* Church decisions could no longer be held hostage by a few people who declared that they would leave the church, or withhold their offerings, if such-and-such an action took place. It was no longer necessary to have nearly unanimous consent to do things. It was not even necessary to have majority consent to do things! And the fact that church unity was no longer based on "agreement" troubled some people immensely. Their quest for doctrinal purity, or politically correct community, or ideological unity had come to an end in New Hope-in-the-Heart Church.

Although some people left the church, accusing it of "watering down the gospel" and "wishy-washy social action positions," the church took steps to help people see the real opportunity that was being presented.

1. *There was still a place for consensus.* Consensus was crucial in two areas of church life. First, there had to be consensus about the energy field of basic vision, beliefs, and values. Second, there had to be consensus in the activities of the small groups. There did *not* need to be consensus for any mission generated through the small groups and large groups. And there did *not* need to be consensus about the management of the church entrusted to the administrative team.

2. *Freedom replaced factions.* In the old system, the quest for consensus had resulted in political factions. Each special interest group competed for control of the church agenda in order to force everyone else to accept its position.

This self-destructive behavior resulted in nothing getting done. *Now* participants of any special interest group were free to pursue their mission in the world, without having to waste energy defending themselves to the institution. Others might not agree with them, but at least the institution would not block them. The biggest hurdle, of course, was to help people understand that the unity of the church was not really based now on *agreement!* At the deepest level, the real unity of the church lay in *the common experience of the transforming power of God touching individual lives.* How individuals interpreted the touch of God would vary; but that they all were experiencing that touch of God was never in doubt.

Chapter 11

Stage 5:
Birthing the New System

New Hope-in-the-Heart Church has come a long way. A vision that became a team vision has transformed spirituality and worship, ordered and lay leadership, and the entire organization of church life. They have experienced and overcome many stresses. On the one hand, the severity of these stresses was resolved before the church moved forward into the next new stage. On the other hand, the church became familiar with working in a stressful environment. They have come to understand that stress is a vital, creative component for church life. Hard as it is to affirm, *they know that they never, ever want to be stress-free,* for that will be a sign that addictions have again enslaved church life and death lies ahead.

The time has come to finally establish the growth system of

transforming . . .
gifting . . .
calling . . .
equipping . . .
and *sending people*

as the routine experience of the church every day, week, and year. This is the purpose for which New Hope-in-the-Heart Church exists.

STAGE 5: BIRTHING THE NEW SYSTEM

GOALS

1. Regular Multi-Track Worship
2. Visionary, Motivating Leadership

3. Diversified and Equipped Discipleship
4. Create a Unity of Faith-Sharing and Social Action

De-construction	Re-construction
1. Do not define identity by heritage.	1. Define identity by vision values and beliefs.
2. Eliminate any "descriptive" small group expectations.	2. Use only "proscriptive" small group expectations.
3. Eliminate all committees except human resources.	3. Rely on P.A.L.S. strategies for small groups.
4. Eliminate the official board.	4. Establish a "futuring" team.
5. Eliminate the board executive.	5. Establish an administration team of 7 to 10 gifted, called, equipped people elected for set terms.
6. Merge the trustees board.	6. Unite trustees and administration team.
7. Do not staff "offices."	7. Discover and train "charisms."
8. Do not "front load" educational or orientation requirements for newcomers.	8. Do direct newcomers to cell groups after experiential worship.
9. Surrender single Sunday worship service.	9. Create multiple worship opportunities.
10. Do not hire professionals to do ministry.	10. Professionals train laity to do ministry.
11. Do not seek traditional clergy leadership.	11. Seek leaders who are visionaries, mentors, motivators, and faith-sharers.
12. De-prioritize visiting, counseling, advocacy, and program development from the clergy agenda.	12. Prioritize visioning, leadership training, adult faith development, worship and motivation for clergy agenda.
13. Reduce "life-cycle" pastoral care by clergy.	13. Train P.A.L.S. group leaders intensively.
14. Don't dwell on financial costs.	14. Count the whole cost of church development.
15. Eliminate institutional budgets.	15. Create mission support budgets.
16. Eliminate generic mission offerings.	16. Initiate designated giving opportunities.
17. Stop talking about mission.	17. Do it.
18. Don't just "do it."	18. Always explain why you do it.
19. Stop relying on printed information.	19. Expand communications media.
20. Surrender the idol of property.	20. Renovate or relocate.
21. Stop sharing "wilderness journeys" and "slow growth."	21. Start sharing personal transformations.

Stress Points

1. Congregation becoming "future"-oriented, not "past"-oriented
2. Forgiveness and humor for inevitable small group mistakes
3. Disagreement about ideology or doctrine allowed
4. Clergy becoming crucial to the vision
5. Disappearance of the bureaucratic "safety net"
6. Eldership now doing ministry, trusting others to do management
7. No such thing as spirituality without social action
8. Social action requiring faith sharing
9. Adult baptism more important than infant baptism
10. Creativity in the design of cell groups taxed to the limit
11. Leadership for holy communion, weddings, and funerals shifted to the laity
12. Crisis intervention for those with old clergy expectations requiring individualized, creative responses
13. Members no longer expected to know everyone by name
14. Disorientation for inactive members, as congregational life has seemingly been turned "upside down."

Regular Multi-Track Worship

The church had previously transformed its Sunday morning worship service into a "motivational" event linked to service, study, and prayer through the week. They had also begun to experiment with alternative services through the week, conscious that much of the public slept in on Sunday mornings. These experiments used various kinds of music and liturgical styles and sought to include various demographic segments of the public. They had a growing awareness of what worked and what did not work, of what musical resources existed in the community, and of what groups of people responded most favorably to their invitations.

By this time, New Hope-in-the-Heart Church had outgrown the initial euphoria of just "doing worship differently." They had a deeper awareness of what was essential in worship for their ministry. They also discovered that some continuity needed to be maintained from service to service—and that every participant had his or her own personal limits as to what helped or hindered the experience of healing and missioning. A plan for creating multiple options for worship needed to be initiated.

A weekly routine of multi-track worship dramatically increased the participation of diverse publics in church life. Each "track" of worship was dramatically different from the others in music, style, and format. At the same time, each track had an "inner continuity" of style and format, so that participants could generally anticipate what would happen in future services.

Each track of worship tended to involve its own "public." However, the church was surprised to discover that age and gender did not usually determine participation in a service. Elderly people would become involved in "experimental" services, and young people might come to traditional services. Men and women participated equally in all services. In fact, even within ethnic groups from the community, cultural and racial representation spread through all services as changing generations associated with the surrounding culture.

Despite multi-tracking, all worship services were linked to the system of thriving church life.

They emphasized "healing" and personal transformation.
They all emphasized "listening" and discernment of personal mission.
They all were "motivational," inspiring people toward mission with excellence.
They all linked people to the small groups or disciplines of faith development through the week.

Eventually, specific small spirituality cell groups (P.A.L.S. groups) began taking over the design and implementation of each "track of worship." The worship teams all included a faith-sharer, drama coach, and music coordinator, and were trained by the pastoral leadership team of the church.

Visionary, Motivating Leadership

The church had previously redeployed its pastoral leader ("the minister") to emphasize the training and equipping of laity to do ministry. This necessarily involved spending more and more time amid the public, to discern the spiritual yearnings and physical needs the laity needed to be trained to address. Finally, this redeployment of energy required the pastoral leader to develop "motivating" worship that transformed the heart, and a "mentoring" leadership style that authentically shared faith.

By this time, the leadership of New Hope-in-the-Heart Church had outgrown the excitement of simply doing something different. They had begun to test the depths of new leadership expectations, and had identified ways in which they needed to be retrained. Even as a new attitude toward ministry emerged in their behavior, a new sense of identity emerged in their leadership. These "pastoral leaders" realized that, although the traditional role of the "clergy" no longer suited the new system, their pastoral leadership had taken on a whole new vitality and importance.

They had become "visionary motivators." Training and equipping was what they *did*. Visionaries and motivators were *who they* were. They needed the spirituality of Moses and Miriam, in order to see the "pillar of smoke by day" and the "pillar of fire by night." They needed to experience the same immersion with the public that Paul and Priscilla and Lydia had with the Gentiles. They needed to anticipate the distant future, not just react to the immediate present. They needed to acquire the skills that would move the heart and bend the will. They needed to have more than a command of knowledge, and gain the power to persuade, encourage, and inspire. Like John the Evangelist, they had to be able to describe the New Jerusalem. Like Nehemiah, they needed the ability to inspire people to rebuild the walls of Jerusalem even as they defended the work from hostile critics.

Many and varied spiritual gifts were given by God to people in New Hope-in-the-Heart Church, but the pastoral leaders of the church needed to receive one gift above all: the gift to "discern between spirits." They had to be able to tell the difference between authentic visions and destructive addictions. They realized for the first time that this was not a prophetic ministry, a teaching ministry, or even a pastoral ministry. Leadership in New Hope-in-the-Heart Church had become *an apocalyptic ministry*. Like the sentinels of Habakkuk, they needed constantly to declare and refine the vision that lay over the horizon—that awaited its own time to be revealed; that would transform the individual and the world. They declared the vision over and over again, so that those who were running with the risen Lord would not faint.

Diversified and Equipped Discipleship

The church had previously initiated a process for spiritual gifts discernment, and established multiplying P.A.L.S. groups to help people grow in faith and discover callings into personal mission. By this time, the rush of excitement gifted and called individuals experienced upon embarking into mission had begun to dull. Now the quest for excellence began in earnest.

The Stability Triangle of church life began to mature. The administration team became accustomed to facilitating creative ideas, without being tempted to presume permission-giving powers. The human resources team developed standards of excellence for church leadership, and became more adept in finding creative ways to train people and to implement "crazy" ideas with integrity. As the small group strategy and process for discerning spiritual gifts began to expand, and as the new "proscriptive" organizational structure gave creative energies every opportunity to grow, now the church needed to provide short-term and long-term training opportunities to equip people for mission.

The church had previously initiated a communications strategy designed to keep people informed of the transitions and stresses within the church. Now that same communications strategy was revised and upgraded. It now helped coordinate and publicize the growing diversity of mission interests in the congregation. The new communications strategy was aimed both internally among church participants and externally to the community as a whole.

Finally, the burgeoning mission activity of the church outgrew the financial support system of a unified mission fund. This was replaced with multiple opportunities for people to contribute to the missions of their choice. The church discovered that generosity inspired more generosity, so that financial support for one mission tended to encourage financial support for other missions.

Create a Unity of Faith-Sharing and Social Action

Previously the church had organized itself in such a way that the diverse mission energies of the people could be released quickly and efficiently. Church participation was not ultimately complete unless it was fulfilled in mission beyond the church. Mission multiplied. The quest for excellence, however, included the challenge to send people into mission who could do "good works" *and* share "deep faith" in a single mission activity.

This meant that skills development and spiritual growth needed to happen together. Training experiences designed by the human resources team included spirituality exercises and coaching to share faith with confidence. The aim of mission was always to transform the *whole person*. Bread for the dinner table was always accompanied by the faith that motivated its being given; and faith-sharing was always accompanied by some concrete, beneficial deed that improved the life of another.

New Hope-in-the-Heart Church discovered that the link between the "mission field" and the "worship service" was the key to the unity of faith and action. No one could be engaged in personal mission without regularly and passionately participating in the worship of the church. If worship participation slipped, the pastoral leaders perceived this as a sure sign that the unity of faith and action had been broken. Without the continuing experience of God's transforming power, any mission activity, no matter how altruistic, would spin out of the church. On the other hand, if personal mission did not evolve from worship, the pastoral leaders perceived this also as a breakdown of the unity of faith and action. An experience of God's transforming power that was not *shared* in ways that gave life to others, would render the church irrelevant.

The chart for Stage 5 indicates some of the strategies for simultaneous de-construction and re-construction that the congregation used. Essentially, the congregation tried to gather a number of loose ends and implement a complete system that routinely functioned through the week and year.

Perhaps the single, most powerful tactic for New Hope-in-the-Heart Church was to relocate its church facility. The old, beautiful, historic building had a number of structural problems, so they knew from the beginning that the facility would need attention. However, they had wisely decided not to make significant changes until the process of church transformation was nearly complete. The emerging mission and identity of the church would guide their decisions about the facility.

At first, they considered renovations to the building but decided this would ultimately be impractical. The cost of preserving the heritage of the property was high, and the result would be a kind of "maze" of corridors and rooms that would confuse newcomers. Their commitment to the future was wholehearted. Next, they considered tearing down the entire structure and building anew. Such a decision would have been impossible in the early stages of church transformation, but their spirituality had deepened enough to overcome even this addiction to property. Nevertheless, this option was also discarded. Their long-range vision of ministry told them that their property was located about half a mile from the right place. They needed to be at the crossroads of community life, and while their present property was once there, it was there no longer. The church needed to be where "the action" was!

In the end, they decided to move. Leased space was not an option for their mission, because they realized God would call them into many different missions. They did not want some "landlord" to veto potential ministries. So they sold the old property, purchased new land, and prepared to build a facility that truly reflected their identity and mission. It would be simple, accessible, and versatile. It would be wired for future electronics and computer needs. It would look much like other modern buildings—except that there would be an enormous, illuminated Phoenix-Rising-from-the-Ashes suspended at the corner and visible a mile away.

It was a big debt, but debt freedom was not their dream. They "lived" in a rented school basement for more than a year, as they raised money. They took some of the stained-glass windows and other historic artifacts with them and eventually incorporated them into the new building. Such preservation of the past was partly appreciation—and partly a reminder of the addictions they had overcome. Old Faithful Church did not die. It had been transformed by a resurrection people.

New Hope-in-the-Heart Church had greater clarity about its future than ever before, and greater motivation to move forward into that future than it had ever expected. Personally and institutionally, people felt they were walking with Christ in the direction God wanted them to go. They were convinced of this. They shared a vision. Whenever they sang "The Song in the Heart," the eyes of the people would glow and their bodies would move to an inner beat. Nevertheless, there was stress in this stage of transition, too! Three stress themes emerged.

"Can We Really Afford It?"

Can We Afford It? The question, of course, was intended as a *financial* question. It had been bubbling up throughout the transition of the church. As worship and spirituality changed, people wondered if they could financially afford to rewire the sanctuary. As leadership expectations changed, people wondered if they could afford to retrain clergy and laity. As organization was transformed, people wondered if traditional stewardship patterns would finance the new system. Now, of course, they wondered if they could afford to relocate and build. The people were highly motivated—but they were not reckless!

The church answered the question in three ways:

1. *They placed financial cost in proper perspective.* The real costs of church transformation included (in order of importance):

—heritage costs (changing the self-understanding of the church)
—attitude costs (changing the behavior of the church)
—leadership costs (changing the expectations of the church)
—organizational costs (changing the structure of the church)

—property costs (changing the facility of the church) and

—financial costs (changing the stewardship expectations of the church).

The church had already "paid the price" of church transformation in many ways. This gave them confidence and motivation to follow through with their calling.

2. *They trusted their leadership.* They identified people of the church who were gifted and called to financial management. They equipped them to understand the unique financial position of the church, and either provided or helped research all the data needed for sound financial decisions. These leaders kept them fully informed and provided solid recommendations. Their pastoral leaders and trusted lay leaders spoke with one voice and shared the team vision.

3. *They became "shareholders" in mission.* Motivated mission calls forth a surprising generosity. The people of the church were prepared to stake their lives on the mission of the church, through personal loans and debentures. Although this represented only a small percentage of the total capital needed, it symbolized a commitment to success that "spilled over" into renewed energy in the spiritual life and world mission of the church. It was no surprise to anyone that, as financial contributions to relocation grew, so also did the financial contributions to all the many missions of the church!

Financial stress continued, but it became a positive stress. People no longer asked, "Can we afford to do it?" but asked rather, "Can we afford *not* to do it?"

"What Do We Do with All These People?"

Newcomers! Even though New Hope-in-the-Heart Church was designed to interact with the public, it was *still* taken by surprise by the positive public response. The spiritual yearning of the public was so powerful, that the church underestimated the numbers of people who would participate in some way in church life. Seating and space became increasingly problematic, especially during the transition stage between buildings. In fact, they had to relocate twice in temporary, leased space. Small groups seemed to multiply faster than the church could train small group leaders. More people became involved in spiritual gifts discernment than the trained counselors of the church could manage. Parking, nursery space, and coffee cups all required creative planning!

Worried that people might turn away in frustration, the church did three things.

1. *They developed an intentional, exaggerated sense of humor.* The church was unafraid to poke fun at itself, and the good-humored folks laughed at the inevitable frustrations. Newcomers felt they were being included in an "impromptu party" and were invited just to feel at home.

2. *They trained a cadre of "guides."* Gifted laypeople, with readily identifiable clothing, were trained specifically to seek out people who seemed "lost" or "confused." They were trained to do more than give information about the church or give directions to meeting rooms and coatracks. They were trained to listen for the real needs of the newcomers and help the pastoral leadership prioritize their responses. In this way, the curious were welcomed, but people with more urgent needs did not get lost in the shuffle.

3. *They produced a quality video about themselves.* Conscious that leaflets and brochures would not receive much attention, and that most people owned videocassette systems, the church produced free videocassettes, which were given to newcomers. (They were invited to return and "recycle" them if they wished.) These videocassettes not only provided "information," but communicated something of the attitude, spirit, and vision of the people.

Newcomers tended to stay with the church, even if things seemed rushed and disorganized. They felt they had the freedom to be spontaneous, and that there was no pressure on them. And they seemed to catch a spirit of adventure in the air!

"I Just Don't Get It!"

Despite all the efforts the church made to build team vision and communicate the changes being made in each stage of transition, there were still well-meaning folks who sincerely "didn't get it." They kept reverting back to old expectations of the clergy, or reverting back to organizational assumptions no longer valid. When they were gently corrected or reminded, they didn't get angry. They just looked confused and occasionally panic-stricken.

The church had always known that addictions to certain habitual behavior patterns run very deep, and they tried to be very patient with people who required longer to identify and overcome them. Now, however, New Hope-in-the-Heart Church realized that there was an addiction deeper than most. *It was the addiction to "safety nets."* People desperately wanted organizations to be tidy, absolutely consistent, simple, and secure from failure. They would sacrifice their own health and opportunity for personal growth to be in such an organization!

Yet New Hope-in-the-Heart Church realized that one could not be associated with the God revealed in Jesus Christ and have such an organization. Their organization simply tried to manage a sprawling, seething, sometimes contradictory sea of spiritual ferment, in which occasional failure was expected rather than feared. However, the church reached out to those who still looked confused and panic-stricken.

1. The church continued to train *credible mentors* (or "midwives") to reassure people who were confused. They realized that for some addictions, a trusting relationship is more important than a reasonable explanation. The former "elders" (now pastoral "friends") were trained to seek out, and be especially sensitive toward, those who were confused. Their own integrity reassured others of the new direction of the church, even though they were still "systemically confused."

2. Credible mentors were the only ones who could ask people who were still systemically confused to *take it one day at a time!* Their assurance to "walk together" spoke volumes. Are you feeling God's healing touch in your life? Is your church experience inspiring and supportive? Are you enjoying yourself? Are you glad you came to worship? Have you grown personally in faith? Have you engaged in personally satisfying mission? Then don't worry about understanding everything. Don't invent future cataclysms for the church. Let the day's own joys and troubles be sufficient for the day. Take one day at a time!

Most of the people who "just didn't get it" continued to be active in the church. They were not judged. They were loved. After all, everyone was an addict. Each person struggled with institutional church addictions in his or her own way. Perhaps the greatest moment of joy came for many leaders of New Hope-in-the-Heart Church when such a confused person awakened one day and said, "I get it! I see what we're trying to do here! I understand how it works! Finally . . . I get it!"

Insight into this deepest of all addictions, the addiction to the "Safety Net Church," has pushed New Hope-in-the-Heart Church to a new self-discovery. *The five-stage transition might be over—but the struggle to overcome church institutional addictions will never end!* They are, and always will be, addicts. They will never be completely free until the return of the Garden of Eden. The structures of today all too easily become the addictions of tomorrow. They will have to do what the church has always done. *They will have to take each day, each decade, each century, each millennium, one at a time.*

Part 4

WELCOME RELIEF!

The Emerging Theology of the Thriving Church System for the Twenty-first Century

The single, most radical change in the religious attitude among people "at the grassroots" and "on the sidewalk" in North America is that *the gospel is not Good News.* The gospel is "Welcome Relief." At some time in the late 1980s or early 1990s, North American culture took a sharp turn off the ecclesiastical "Information Highway" and onto the "Damascus road." They seem to have silently and collectively decided that all the conflicting interpretations, competing demands, alternative liturgies, and diverse advice on how to lead a good life, are essentially meaningless, unless their own lives can be somehow changed, touched, and transformed through some authentic connection with divine power.

Though the genesis of this shift can be traced to changes in the 1960s, it is apparent that North American denominations have all been taken by surprise by this change of direction. In the midst of numerical losses, denominational leaders of all persuasions, whether "liberal and mainline" or "conservative and evangelical," have all been standing farther down the Information Highway with their portfolios brimming over with "politically correct" or "righteously pure" information, looking back and wondering where the people have gone. Not only are fewer people following them, but even fewer people care about their continuing quarrels with each other.

At first, denominational leaders and many academic theologians thought that people had simply "gone secular." They assumed that the temptations of modern culture had spirited people away into rampant materialism, capitalism, selfishness, atheism, and a general pursuit of personal privilege and pleasure at the expense of the planet, the church, the developing world, and their next-door neighbor. They devised a variety of "Righteous Remnant" theologies to explain the situation. Loosely associated with the prophet Isaiah, such theologies convey a self-image of prophetic voices crying in the "wilderness" of the cultural wasteland, calling vainly for people to turn obediently back to their particular "information portfolio" on right living. Whether "liberal" or "conservative," "Righteous Remnant" theologies are usually accompanied by vague suggestions that one day, when the ozone layer disappears and "the Oppressed" rise up, or, when world economies go bankrupt and hordes of "Enemies" threaten national security, people will recognize the wisdom of the prophets and return to the right way. The fact that the numbers of the "righteous few" steadily decreased only reinforced the "Righteous Remnant" theory. After all, they expect to be a "remnant."

Survey after survey of the North American public has revealed, however, that such an interpretation of religious and cultural life simply cannot be sustained. The public is more interested in "spiritual matters" than ever before. More people believe in God, more people seek spiritual truth, more people view the Bible as "special," and more people want to shape their living in accord with the will of the Divine, than anyone seems to have expected. We have discovered that the North American public has left the ecclesiastical "Information Highway" not out of spiritual disinterest, but motivated by a zest for spiritual discovery.

Chapter 12

The Theological Debate

A new theological sensibility is emerging at the hinge to the twenty-first century that is radically different from the respectable denominationalism of the twentieth century. The principles and processes of this new theology of the church are being developed even as this is read. Some churches intend to be in the middle of it, some churches intend to have nothing to do with it, and many addicted churches simply are unaware that it is happening.

At the end of the twentieth century, the continuing and sometimes venomous quarrel between "liberal" and "conservative" churches of North America has been judged by increasing numbers within and beyond the church to be a great hypocrisy. The extremes of the theological continuum are not nearly as different from each other as they claim to be. They are both pulling their constituencies down the same "Information Highway"—a highway which, for more and more people, seems to lead nowhere. They behave like competing, door-to-door typewriter peddlers, utterly absorbed in arguing about the relative merits of a Royal versus an Olivetti, and taken by surprise that the culture is now buying computers. They may even set aside their previous disputes, in order together to persuade people that computers are, after all, nothing more than fancy typewriters. Increasing numbers of people, however, are no longer deceived. They know they are in a whole different religious paradigm.

Liberal or conservative, Protestant or Catholic, North American denominational theology has uniformly shared the assumption that "God" and "the World" have little to do with each other. The one is pure, the other is sinful. The role of the one is to judge, the role of the other is to be judged. "Godliness" may be defined differently, by different denominations, with different principles of behavior, but the one thing about which everyone agrees is that it is different from "worldliness." The church is called to be "in" the world, but not "of" the world.

Behind this assumption is a debate which has shaken the church from New Testament times forward. It is a debate about whether it is possible for human beings, through their own efforts and reflections and cultural strivings, to glimpse or grasp something of the divine; or whether insight and reunion with God can be accomplished only by revelation "from above." Is culture transparent to the divine, a potential vehicle for the discovery and celebration of eternal meaning? Or is culture merely a necessary encumbrance to daily living, and an obstacle to the receiving of eternal meaning?

This historical debate has been an argument regarding the "forms of love": *agape* and *eros*. North American denominational theology has generally come to assume that agape and eros are fundamentally antagonistic principles. Agape refers to that love which is entirely sacrificial, spontaneous, and unmotivated by any merit within the object loved. It is through such love, and *only* through such love, that human beings can be reunited with God. Indeed, such love is the very essence of God, and, insofar as it can be approximated by human beings through selflessness, sacrifice, and absolute compassion, it is the only "love" that brings authentic eternal or spiritual meaning. No human activity, behavior, cultural construction, or endeavor can reach "upward" to bring reunion with God. Only the "downward" rush of God's love can accomplish salvation.

Eros, on the other hand, refers to that love which is self-affirming, acquisitive desire and longing. It is not spontaneous, but is evoked by the beauty or other merit within the object. It is emotion and passion and the creative energy of culture itself, which strains toward unity with all that is eternal. Where agape is all mind and spirit, eros is all flesh and blood, form and content. While agape rejoices in the universal, eros celebrates particularity and uniqueness. Eros is the conviction of the greatest scientists that they can discover something of eternal Truth, and the passion of the greatest artists that they can create something that reveals eternal Spirit.

In the history of Christian thought, agape and eros have not always been seen as fundamentally antagonistic principles. There is no room here to trace the historical interaction of these themes. Let it suffice to urge the reader to consider Origen of Alexandria, Tertullian the Montanist, Bonaventure, Erasmus the "alternate" Reformer, Pascal, Boehme, Bergson, and many others. There is a rich tradition, among both Christian mystics (male and female), and classical theologians, in which both principles were affirmed.

It is significant that a resurgence of interest in the thought of Paul Tillich parallels the shift of North American culture away from the "Information Highway" and onto the "Damascus road." After all, this is the theologian who argued with Karl Barth specifically over the unity of agape and eros. Influenced by the mysticism of Jacob Boehme and the ontology of Friedrich Schelling, Tillich has been the primary spokesperson in this century for the unity of the "Power of Being" and the "Ground of Being," the value of the erotic and the irrational, and the eruption of the infinite in the finite that simultaneously employs and shatters all cultural forms. His insights into our need to control the world, and the power of the demonic that in fact controls us, interpret the realities of addiction for the twenty-first century. His famous statement, "Religion is the substance of culture, and culture is the form of religion," lies at the heart of the theology of culture today. Those North Americans who have given serious thought to exiting the denominational "Information Highways" will likely agree with Tillich: "The church and culture are within, not alongside, each other. And the Kingdom of God includes both while transcending both" (from "Aspects of a Religious Analysis of Culture").

Given the debate in academic circles, churches in North America have widely shared the unconscious assumption that agape and eros are fundamentally antagonistic principles. Karl Barth, Anders Nygren, and the perspectives of Neoorthodoxy dominate denominational thinking. Any step toward reconciliation or reunion with God must be accomplished only by the divine, and never by the human. There is a radical separation between human culture and divine will, such that no human yearning can overcome the gap and no cultural creativity can bridge the gap. Insofar as eros can be identified with any and all forms of self-affirmation, it is seen as at best futile and irrelevant, and at worst demonic. Self-sacrifice, self-denial, and the penitent response of absolute obedience to divine will is the only way to personal (or social) salvation.

Definitions of the divine will that demand obedience may vary, but the assumption remains the same. Self-fulfillment is "sinful" or "middle-class," while self-sacrifice is "holy" or "politically correct." The fundamental attitude of the believer must be one of apology; the spiritual response must be obedience to a specified agenda; and the church agenda is an abstraction of correct doctrine and denominational policy that is taught and memorized on the ecclesiastical information highway. The whole mission of the church is to issue the prophetic call to repent, and turn back to the true and holy information portfolio. The only model of discipleship is self-denial and self-sacrifice.

Even as the church continues to decline in numbers, the theological assumptions that feed its "righteous remnant" image motivate the church to continue to devalue culture. The church is always the adversary of society. Culture in itself is either spiritually neutral or a contaminating evil. Aspects of self-affirmation (artistic expression and perception of beauty, personal spiritualities and interfaith conversation, sexual identity and intimacy, invention and technology) are considered fundamentally irrelevant to the core of faith and belonging. Those denominations which are ideologically "right" fashion a "fortress" church around confessional dogma; while those denominations which are ideologically "left" fashion a "minority consciousness" around sociopolitical policy.

In either perspective, the denominational church is the adversary of culture. The church maintains a "theology of struggle" with the world beyond its doorstep. They see themselves as "opting for exile" in the manner of the Essenes preferring to leave their country for Qumran rather than live in a contaminated society. The official role of the church (liberal or conservative) is always to criticize, never to appreciate; always to teach, never to learn; always to lament, never to celebrate. As a result, it becomes increasingly impotent for cultural change and irrelevant to the universal quest for reunion with the divine, which has become the primary religious goal of the many publics of North America. For them, the denominations have become clubs for the opinionated, rather than vehicles of discovery.

The emerging theology of the twenty-first century, which is growing and expanding largely outside the old denominational framework, no longer assumes agape and eros to be fundamentally antagonistic principles. Suddenly the passionate desire for reunion with God is not only possible but legitimate. It might be personal, as Spirit awakens infinite passion for God; or it might be corporate, as Spirit awakens the mystical quality of community and interpersonal relationship. Ecstasy and intimacy, long treated with suspicion by the denominational churches, become central to religious experience.

Culture itself can become a vehicle for meaning, rather than an obstacle to meaning. To be immersed in culture is no longer to be lost to faith. Culture becomes a two-way vehicle, not only for the communication of the divine to the human, but for the questing of the human toward the divine. It is not eros that is demonic, but cultural forms that make exaggerated claims to encompass the fullness of God. Self-affirmation and self-fulfillment are no longer ignoble goals but gain new religious worth in the arena of responsible community.

The reunion of agape and eros changes everything. Individuals and congregations that consciously or unconsciously make such a shift in their theological assumptions, find themselves in sharp contrast to their own denominational partners. Indeed, they are often criticized by their own denominational brothers and sisters, from both the "liberal" and "conservative" perspectives. They are accused of being "worldly" or of "watering down the true gospel." Yet for this new breed of believer, the fundamental spiritual attitude is one of yearning, not apology. The spiritual response is one of searching, not obedience to the dogmatic or ideological agendas articulated on the ecclesiastical information highway. The mission of the local congregation is no longer to issue prophetic calls to repentance, but to proclaim a vision of the mutual participation of the infinite and the finite, which can be discovered through culture, even if it cannot be described by any one cultural symbol.

The heart of the emerging twenty-first-century theology is not responsibility, but joy. Such joy is "erotic," because it is not merely self-sacrificial but self-affirming. Individuals allow themselves to be touched and transformed by the Spirit. Their "salvation" does not depend on assent to a particular list of dogmatic propositions, or on the adoption of a uniform behavior pattern, but rather it depends on their experience of daily unity with God. The denominational theology of the twentieth century tended to be very conscientious, often intolerant, always worried, merely friendly, and never, ever ecstatically happy. The emerging theology of the twenty-first century is extraordinarily caring, often irreverently humorous, always curious, profoundly intimate, and never dull.

Five Theological Motifs in the Thriving Church System

The theology emerging from the ferment of public interest in "spiritual matters" is not in any sense systematic. It is filled with inconsistencies, paradoxes, surprises, understatements, emotional nuances, and even exaggerations. It is the eruption of eros itself into religious life, with all its ecstasy and wildness. Paradoxically, religion among the public today has never been discussed so freely and with such animation, and yet, at the same time, it has not been so "unreasonable" since the intertestamental period of biblical times. The North American denominational church is discovering that the cornerstone of religious experience for the twenty-first century *is no longer ethics!* The cornerstone of religious experience has become *apocalyptics!*

It is not that people are unconcerned about the reasoned, moral edification and correction of society. This is just not the cornerstone of their religious sensibilities now. They are concerned about turning society upside down or inside out, by means of the "supernatural" or "irrational" power of God. While the twentieth-century denominations are busy creating the "Just Society" or the "Moral Majority," the public is anticipating the New Jerusalem! These are radically different expectations.

There are at least five theological motifs emerging in the apocalyptic religious consciousness of the public on the brink of the twenty-first century.

Sentinel Theology

There is a change emerging in the "major metaphor" that defines the identity of a church, church leaders, and committed Christians. For years the "major metaphor" has been "the Prophet." The church *was* Amos, called from among the shepherds of Tekoa, rebuking the nations and calling for "justice [to] roll down like waters, / and righteousness like an ever-flowing stream" (Amos 5:24).

Church leaders and committed church participants saw themselves in a confrontational relationship with society, advocating unpopular sociopolitical agendas in behalf of oppressed minorities, from a community base with an essentially rural memory. The core of committed Christians tended to be a grim people, a serious people, troubled by the urbanized wilderness and the industrial or technological evils of the land. Religion was "serious business." Pastoral "workaholism" was praised. Driving a beat-up Chevy, wearing somber or unfashionable clothes, and contentment with poverty-level wages were all appropriate to religious life as "prophetic witness" or "solidarity with the oppressed."

"The Prophets" spoke of exile, journeys in the wilderness, and the trials of the righteous. They sought to be "other" than their neighbors, and "different" from the world. They praised agapic love (self-sacrifice, self-denial, and obedience to divine initiative through which alone salvation could be obtained) and shamed erotic love (self-affirmation, self-fulfillment, and creation of human initiatives to discover eternal meaning). However, as fewer and fewer people listened, and as society seemed to continue unchanged, the "prophets" became pessimistic, isolated, and depressed. At the close of the twentieth century, the zeal of Amos has been transformed into the lamentation of Jeremiah.

A new "root metaphor" is emerging, however. It is equally biblical. One might say it is a blend of wisdom literature, apocalypticism, and prophecy. It is the metaphor of "the Sentinel." It is the "watchman" on Habakkuk's rampart, proclaiming a vision that awaits the right time. The sentinel proclaims an experience of proximate holiness that is just over the horizon, a message of destiny to keep those who are running (i.e., most highly stressed, modern people) from fainting. Whatever the chaos of society, the spirit must be right within the individual human being, for "the righteous live by their faith" (Hab. 2:1-4).

Life and living is what the sentinel is all about. Religious people begin to see themselves in conversation with society, sharing a dialogue of faith and meaning, in a postsecular age in which "spiritual matters" are uppermost in the minds of people, but in which true majorities of doctrinal agreement no longer exist. They tend to be a good-humored people, perhaps even irreverent. They are open to ecstasies, in addition to knowledge. They prize irrationality and emotion, flexibility and tolerance, leisure and quality of life. They are not at war with technology and industry, nor are they entirely at peace with it. They are simply aware that personal transformation precedes lasting social change.

Like Habakkuk, these are people who have truly learned to be at home in the city, the very epicenter of human culture, construction, and creativity. They are not trying to bypass the city, on some wilderness journey to chase a mirage of "political correctness" or "doctrinal purity." They are preoccupied with the continuous discovery of meaning in an ambiguous, urbanized oasis. Curiously, when under stress, such religious sensibilities tend not to burn out in moral despair and lamentation, but find strength from some inner source of the heart to harmonize with the "Song of Songs." David and Solomon, two of the most earthly spiritual mentors of the Bible, would be pleased.

Healing

A second theological motif emerges from the Gospel of Luke and the Acts of the Apostles. The theme of "healing" contrasts sharply with the denominational theological emphasis on "obligation." Especially with the rise of the Social Gospel movement in the latter half of the twentieth century, the church has dwelt upon the calling of sinners to repent, take up the cross, and follow Christ. The hymns, liturgies, sermons, devotional guides all repeat the theme of "obligation": taking responsibility for the ills of the world, obedience, dedication, hard work. The Gospel stories of the calling of the disciples are told and retold, usually in connection with being sent out with only one pair of sandals, to face hardships and trials which may well end in persecution or death. Indeed, the most powerful christological theme of the twentieth century has been to "be Christ-like" by imitating Christ's example of moral living, even to the "cross." The more one suffers for others, the more spiritual one must be.

This is no longer the world of public experience on the edge of the twenty-first century. People today hear the demands of ecclesiastical religion as simply one strident voice among many. They are already burdened by the obligations of their employer, their federal government, their school board, and innumerable charities. From their perspective, the kind of discipline and self-sacrifice required by denominational religion is exactly parallel to that of the "Suzuki" musical education program and sports for their children. Moreover, for the same expenditure of energy, they will find more fulfillment in the latter activities than in attending church on Sunday morning.

If the religious emphasis on "obligation" no longer motivates public interest in religion, what does? Clearly, it is the longing for "healing." While most people have no clear notion of what "sin" is, and why it is so bad, everyone is intimately familiar with addictions and their destructive power. They know that addictions come in many forms, that every single person is in the grip of more than one, that these addictions are robbing them of life and meaning, and that no amount of learning or education will ultimately rescue them from such living death.

The public today does not yearn to be "called," but yearns to be "healed." They cry out to be different, changed, transformed, free from the addictions (whatever they might be) which shackle them. To see this, one only needs to listen to the music of today. One can sense in lyrics and melody the frantic pressure, hurried lifestyle, hopeless inevitability, and addiction to behavior patterns beyond an individual's control, which not only mark North American public life, but which explain why the public has little time for one more message of "obligation" delivered from one more public institution. It is no accident that "erotic" images of lovers meeting together are often coupled with the themes of being personally touched by the power of God. Images from Habakkuk ("Those who are running will not faint") and images from the Song of Solomon ("My beloved speaks and says to me, / 'Arise, my love, my fair one, / and come away . . .'" [2:10]) are unmistakable.

Stories from the Gospel of Luke and Acts of the Apostles have evoked particularly positive responses from the public. This is because the Christology of the Gentile mission is more relevant for the twenty-first century than the "moral example" Christologies often associated with the Gospel of Mark. The transformations of Cornelius, Lydia, the Ethiopian treasurer, and the nameless jailors, centurions, and commoners recorded in the Acts of the Apostles are stories in which modern "seekers" discover new meaning and purpose through encounters with Christ. The healings of Legion (Luke 8) and the blind man at the temple gate (Acts 3) are received as stories of liberation from destructive addictions through one's connection with a Higher Power. The "Gentiles" of the twenty-first century are the spiritually yearning, institutionally alienated public. They find the stories of a holy family displaced by bureaucratic whim (Luke 2), finding the infinite revealed in the ordinary, powerful symbols of hope. In the Gospel of Luke, the faith of Israel is found in a Gentile soldier (Luke 7), the most intense grace is given to the most prodigal son (Luke 15), and individuals are constantly surprised by visions (Luke 1, Acts 7, 10, and 16).

The key to the popularity of Luke-Acts is not simply that it personalizes the Christian experience. Indeed, part of the appeal of the Gospel is that it motivates people into greater activity for social justice by providing them with a sense of personal mission. The real key to the popularity of Luke-Acts is that it describes a salvation that does *not* depend on the "imitation of Christ," but rather depends on "being with Christ." It is the association with Christ, or the unity with Christ, that brings meaning and purpose. Seekers on their own "Emmaus roads" of spiritual yearning suddenly find themselves accompanied by the incognito Christ, warming their hearts and opening their minds to new insight. Therefore, contrary to the theology of "obligation" as it is most often denominationally expressed, the energy of the individual is no longer primarily directed to "doing," but to "being." The ethical action has become secondary—important, yes!—but secondary. The key to religious experience is what happens on the road, and that the Lord is made known in ordinary things (Luke 24:35). And, by God! the public longs for that coffee break to come.

Such healing, or personal transformation, cannot be obtained simply on the ecclesiastical information highway. This is not a matter of education. It is not a matter of corporate action. It is a matter of personal change, without which the discipline of education and the rigor of corporate action will merely end in guilt and pessimism. It may be that, in a time when "Christendom" still described North American society and people already had some experience of the healing touch of God, the church could motivate its members through emphasizing "obligation." No more! Today the public that has embraced 12-Step programs, New Age experimentation, mysticism, and small group intimacy, has also discovered something of extreme significance: "Healing" must come before "obligation."

Walking with the Risen Lord

The third powerful motif for the twenty-first century public follows from the second. Just as meaning and purpose in life are anchored in the "healing association with Christ," rather than in the "ethical imitation of Christ," so also the public is less interested in "taking up the cross," and more interested in "walking with the risen Lord." The "Good Shepherd" symbolism and the promises of Jesus to "come again" (John 10 and 14) are coupled with the Emmaus resurrection story (Luke 24) and the promise "I am with you always, to the end of the age" (Matt. 28:19). The theological key for public interest in the church is not the hope of pursuing Christ toward a distant goal of social or spiritual perfection, but the dream of being with Christ in daily living.

The "cross," as a symbol, has lost serious meaning for the public of the twenty-first century. First, it has been trivialized to become no more than glittering jewelry and a good luck charm. To follow the cross today is an invitation to shallowness, or a perpetuation of the addiction to materialism with which all people suffer. At a deeper level, however, the cross has ceased to be a symbol for liberation. It has become, instead, a symbol for ever-increasing obligation. The long ideological or doctrinal agendas with which the denominations ("liberal" or "conservative") have burdened this symbol, have transformed it into a sign of drudgery, guilt, and enslavement.

People have learned that *no one* can follow Christ. No one can bear such a cross. In their eyes, the imitation of Christ is a pretension and an arrogance assumed by elitist, ecclesiastical church "members" to signify that they are not only "other" than the world, but "better" than their neighbors. The cross has become a vehicle for adding to the already overpowering "guilt-load" experienced by people who are all too aware of the addictions that shame and shackle their lives.

It is no accident that North American publics largely ignore Lent and fill the church at Easter. Nor is it any accident that, in those churches or centers of worship where increasing numbers are worshiping, the cross is often inconspicuous as a symbol or missing from the room altogether. The denominations tend merely to lament the lack of "faithfulness" or "discipline" of society, and tend not to understand the significance of such behavior. The public has had enough crucifixion already—they yearn for resurrection.

The proximity of the risen Lord to one's individual daily living continues the theme of the healing presence of Christ. It is the recognition that a healing association with God, which transforms life, cannot be momentary but must be a lifelong and daily experience. It is the same thinking that keeps an alcoholic regularly attending Alcoholics Anonymous long after having actually stopped drinking. Unless they have a sense of the proximate support of the risen Christ each day, their addictions will reassert themselves.

What does the yearning to "walk with the risen Christ" mean? First, it is an experiential "walk." There may be a structure of liturgy, prayer, Bible reading, or meditation exercises associated with the experience, but these are meaningless without some expectation of a higher, deeper spiritual consciousness of the divine presence. Most people will acknowledge that there are "dry" periods in which they do not feel such "closeness," but the very fact that they recognize this state as undesirable, and have confidence that it can be corrected, provides a different motivation for the organization of the daily routine. This is not an intellectual certainty, a body of knowledge, or a specific activity. Indeed, it may not be entirely "rational" or "controllable" at all. It is a heartfelt confidence in the immediate presence of the Holy. It takes personally the promise in Isaiah: "But you, Israel, my servant, . . . / the offspring of Abraham, my friend; . . . / do not fear, for I am with you, / do not be afraid, for I am your God; / I will strengthen you, I will help you, / I will uphold you with my victorious right hand" (Isa. 41:8-10).

Second, it is a daily "walk." It is a seven-day-a-week experience that embraces the whole routine of living. Work, leisure, illness, wellness, divorce, marriage—everything that happens in an individual life carries the potential revelation of the presence of Christ. More than this, the individual lives with a sense of daily expectation or readiness for the coming of the Holy. They have an "early church consciousness" that "this Jesus, who has been taken up from you into heaven, will come in the same way as you saw him go into heaven" (Acts 1:11). A life lived in such expectation is not simply waiting for a final, cataclysmic "Second Coming," but rather anticipates each day to be a "Kairos" moment in which human experience becomes surprisingly transparent to the divine. Christ comes, and comes again, not so much as a "thief in the night," but as a "lover in the evening." Fresh waves of insight, fulfillment, or joy periodically transform the routines of life from the mundane to the cosmically significant.

Finally, it is a purposeful "walk." The risen Lord is going somewhere in particular, to do something which suits one's individual gifts perfectly. One accompanies Christ, not out of obligation to fulfill someone else's mission, or some institution's mission, but out of eagerness to fulfill "my" mission. It is a mission that uniquely matches the very spiritual gifts, personality traits, and inner talents with which God equipped me. Such a personal mission may not be immediately clear. The "walk" with the risen Lord will involve a journey of personal discovery that will discern just what one's gifts, personality, and talents might be. Discernment may, in turn, lead to changes in career, lifestyle, and even marital status. In the end, however, to walk purposefully with the risen Christ means devoting all one's time and energy to doing that which one enjoys doing most of all, and does with excellence.

Return to Eden

The fourth powerful motif for the twenty-first century public flows from the consciousness of the purposeful walk with the risen Christ. It is the theme of "personal destiny": a vision of ultimate fulfillment, final victory, or homecoming. It is a destiny which combines final and complete insight into one's own unique selfhood, affirmation, and cleansing of that selfhood, and taking one's appropriate place in the eternal scheme of the universe. It is the final, real answer to the impulse to "belong." Such an impulse never could be fulfilled merely through membership in an institutional church. So shallow does such a "belonging" become, that the twenty-first-century spiritual seeker would feel shamed to settle for it. It is not an institutional belonging, nor even a community belonging, but a cosmic belonging. It is not leaving the world, nor is it rejecting the world, but it is being "right" with all creation.

There are many salvation metaphors in the Bible: the New Jerusalem (Revelation 21), the Heavenly Banquet (Matthew 22), the Eternal Awe (Hebrews 9), the Final Battle (Ezekiel 37), the Rapture (Matthew 24, 25), and others. The most powerful metaphor for the twenty-first-century public, however, is the vision of Paul of the return to Eden:

> I consider that the sufferings of this present time are not worth comparing with the glory about to be revealed to us. For the creation waits with eager longing for the revealing of the children of God. . . . We know that the whole creation has been groaning in labor pains until now; and not only the creation, but we ourselves, who have the first fruits of the Spirit, groan inwardly while

we wait for adoption, the redemption of our bodies. For in hope we were saved. Now hope that is seen is not hope. . . . But if we hope for what we do not see, we wait for it with patience. (Rom. 8:18-19, 22-24, 25)

Following the metaphor of Paul, just as through Adam the eviction from Eden led to the struggles and pain of life, so now, through Christ the "new Adam," the fulfillment and harmony of all creation can be regained by a return to the original perfection of Eden.

At first glance, such a metaphor speaks powerfully to the present public who are so sensitive to environmental issues and the preservation of the planet. At a deeper level, however, such a metaphor heals the theological rift between God and the world. The very particularities of each existing thing, animate or inanimate, find their appropriate place in a purified harmony of the universe. Humanity, the environment, and the divine, are all at one. Wholeness of heart and mind, health restored through freedom from all destructive addictions, reunion with God—all are achieved in the perfected beauty of the Garden of Eden.

It has often been observed that the central themes of religious behavior are designed specifically to reflect in miniature the metaphor of salvation toward which a religious system points. If the metaphor of salvation is the Heavenly Banquet, for example, religious behavior may be constructed around the sacrament of Holy Communion. Or, if the metaphor of salvation is the Just Society, religious behavior may be built around social activism. Or, if the metaphor of salvation is the Righteous Remnant, religious behavior will emphasize membership in an institutional church or organized cult. In this case, the central salvation metaphor leads to a very different religious behavior. It glories in the idiosyncratic, the individual, and the personal expressions of eternal meaning that are as varied as the species of flowers in the garden. Public concern for the environment takes on a deeper, more cosmic significance. Personal disciplines in self-awareness that seek "wholeness" for the human spirit, or disciplines that combine meditation and physical exercise to achieve "wholeness" with the universe, both connect easily with a "Garden of Eden" metaphor about overcoming all alienations.

The Damascus Road

At the close of the twentieth century, the public has taken the exit ramp off the ecclesiastical "Information Highway" and made a sharp turn onto "the Damascus road." The story of the life-change of Paul has become a model for spiritual life today, but it was never rightly understood by the denominational churches.

Denominational theology always tried to describe what happened as the "*conversion* of Saul." "Conversion" was then assumed to be the adoption of a completely different set of beliefs, dogmas, or ideas. It was a matter of the mind. It was the assimilation of "new information," which, once properly understood, changed the behavior of Paul from bigot and murderer to benevolent caregiver. Modern critics of Paul who accuse him of patriarchal or anti-Semitic prejudices still never doubt that what seemed to happen to Paul was just such a "conversion." The problem of the liberal institutional church is simply that Paul failed to understand the new information properly, a state of affairs the denomination will make sure does not happen for modern believers by providing correct, updated "information." Denominations may disagree about the exact content of the correct information (dogma, beliefs, ideas) to which we, like Paul, must be "converted," but each denomination will articulate its list of doctrinally pure or ideologically correct assertions. More than this, each denomination will deploy, in subtle or crass ways, its own magisterium to police the thoughts of its constituency.

It is no accident that the rapidly accelerating rejection of institutional religion at the close of the twentieth century parallels the rapidly accelerating adoption of computer technology. Computer technology has helped the public to perceive something about religion with greater clarity than ever before. *Authentic religion is not about information. It is about experience.* Insofar as the denominations continue to assume that the religious life is essentially a matter of processing a certain kind of data correctly, they have all uniformly made what philosophers as historically distant as Immanuel Kant called "a category mistake." They mistakenly think they can treat religious experience the same way a computer organizes and interprets data bits. They devote their energies to designing ever more efficient "software" (educational materials) with which they can "program" their followers to "process" social experience in such a way as to emerge with "correct" answers or behavioral responses.

The public, newly sensitized by computer technology to the full meaning of "information," has recognized that the gospel is not a "data bit." As Kant pointed out long ago, religion is *not* simply a different kind of information. It is not "information" at all! Computer awareness has helped the public realize this, but it has not brought about the subsequent rejection of religion that Kant might have imagined. The public, which has also been bombarded and overwhelmed by "information" through computer technology, has discerned that there is more to truth than is revealed on the Internet. Truth is more than ideologically correct information, more than doctrinally pure information, and, in the end, it is not "information" at all. They will continue to embrace computer technology, because the computer helps them in their "doing." Yet they will explore religion with renewed fervor, because only this will help them in their "being." And they will reject denominational institutions, so long as they continue to make a "category mistake" by confusing "faith" and "information."

For the twenty-first-century public, what happened to Saul on the road to Damascus becomes a paradigm for the potential experience of every person. Saul truly is not the "unique case" the institutional church has thought him to be, but is a kind of "Everyman," the archetypal spiritual seeker. Moreover, there is every reason to believe that it is precisely because Saul's experience can be universalized, that early Christians decided it was absolutely essential to include the story in the Bible.

The story of Saul, wrongly identified by the institutional church as the "conversion" of Saul, is more properly understood as "the transformation of Saul" or "the re-missioning of Saul." Saul is not different from the average citizen. He means well, he intends good, he tries his best. He believes in law and order and generally respects authority, but he is not blind to injustice and works hard to make the system work better. He has studied with the best teachers, and been educated in the best colleges. He seeks not only to be a good person but to understand the moral life. He seeks to follow God's will and live in fairness and compassion with his neighbors. If necessary, he will sacrifice his life for his country or his beliefs, but he realizes that there is plenty of room for negotiation before that should be necessary. Saul is not a fanatic, but a seeker. He is not mentally ill, nor emotionally disturbed, but simply a good man trying to be the best he can be, under the conditions of his culture and society. He could easily be anyone's good friend.

What is decisive for Paul is the recognition of his profound addictions. The good he intends to do, somehow he can never fully achieve. The evil he does not want to do, he seems compelled to do anyway. This profound consciousness of addiction (named and unnamed) to forces, attitudes, destructive habits beyond his control, drives him to despair. He is well-intentioned, but good intentions are not enough. He is well-educated, but education cannot help him. He has many friends, but his friends are all in the grip of the same addictions. He is, in fact, no different from every decent man or woman, no different from you or me, no different from the successful middle-aged adult who suddenly confronts an addiction. "Wretched man that I am," Saul says about three in the morning every wakeful night. "Who shall save me from this living death?" Even local "12-Step" programs, a whole library of self-help books, and the serious discipline of tai chi all fail to liberate him from final meaninglessness and ultimate personal failure.

Then occurs the fateful journey to Damascus. First, there is *the blinding light.* Note that Paul was not looking for it. It happened unexpectedly—and it hurt. It changed him inside, but in itself it imparted no particular information to his mind. In a twinkling, as if the last trumpet had sounded heralding the end of one day and the beginning of a new day, he was a changed man. He was different. He didn't know how different, but only that he was different. Somehow the addictions from which he could not escape (which the later institutional church would call "sin") had been overcome. Physically blind and confused, humiliated at no longer even being able to feed himself, nevertheless Saul had a hope he had never experienced before. It was not that Saul had gained some new "information." He had gained a new spirit. *It was not that Saul had "changed his mind" about important subjects, but that he had gained a whole new identity.* It was at that millisecond, when Saul became a "new creature," that his name was changed. He was no longer Saul . . . he was "Paul."

Second, *he hears the voice.* Once again, no particular information is communicated. Hearing the voice makes Paul's encounter with the divine *personal.* He is called by name, and God is revealed by name. There is a personal connection between the individual and God. God is not an abstract power, and the meeting on the Damascus road is not a chance coincidence. It is part of a plan, because God has a vested interest in the individual. God has perceived the destructive, addictive behavior of the individual, and takes initiative to rescue him. To be sure, there is the promise that there is much to be learned, and that there is information to be gained. Yet this comes later. First, there must be healing. Second, there must be established a personal connection between the individual and God. Only then will new information have meaning.

Significantly, the biblical story states that Paul's companions hear a voice but do not perceive the identity of God. This reinforces the importance of the personal connection between the individual and God. It does not happen as a group, as an organization, as a congregation, or as an institution. One's companions see the transformation occur, and may even be aware of its healing significance. They may be encouraged to seek such a personal, transformative connection themselves. It gives them hope. Nevertheless, the Light and the Voice come unexpectedly, as the depth of individual despair matches the power of God's grace.

Third, *Paul befriends Ananias.* Only now does the religious experience have an "informational" content. Note, however, that it is only shared *through a mentor.* Ananias is not a traditional preacher, teacher, or educator. He is a mentor. The biblical story clearly indicates the *five characteristics* of a mentor, which are suggested in many other stories in Acts (e.g., Peter and Cornelius), and which Paul himself will later demonstrate in his relationship with Timothy, Prisca, Aquila, and Lydia:

1. The spiritual bond that unites the mentor and apprentice, in which the integrity of their relationship is grounded in a mutual connection to God.
2. The personal bond that unites the mentor and apprentice, through which truth is communicated by the spontaneity and authenticity of shared life experience.
3. The courage by which the mentor shares himself or herself, becoming vulnerable to another who is not fully known and perhaps not even well liked.
4. The mutual confirmation and celebration of healing, and the readiness to discover the hidden meaning and purpose behind it.
5. The vision of the mentoring relationship that points beyond itself, toward the unique destiny of the apprentice.

The relationship between Ananias and Paul is simultaneously uncomfortable and profound for each of them. In the end, each one is changed, equipped, and motivated to walk with Christ in ways neither anticipated in the beginning.

Therefore, once Paul experiences the mentoring of Ananias, the fourth step on his journey is *to go public with his faith in the synagogue.* As mentioned earlier, this allows Paul to finally articulate his faith, confirm permanently his new identity, and thereby complete the healing process. The Bible story makes it clear that "going public" involved both risk and personal growth. On the one hand, it offended many people, for a variety of reasons. On the other hand, the very debate that resulted forced Paul to think carefully about his experience, leading both to the intellectual clarity and personal courage which would mark his later career. In a sense, it is personal growth through trial and error, experimentation, and passionate dialogue.

Finally, the road to Damascus reaches completion as Paul *climbs over the wall* to embark on his personal mission. Paul now has a sense of life purpose and personal destiny that he never had before. He will not "burn out," and, although he will have many bitter experiences, he never again comes to the brink of despair. His hope will be rooted in the transforming experience of healing by God's power, a healing he believes is possible for every human being. His confidence will be rooted in the personal connection achieved through the hearing of Jesus' voice, and his confidence will never be shaken even when his own church doubts his right to be an apostle. His faith will be rooted in the mentoring he received, and in the fiery struggle of clarifying his experience through dialogue with the world. That faith will undergo many changes and evolutions, but it will never be lost.

In short, the "Everyman," Paul, has discovered meaning and purpose for his life. He has experienced ecstasy and intimacy (experiences which he continues to share throughout his life), and he has a sense of personal destiny that banishes his fear of death. The life that has been routine and meaningless, is now purposeful and rich. The daily alienation he felt has been replaced by a seven-day-a-week consciousness of the personal presence of Christ. His addictions have not disappeared, but he has been empowered to combat and overcome them. He finds himself motivated to take compassionate risks for the sake of other people. And *that* is what religion is all about.

It's a First-Century World!

Futurists of every kind—sociologists, historians, and theologians—have been saying that we live in a "postmodern" world. The industrial, labor-intensive world of distinct nations and multiple economies is passing away. It is, indeed, being replaced by a technologically supported information and communication network that has transformed the world into a neighborhood with a single, complex economy. People have more private time than ever before.

The identification of the postmodern world, however, is not enough to explain our strange and diverse culture. If people have more private time than ever before, they have also discovered in that private time a meaninglessness and futility about life that past generations were perhaps too busy to realize. The truth is that we are also living in a "postsecular" world. The modern penchant for atheism, and agnosticism, and skepticism is also passing away. There is a ferment of religious interest and spiritual experimentation that surpasses anything we have known for 2,000 years.

The past 2,000 years have brought us full circle back to intertestamental times. It is an "in-between" time, a transition from the known to the mysterious, a time with special attributes like these:

apocalyptic expectations
alienation from authority
cultic, mystical, and religious experimentation
a highly competitive and diverse religious "market"
ambiguity and experimentation regarding gender, intimacy, and family life
migrations of races and peoples, cross-cultural communication
fascination with the irrational and supernatural
"feast or famine" economic changes
popular "powerlessness" at the hands of hidden, competing "tyrants"
messianic expectations and powerful spiritual yearnings

The first century was also a "postmodern" era in the experience of the people of that time. They, too, were conscious that attitudes and behavior patterns that had dominated daily life for hundreds of years were disappearing. They, too, experienced an overwhelming burst of information and communication, encouraged by opportunities in transportation and improved technology. They, too, had more time to pause, look inward, and discover their lives addicted and trapped and meaningless. Then as now, the Magi searched the skies; the Zealots led revolts; the philosophers divided into countless schools to debate the One and the Many; the religious institutions lamented the erosion of their constituencies; and even the shepherds were prepared to risk their flocks, to charge out into the night, on the mere rumor of angels.

In a profound sense, the church of today faces the same dilemma of the early Christian believers and the Essenes who formed the Qumran community. The church can respond as did the Essenes. Stung by the rejection of their message, filled with righteous indignation, convinced that their way was the only way, questing for doctrinal purity and ideological correctness, they identified themselves as a "Righteous Remnant" and chose exile. Withdrawing to the desert in order to be uncontaminated by the world, they built a fortress in the caves near Qumran. There they worshiped in the *right* ways, and no doubt held group discussions long into the night around the campfire to discuss the folly of the world. They meticulously wrote everything down, confident that the pendulum of history would shift in their direction and one day they would emerge again justified. Despite all their self-sacrifice, they perished.

On the other hand, the church today can respond as did the early Christian believers. Accused of being worldly, they remained in conversation with culture, changing and shaping and perfecting their glimpse of truth. Accused of "watering down" the Torah, they addressed the spiritual yearnings of the public with an opportunity for personal transformation and healing. Accused of undermining traditional religious institutions and moral practices, and of subverting political authority, they were attacked by both the liberal "left" and the conservative "right," but their gospel was so effective in meeting the spiritual crisis of the public that, in the end, none of the adversity mattered. It is true that culture changed the church. It is also true that the church changed culture.

The denominations of today are like the traditional religious institutions of the Roman Empire. They are speeding down the ecclesiastical information highway, ready to instruct the people in the doctrinally pure forms of worshiping Artemis, the theological intricacies of understanding the Athenian "Unknown God," and the ideologically correct ways of reforming the social fabric of Galatia. As Paul would discover, any "mission to the Gentiles" will always draw criticism from those who insist on certain rules of membership and the sacrifice of self to the obedience of hierarchy. What a surprise it was to the traditional institutions of the Roman world to discover that the public had left the information highway—and detoured onto the Damascus road!

The time is running out for the denominational churches of today to awaken. Membership decline, diminishing community interest, and rapidly declining resources, are already pushing many churches beyond the mysterious "critical mass" of potential recovery. Many other congregations, however, are embracing the Acts of the Apostles. They are literally being repotted, reborn, and transformed, thriving amid renewed and accelerating interest from the diverse publics of North America. They have discovered that for millions of spiritually starving people today, the gospel is *not* Good *News,* but it is *Welcome Relief!*

Index